The Successful Student's Handbook

A Step-by-Step Guide
to Study, Reading, and Thinking Skills

The Successful Student's Handbook

*A Step-by-Step Guide
to Study, Reading, and Thinking Skills*

RITA PHIPPS

UNIVERSITY OF WASHINGTON PRESS
Seattle and London

*The Successful Student's Handbook: A Step-by-Step Guide
to Study, Reading, and Thinking Skills* is a revised and
expanded version of *For Students—about Studying*
(Copyright © 1977 by Rita Phipps).

Library of Congress Cataloging in Publication Data
Phipps, Rita.
  The successful student's handbook.

  Rev. ed. of: For students. 1977.
  Includes index.
  1. Study, Method of—Text-books. 2. Universities and
colleges—Examinations—Study guides. 3. Report writing
—Text-books. 4. Note-taking—Text-books. I. Title.
LB2395.P54 1983   378'.1702812   80-54427
ISBN 0-295-95802-2

Contents

Preface   xi

1. To the Student—Before You Do Anything Else   3

A. You as a Better Student   3

B. How This Course Works   4

C. How to Take Lecture Notes: A Brief
Introduction So That You Can Start Today   7

D. Asking and Answering Questions   10

E. Problems with a Teacher?   11

F. What If You Are Absent?   12

G. Your Own Shorthand Technique
and Abbreviations   12

H. Concentrating   12

I. Procrastinating   14

2. Motivation   15

A. You Must Have Motivation   15

B. There Are Many Different Motivations   15

C. When You Have No Motivation   16

D. Increasing Your Motivation   17

E. Your Own Efforts
Can and Will Make a Difference!   17

F. Motivational Pep Talk   17

3. Scheduling   19

A. Finding the Time   19

B. What to Do with the Time   29

C. Where Will You Study?   31

D. Getting Ready to Study   31

E. Suggested Menu Item
for Students in a Hurry   32

F. Suggested Shopping List
for Students in a Hurry   32

4. Your Memory   35
Proper Storage, Firm Storage, and the Copy, Check, Correct Method

A. **Proper Storage**   35

B. **Firm Storage**   38

C. **Trying to Remember Something:
A Real Life Story**   41

D. **Sabotaging Your Own Memory**   42

E. **The Copy, Check, Correct Method**   42

5. The Reality Check   47

A. **Is It True or False?**   47

B. **How to Make a Reality Check**   47

C. **The Words We Use and the Real Things
in the World**   48

D. **Familiar and Unfamiliar Information**   49

E. **Reality Checks Are Important
for Learning**   50

F. **Checking Reality
Makes Life More Interesting**   50

6. Making the Most of Your Memory   52
Cross-Referencing and Page-Flipping

A. **Cross-Referencing**   52

B. **Page-Flipping**   57

7. Taking Tests   59

A. **Yes, You Can Learn How
to Take Tests Well**   59

B. **Why Tests Are Useful**   59

C. **The Different Kinds of Test Questions**   60

D. **Several Questions at One Time**   61

E. **You, the Test, the Teacher,
and the Grade**   63

F. **How to Overcome the Fear of Tests**   65

G. **Practice Your Test-Taking Skills
in This Course**   66

8. Self-Testing: The Dress Rehearsal   68

A. **Why You Need a Dress Rehearsal for a Test**   68

B. **How to Have a Dress Rehearsal: Give Yourself a Test**   68

C. **How to Answer and Correct Your Self-Test Questions**   68

D. **When Should You Have Your Dress Rehearsal Self-Test?**   70

E. **Is All This Trouble Worth It?**   70

9. Using the Material   71

A. **On Tests**   71

B. **For Other Purposes**   71

10. Checklist—Where You Are So Far   73

The Study Skills and Procedures You Should Now Be Practicing and Using

11. The Words and the Sentences   74

A. **Understanding the Words**   74

B. **Understanding the Sentences**   74

12. The Paragraphs and Their Main Ideas   77

A. **Understanding the Paragraphs**   77

B. **Finding the Main Idea**   77

C. **The Three-Step Method for Finding Main Ideas**   78

D. **Examples of How to Use the Six-Question/Six-Paragraph Method**   79

E. **Main Ideas: Review**   82

F. **Paragraphs with More Than One Purpose (Which Are Two or More of the Six Types)**   84

G. **Some Problems with Finding the Main Idea**   86

H. **Where to Write Down Your Main Idea Statements When You Are Reading an Assignment**   89

13. Underlining the Supporting Material   90

A. What Is in a Paragraph   90

B. How to Underline   90

C. How to Summarize   100

D. How a Whole Article
Is like a Single Paragraph   102

14. General Categories and Specific Examples   103
Outlining

A. How to Get a Lot of Work
under Control   103

B. How to Write Out an Outline   105

C. Outlining Helps You Remember
Your Material   109

D. Outlining Skills Help You Answer
Test Questions   112

15. More on Note-Taking   117
Using the Left-Hand Margin of Your Notebook

A. Why You Should Use the
Left-Hand Margin   117

B. How to Put Material in the
Left-Hand Margin   117

C. What Studying Really Is   120

D. How Cross-Referencing/
Reality Checks Fit In   121

16. Preparing Textbook Notes for Proper Storage   122

A. How to Study Your Textbook Notes   122

B. An Example
of How to Study Your Textbook   125

C. How to Skim and Scan   127

17. Writing a Research Paper   130

A. What Is a Research Paper?   130

B. What Is Research?   130

C. Reporting Your Findings   130

D. How to Conduct Research   130

E. Finding a Topic   130

F. Limiting Your Subject   131

G. Doing the Research   131

H. Other Library Services   133

I. Reading Resources Material/
Doing the Research   137

J. Taking Notes   137

K. Writing the Paper   138

L. Notes and Bibliography   141

18. Consolidating the Paragraph Summaries   144

A. Making Paragraph Summaries
in Your Textbook   144

B. How to Consolidate Paragraph
Summaries   145

C. How to Consolidate Summaries
of Several Pages   152

19. Consolidating Lecture Notes and Outside Reading Notes   159

A. How to Consolidate Outside Reading
Notes   159

B. How to Consolidate Reading
and Lecture Notes   167

20. Checklist   170
What You Should Be Doing from Start to Finish

Index   171

Preface

This book was written to help students increase the strength and sharpness of their minds, and to help them improve their abilities to concentrate, read, remember, take tests, and, in general, succeed in college. I hope it helps you.

If at all possible you should definitely enroll in a study skills course. Working in a class with a teacher as your guide, to answer your questions and give you a fuller understanding, will be the best way for you to improve your study skills.

But if you want to improve your skills without taking a study skills course, this book can help you. You may not want to do all the suggested exercises. Then don't. One suggestion that is important, though, is that you don't skip around in the book, trying to read later chapters before you read the earlier ones. The reason is that each chapter is based on what went before. If you don't read and understand the first chapters, you may not have an easy time understanding the terms and procedures used in later chapters.

An exception can be made, however, if you believe that you need immediate help with reading and understanding your textbooks. In this case, you would want to start with Chapters 5 and 11. If you do this, though, be sure you do not overlook the earlier chapters on note-taking, motivation, scheduling, and memory. These chapters will provide you with a firm foundation for your study activities.

Please take note of these special points:

—This book is intended mainly for college students.

—The style of the book is repetitive, but is so for a reason. The repetitious style is used for *teaching* purposes. *Repetition helps people understand and remember.* This is especially important in a skills-building course like this.

—This course is a *skills-building* course. There is really no course content other than the teaching of skills. Or, from your view, the *learning* of skills.

—The major homework for this course is to use what you learn here to help you in your other, subject-matter courses. The homework is to apply and use and practice what you learn in this course as you attend and study for other courses.

I always know my students are doing their homework well when they say, "I did a good job on my history test because I used the skills and methods I am learning in *this* class!" And that is one of the two major purposes of this course and this book.

The other major purpose is to help you learn how to think, to use your inborn, good mind.

Thus, as you read these pages and go to your study skills class, you should be both (1) learning the actual study skills, and (2) learning how to use your inborn intelligence to its very best advantage, that is, how to think at a high level.

Special thanks go to my colleagues who taught earlier versions of this book and gave me excellent suggestions: Sylvia Lovelace, Thirza Smith, Americ Higashi, and, especially, Mark Palek. I have incorporated most of their suggestions in this revised text. Also, my own students have given me many ideas about how to improve the book. These ideas are all now in this edition. Dale Chase is also thanked for his help with the information and materials concerning library use.

Thanks are also due to the Seattle Community College Curriculum Development Committee for awarding me a grant to write the original version. And I want to thank our union for negotiating the development grants into our collective bargaining agreement, providing many of us faculty with the opportunity to improve our courses for our students.

Finally, I want to thank my loved ones, some of whom, especially Susanna, helped with the typing, and all of whom encouraged and cheered me on. Thank you, Jessica, Susanna, Diana, Georgia, Elaine, Barbara, Dale, and Mom.

Seattle, Washington
April 1983

The Successful
Student's Handbook

A Step-by-Step Guide
to Study, Reading, and Thinking Skills

CHAPTER 1

To the Student—
Before You Do Anything Else

A. You as a Better Student

If you really want to become a better student you can. There is no doubt about it. This study skills course will give you the opportunity to learn how to become a more successful student. All it takes is for you to come to class every day, do the work conscientiously, and have the confidence that you can do it. You *can* do it.

While some of you may be taking this course simply to brush up on or improve the study skills you already have, others of you may be taking this course because you feel at a loss. Perhaps you don't know how to take good notes, read and understand a textbook, study for a test, remember what you have studied, get good grades on a test, etc. The rest of this first section is for those of you who feel more or less at a loss.

There are several reasons why you may not be the kind of student you wish to be. One reason may be that you did not take high school (or even elementary school) very seriously. Perhaps you sluffed off and had more interest in your social life than in your classwork. Or perhaps at some point early on, maybe even as early as the second or third grade, you began to fall behind and not only missed out on important learning experiences but also lost confidence in yourself. Perhaps you have been out of school for many years and do not feel sure you remember how to study. Perhaps you are a restless, impatient sort of person who is not very self-disciplined. These are all problems that this course can help you overcome.

Another kind of problem could be emotional. Sometimes it happens that a student thinks he or she is serious and yet begins to cut class, doesn't do assignments, and has lots of reasons (excuses) for why this is happening. Cutting class, not doing assignments on time are danger signs. If you notice these danger signs occurring with you, talk to your teacher right away. You may be suffering from one of several problems that prevent students from succeeding. These problems *can* be overcome.

For example, you may be so used to failure as a student that you can't break the habit. You have all the best intentions and yet the next thing you know you are back in the same old rut. You may hate that rut and you may have tried to get out of it, but it is familiar; it is a habit. There is nothing easier than falling back into a familiar rut, no matter how much you think you want to get out of it. You need to break the old habits of failure, of not working hard, of letting things slide. One way to break them is by making new, better habits. Do not underestimate the power of bad habits. They can defeat you. This course can help you learn how to make new, better habits.

Some people, on the other hand, because of some emotional problem, cannot accept success, as strange as that may seem. They do well and then, just as they are beginning to achieve success, start sliding. All kinds of excuses crop up, like, "I'm doing so well now I can relax for awhile." See your teacher right away if you recognize this pattern in yourself. There *are* ways to overcome the problems that hold you back.

Yet a third kind of problem could be physical. Some people are born with the physical inability to see words correctly. As a result they cannot learn to read well and are very poor spellers. People with this type of problem often begin to fear their intelligence is low. But this is *not* the case. It is a physical problem and it can be dealt with. If you believe you have such a problem, discuss it with your teacher, who will be able to suggest how you can go about getting the condition diagnosed and overcome.

But whatever it is that has kept you from the success you desire, it can begin to be overcome. It depends on the amount of effort you yourself put into taking charge of your own life, which includes putting a real effort into this course. Unfortunately, your teacher cannot work a miracle on you. Your own efforts are needed if you want to make the most of the opportunity that this course offers you.

B. How This Course Works

1. Besides helping you to become a better student in general, this course can help you do well in your courses *right now*. In other words, you should begin *immediately* to apply what you learn here in the other classes you are presently taking. If you aren't taking any other classes now, the material you will learn in this course can be used in the future, should you decide to take other courses then.

2. *The material in this book is presented in a deliberately repetitive way. If you believe you understand an idea the first time it is stated, then skim over the rephrasings and further statements of that same idea.* However, as the book progresses and the material gets more difficult, you may want to read every repetition because in that way you will get a fuller and clearer understanding. Be sure you do not start to skim and skip if you only partially understand an idea. *Do not be in a hurry.* Reading the same idea over and over isn't going to hurt you. You may feel bored sometimes and you may think you don't need all the repetition. *But almost everything is repeated more than once because for every idea there is going to be at least one student who needs to hear it several times before gaining full understanding. I'm doing it for their sake.* It may be for your sake, too, with some of the ideas.

3. The first three chapters of this book are by way of an introduction. They are for the purpose of making sure (1) that you have a good general approach to the subject and the course; (2) that you have the drive or motivation to put forth the effort to learn the study skills; (3) that you know how to schedule the time you will need to study these skills (and also the materials in your other courses) so that you can truly learn them.

The next six chapters (4–9) teach you important basic skills. These will be the foundation for the more advanced skills that come up later in the book. Chapter 10 is a summary of the book up to that point. By then you will be able to take notes in lectures, study them for tests, and take tests.

The next three chapters (11–13) teach you how to read, understand, and underline your textbook assignments. Chapters 14–16 teach you how to organize and outline your lecture notes and your textbook notes. The next chapters (17–19) are the most difficult chapters of all, and in order to learn the skills taught in these chapters you will have to have learned the material in the previous chapters. The last chapter (20) reviews what you have learned in the entire course.

Thus, if you come to class every day, do your work conscientiously, ask questions when you don't understand something, have the confidence that you can do it if you just keep plugging along, you will learn these study skills and find that you *have* become a better student. Other students have been able to do it. And you can too.

It will not end there, though. In order to keep improving your skills so that you can become an even *better* student, you will have to keep practicing these skills in all the courses you take as you continue your career as a student. And, as you gain experience, you will modify the methods you are learning here and will develop your own personal methods of studying.

4. Since reading is such an important skill, let me go over one helpful method right here. This way you can have a head start on your reading skills, even before you start the course.

A commonly used name for this method is the *SQ3R* method.

S = Survey

This means you check over the whole book before you begin reading it. Look at the table of contents to see what the book is about. Then glance over the chapters, looking for the kinds of headings, diagrams, chapter-end questions they have. See whether there are little summaries at either the beginning or ending of the chapters. You should take only a few minutes to do this. The purpose is to *orient* you to the book. It is like looking at a map briefly to give you a feel for the new place you just moved to.

Q = Question

This means you are supposed to turn every chapter title into a *question*. For example, the title of a textbook in your new political science course is *The American Political Tradition*. Change this, in your mind, to "What *is* the American political tradition?" Now you are going to read the book with curiosity, seeking answers to a question.

As you will read in Chapter 2, one of the best motivations to get you going as a student is *curiosity*. Einstein said that he didn't have any special talent, that he was just tremendously curious about things.

Or, let's say the first chapter heading in that political science text is "The Founding Fathers: An Age of Realism"; you need to turn it into a question so that you can approach the chapter with curiosity, seeking an answer. You might turn the heading into "Who *were* the founding fathers? What *are* the founding fathers anyway? *Why* was this called an age of realism? What does the author mean by 'realism' anyway?" And so on. Thus, by turning the headings into questions, you can see that the chapter suddenly becomes something you want to jump into and search around in to find answers to satisfy your curiosity. (What if the questions do not arouse your curiosity because you aren't interested in the subject? Read Chapter 2 to find out!)

3R = R for Read, R for Recite, R for Review

R for Read

This means you go ahead and start reading now, but for the purpose of trying to find answers to the questions you have asked. Chapters 10, 11 and 12 will help you improve your reading.

R for Recite

Reciting, as used in the SQ3R method, is basically the same as the method I call the *Copy, Check, Correct* method (Chapter 4). Reciting, or *copying, checking, and correcting*, means that after you have read or studied a chapter or some material, you then try to recall it without looking at the book or the material. Can you remember the material you have just read or studied? Chapter 4 will teach you how to do this.

R for Review

This is a combination of the *copy, check, correct* method and the self-testing skills covered in Chapter 14. It helps you to nail down the material so that you have it secure in your memory. Chapters 4, 13, 17, as well as other parts in the book, help you understand how your memory works and how to use it to your best advantage.

Do **For Practice** on page 6.

All the questions in this **For Practice** are part of S (Surveying). Check your answers with your neighbor or in a small group in your class.

You are about to start on the important and challenging adventure of becoming the kind of successful student you have wanted to be. You ***can*** *be it!*

5. There are certain qualities of mind that you must have if you are going to be a good student. *You need to develop a mind that pays attention. That is, you need to develop a mind that thinks with precision, exactness, accuracy. Which means your mind needs to be able to focus sharply on the exact point.* You need to develop carefulness and mental discipline. Without these qualities of mind you will find information going in one eye and out the other. Or, if you are in a lecture, in one ear and out the other.

This course is going to give you the opportunity to develop these qualities. *But, most important, you yourself must consciously strive to be careful, precise, exact.* You need to brainwash yourself with such self-orders as: "I must be careful about this." "I must focus sharply on this and try to understand it exactly." "I must be sure to copy this accurately." If you are, for example, generally careless or a bad speller, you can even go so far as to painstakingly copy one letter at a time as you copy the words from the blackboard into your lecture notes. This can help you become more focused and careful.

6. Again, the book and your teacher cannot magically zap knowledge and clear thinking and mental discipline into you. The only way you can gain knowledge and learn skills and achieve success as a student is to constantly work on improving the quality of your thinking, of your

For Practice

Using this book, answer the following questions; then compare your answers with your classmates' answers.

1. What is this book all about? (To answer, look at the title and read the names of all the chapters.)

2. Is there any way to find out where a certain study skill is discussed in this book? (To answer, try to find out, for example, where you can find the skill of how to take tests. Where did you look to find out?)

3. How does this book get its information across to you? (To answer, see whether the author is presenting information to you or whether it is basically a workbook in which you do all the work to teach yourself? What will you do to check this out?)

4. Does this book have the latest information? (How will you find out? Where will you look in the book to find out very quickly and easily?)

5. Do you think you will like this book? Will you be able to understand it and learn from it? (How will you find out?)

mind. It may take hard work and may wear you out sometimes. But the reward will be worth it. Where do you want to be next year? In the same rut you are in now or functioning as a successful student? It is up to you. And you *can* do it.

7. Think positively! Look for all the good you can in the course, the teacher, the work. Be proud of yourself and the knowledge you are gaining, however slowly you may be gaining it! *This attitude will help you; a negative attitude will hold you back.*

C.   How to Take Lecture Notes: A Brief Introduction So That You Can Start Today

1. Draw a line down your notebook page so that you divide the page into two sections. Have about two-thirds of the page on the right side of the line and one-third on the left. Leave the left one-third blank until you get to Chapter 15 when its purpose will be explained and you will then begin to use it.

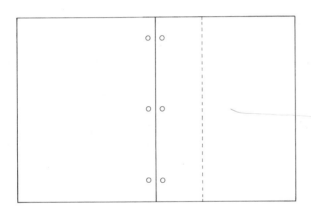

What should you write in your notes (in the right two-thirds of your note page)? First, put down a heading or title for each set of notes or each day's lecture. For example, if your teacher says she or he is going to lecture on how to take notes, you immediately write that down in your notebook and underline it. (See next illustration.)

Then you write down the following three sorts of things:

a.   Whatever the teacher writes on the board. (Copy this *exactly*; especially be sure that you copy the correct spelling of the words on the board.)

b.   Whatever the teacher repeats or emphasizes or says is important. You can write this in your own words; this translating what someone says into your own words is called *paraphrasing*. For example, your teacher might say, "It is very important to remember that you must focus your attention carefully and concentrate." You can write this in your notes in your own words: "Pay attention, concentrate, be careful!" In this *paraphrase* you have caught the teacher's meaning but said it in your own words.

c.   Whatever you think is important—you have to use your own judgment, which will increase as you gain experience. (Remember, you can paraphrase what the teacher says.)

In order to do the above you will need to pay careful and close attention. You will need to strive to be accurate, exact, precise. If you do not understand something or feel your notes are getting confused, *be sure to raise your hand and ask a question.*

You do not have to write in sentences. You should not try to write every word as you take down what the teacher is saying. You can have diagrams and arrows and circles, and your notes do not have to be perfectly neat—as long as somewhere in them are the three things listed above. *You should try to be orderly,* but getting down the three things is more important than trying to organize and outline and neatly write the notes as you take them in class. The space on

Leave one page blank. Don't be afraid to waste note paper!
↓

Write on only one page. This makes your notes easier to read.
↓

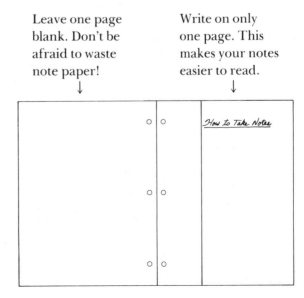

the left will be for the purpose of organizing your notes. More on that later in Chapter 15.

If the above had been a lecture, your notes might properly look like the example below.

Do *not* write your notes from the line on the left to the margin or edge of the paper on the right. Leave spaces and room so that you can add more information later when you read the textbook assignment on the same subject. (See examples on page 9.)

The reason is that as you read the textbook, you will want to go back to the *lecture notes* and check them. You may need to improve them with the help of the textbook. As you add to or correct your lecture notes, the notes will get rather cramped, with the additions squeezed in between the lecture notes. If you have not left enough space for the additions and corrections,

you may have to write between lines and sideways along the edge of the page. *As you add the new material from the text, be sure to include the page number from the text* so that you can go to the text for further reference later if necessary. (See example at the bottom of page 9.)

2. In this course the readings in the textbook and the material in the lectures will be closely coordinated. The purpose of this is to give you the opportunity to learn, in a controlled and perhaps simplified way, how to combine *textbook* and *lecture* materials. Once you begin to get the idea of how to combine these two kinds of materials and practice the skill, you will be better able to handle doing this process in other courses in which the text and lectures are not as well coordinated as here.

---

divide the page ⅓   ⅔

(She'll tell about this in Chap. 15— leave it blank for now

ENG. 090 - 10/30 - p. 1

TAKING NOTES (have a heading)

PAY ATTENTION!
Put in notes on:
1. What is on board (copy exactly)
2. What teach repeats or says is important
3. What I think important (don't need to be in sentences)

paraphrase = saying something in my own words

CAN BE MESSY!

If you write your class notes on loose pages and later put them in your notebook, or if you ever lend your notes, you may want to include the name of the course, the date, and the page. This way your notes can always be kept in order.

In courses in which you read the textbook *before* you have the lecture or in courses in which the textbook and lectures are quite different, you will need to combine the two materials differently. Chapter 19 will teach you how.

3. As you gain experience you will also see whether you are doing a good job at note-taking. The "Moment of Truth" will come after you get your first test back. Assuming the test was fair, you will be able to see whether your

Do it like this . . .

. . . not like this

TAKING NOTES

Be sure to take notes on:
1. What is on board
2. What teacher says

TAKING NOTES
Be sure to take notes on:
1. What is on board
2. What teacher says

divide the page ⅓ / 2/3

ENG. 090 - 10/30 - p. 1

TAKING NOTES (have a heading)

Add material from text (p. 8)
PAY ATTENTION!
Put in notes on:
1. What is on board (copy exactly) — Have page no. from text
2. What teach repeats or says is important
3. What I think important (don't need to be in sentences)

Be sure to leave spaces (p. 8)

paraphrase = saying something in my own words
CAN BE MESSY!

(She'll tell about this in Chap. 15—leave it blank for now)

This is how your notes will look after you have read the text and added information from your reading. Now your notes are as complete as you can make them. *The completion of your notes is one activity you do during your studying time.*

notes were adequate and complete or not. By checking the returned test against your notes, you will see where you slipped up and what you need to do to improve your note-taking. By doing this conscientiously after every test, you will learn the best way for *you* to take adequate and complete notes. *Only practice and experience and self-examination will help you find your own best way to take notes.* Don't expect to be an expert note-taker for a few years yet. It takes a lot of experience. But if you do your work well in this course and follow the directions carefully, paying attention, you will, without doubt, begin to gain the experience necessary for becoming a good note-taker and better student.

Remember, learn this method first, so that you can get the idea of exactly how to take notes. Then, later, as you gain experience, you can modify this method and develop your own, individual way of taking notes. (Flip back to Section B.3 to find an early remark on this topic.)

As you get better at taking notes, it becomes easier and can be done more quickly. So take heart.

4. Some students want to know whether using a tape recorder in class will help. No, it will not. In fact it will hurt if you depend on the tape recorder instead of on your note-taking ability. As you will see in later chapters, it is important for you to write down your notes and think about what you are writing as you write the notes. The important skill of *paraphrasing* is learned as you struggle to take complete and accurate notes. Also, the act of writing down the lecture (either exactly as given or in your own paraphrasing) starts the learning process. For this, just listening is not as effective as taking notes. At first, if you don't know how to take notes, just listening may seem very important. You are afraid that if you start struggling to take notes you will miss what the teacher is saying. But once you improve your ability to take notes (which is bound to happen if you keep trying), you will find that writing will improve your understanding in the long run more than passively listening to a lecture. Handicapped and foreign students, however, because of special circumstances, may need to use a tape recorder.

Now you must begin immediately to practice the skill of note-taking in this and in your other courses. If you practice conscientiously from now until Chapter 15, you will be ready and able to advance to the other aspects of note-taking that are presented in that chapter.

D. Asking and Answering Questions

You must ask questions whenever you do not understand what your teacher is saying. You must ask questions when you do not understand something in your textbook. *Unless you ask questions you will not learn.* (Flip your pages back to page 7 and reread the second paragraph of Section C, part 1c.)

Whom should you ask? Ask yourself first of all. When you ask yourself, you yourself will then begin *to use your mind* to search for the answer. Your own mind, excited by curiosity or wakened by need, will become actively involved. *This active use of your mind will make your intellect stronger and sharper.*

But how do you yourself search for the answer? If it is about the meaning of a word or concept, you can look up the word or idea in a dictionary or encyclopedia.

You can also look in the *index* of your textbook for other places in the book where the same word or idea is used. (An *index* is an alphabetical list of all the topics discussed in the book.) This list, or index, appears at the back of the book. However, not all books have an index. (Try the *table of contents*, at the beginning of the book, if there is no index. It won't be as helpful, but it may give you some indication of where a topic might be found.)

For example, what if you do not really understand what World War II was all about. Your reading assignment in your history textbook is not all that clear or complete. You are curious (the best thing that can happen to you!), or you feel you need to know more about this topic. Look up "World War II" in the textbook's index, if it has one. There you might find an entry like this:

World War II, 44-45, 90, 137, 205-20, 308

Now you just need to turn to all these pages and read about World War II.

Then try to put together in your mind all the different pieces of information you have just read. Flip back and forth several times between these pages; sit and think about how all these pieces of information fit together, what they all add up to, what you think about it all, etc.

This active mental work is an excellent way to exercise and increase the sharpness of your mind!

In this way you can teach yourself a specific topic and, in general, develop a sharper mind at the same time. Actively trying to find out answers for yourself is the best method of finding answers: you make yourself sharper and you are also in control of your own learning.

This method, though, can take time. There may be times when you need to understand a word, concept, or topic very quickly. (Quick is not necessarily good; but sometimes there is a time limit on you.) Then you can ask another student in the class or anyone else who knows the subject. Or you can always ask your instructor (see Section E below).

You can ask the teacher after class or right in class while the lecture is being delivered. You definitely should raise your hand to ask a question even right while the instructor is talking. The teacher will stop to answer your question. This will help you understand the material then and there. (Flip back to Section D and read the first paragraph.)

Chapter 6 on memory (especially pages 52–53) will explain why this last method (questioning while the lecture is going on) will help you get a good, clear understanding of the material. Chapter 6 will also explain that the page-flipping I'm asking you to do is good for studying and learning.

E. Problems with a Teacher?

1. What if your teacher talks too fast or too softly or you can't understand the lecture and, as a result, you are falling behind in your notes? Then you need to raise your hand and say so. It is perfectly all right to say, "Would you mind going a little slower?" Or, "Would you mind speaking a little louder?" Or, "Could you explain that last point again?" Or, "Could you go over that again?" (Flip back to the last two paragraphs of Section D above.)

You can be sure that there are always other people, at least one other person, in class with the same problem or question, and they will be glad someone is bringing it to the teacher's attention. But what if the teacher has a negative response? Or what if no one, including yourself, is willing to speak up in class? Perhaps you would feel more comfortable speaking to the teacher after class. You can also go to the teacher's office and explain what the problem is. *Make an effort to seek out your teacher.*

Should the teacher have a negative response? No, because the teacher is there to serve you. The teacher is in a service profession and you have every right to indicate whether or not you are getting that service.

If you are a serious and sincere student then the teacher ought to respect you and ought to respond in a positive way to your concern or problem or question. But what if, despite this, the teacher still offers you no help? The next step is for several students to speak to the teacher. If the teacher still will not help you, then you should to go the teacher's supervisor.

Another alternative is to consult with a counselor. A counselor might be willing to talk with your teacher for you and help resolve a problem between you and your teacher.

The key is to be polite, concerned, sincere, seriously interested in getting your education.

Most teachers are responsive and will be glad to help students or improve their own teaching methods. But teachers are not mind-readers, and unless students bring their problems to the teacher's attention, the teacher will not be able to help.

2. *In any case, you should take action as quickly as possible because you do not want to waste time. If you are falling behind, immediately seek help.* Besides talking to the teacher, you can also find classmates to study with or you can get a tutor. You are in control of your own life and must, in good time, take your own steps to improve your situation. (Where, in Section D, above, did you read about having control over your learning? Flip back and find that remark.) For example, you are not helping yourself if you wait until mid-quarter to go to the teacher and say that you stopped understanding the first week of school and have been behind ever since. Do not stew and worry and see time and opportunity slipping away. It is up to you to help yourself as quickly as possible.

F. What If You Are Absent?

If you are absent from class (which you should be only if you are very ill or some emergency or tragedy has occurred), then you must be sure to get notes from a classmate. While the teacher will be glad to explain some things to you, you can't expect the teacher to give a fifty minute replay of the entire class that was missed.

You should get the phone number of at least two classmates whom you can call for homework assignments.

Getting an education is serious business. You won't get your education if you're not serious about it.

G. Your Own Shorthand Technique and Abbreviations

Because you may have to take a lot of notes in a short time you will find it useful to develop your own set of abbreviations and your own speedwriting or shorthand technique. Here is an example of my personal technique (these are notes I recently took on a speech about current legislation):

> gov. may call bk.
> for 20 days — start
> prob 14th / only bills
> out of comm. of origin
> + those w/ # ⟶
> 3/4 wl be dead

Translation: Governor may call (legislators) back for twenty days. (They will) start probably on the 14th (of February). Only bills (passed) out of (their) committee of origin and those with money (attached) (will be considered). Then three-quarters (of the present bills) will be dead.

These are all abbreviations I have developed for my own use (gov., bk., prob., com., w/, $, wl). When I am really in practice I write using mainly consonants (I rt sng mnly cnsnts)!

Do **For Practice.**

H. Concentrating

1. If you have a problem keeping your attention focused on your work you have a serious problem!

You can overcome this problem, but it will take effort and determination.

When you have trouble concentrating you are not able to get the most out of your studying. Your memory will not work well. You will take longer than you should to get your work done and will have less to show for it.

2. What causes lack of concentration? There could be several reasons. If you are not interested in the subject, if it is really boring to you, then your mind will wander to more interesting subjects.

If you have a long history of letting your attention wander, then you have a bad habit to break.

Are you afraid you are stupid or a failure as a student? If you have this fear, then you may really be holding back from trying hard enough. Because if you try hard and still fail, you may fear you have to face the fact that you are a failure. People who fear this often subconsciously hold themselves back from studying or trying hard. This way they can avoid having to face thinking of themselves as failures. Or conscious thoughts of fear, thoughts that they might fail, that they are stupid, keep coming to mind, interfering with their work. These people are, in fact, *not* stupid. And if they have failed before as students, they can change this. You, if you have had failure as a student, can change failure into success. (Also see Chapter 3, Section B.3.)

But you must have good concentration before you can become a successful student.

3. Fortunately, the main method depends on your own will power and determination. You have the ability to control your own mind by saying to yourself: "Go away, negative thoughts! I

For Practice

Rewrite the first paragraph of Section F, "What If You Are Absent?" (above), in your own shorthand technique, using different abbreviations (*u* instead of *you*, for example) and symbols (use an arrow—as in the example in Section G above—for *then*), etc. Be inventive!

am going to succeed. I just have to keep my two feet going, one step at a time." Or, "Go away distracting thoughts. I will think about you later." You can even set a time, an hour, when you will just sit and concentrate on the thoughts or daydreams or ideas that are trying to get your attention during your study time. "I will stop studying at 3:00 and daydream about my plans for the weekend. Then at 3:30 I will start studying again." (Above you read about controlling your own learning and your own life. Here you are reading about controlling your own thoughts. For practice, quickly flip back to the remarks about your control over your life and learning.)

It is fortunate that the cure rests in yourself. Because you are in control of your own life. No one else but you is in control of your own thoughts. They are under your own control—but you must learn to practice and use that control. It is there for you if you will take it.

No, it is not easy. It will not happen overnight. But slowly, day after day, you can get better and better at it. (You may have some backsliding. That is natural. The main thing, though, is just to try to keep moving ahead.)

If the subject is boring, try to take more interesting courses. Or can you find a way to make the topic more interesting? Perhaps if you start to ask questions about the subject or the assignment? (Flip back and review the Q part of the SQ3R method, page 5. Also flip to page 10 and reread the second paragraph of Section D.) Try to stir up your natural curiosity. That would be the best thing—because natural curiosity is the best motivator (see Chapter 2) and the best creator of concentration.

I. Procrastinating

Procrastination is another common problem. If you can schedule your time (Chapter 3), use positive thoughts and directions for yourself (as for improving your concentration), and do one little step or part at a time (instead of worrying about the whole task before you), you can reduce your procrastinating. If you find procrastination ruining your chance for success, a college counselor will be glad to work with you further. Don't procrastinate about trying to overcome this problem!

Your Summary

Go back over this chapter and write here the most important, interesting, or helpful things you learned. You should write down the page number(s) for each item you list:

Items   *Page Number(s)*

For example:

Ask questions during class   7, 10, 11

Compare your list with your classmates' lists.

CHAPTER 2

Motivation

A. You Must Have Motivation

Do you know what the word "motivation" means? It is from a Latin word meaning "to move." It is like our word "motor," which is also from this same Latin word.*

Imagine a car without a motor. It will not be able to move. You can turn the key and pump the accelerator and have big expectations—but if there is no motor, the car is not going to get anywhere. People are the same way. They can open their eyes in the morning. They can yawn and stretch and plan to get up and go to school and study and get all their work done. But if there is no motivation, a person can turn over and go back to sleep. Without motivation a person can skip classes, forget to do homework, or do a half-hearted job, and, in general, not get anywhere.

For human beings, a motivation is a purpose or goal or interest or determination. It is anything that gets you up and going, doing and trying and making an effort and not giving up. It is your driving force.

If you don't have a motivation (a driving force) for being in school, for doing well in school, then you are not going to do very well. You may even drop out. But if you have a motivation, a motor to keep you going, nothing can stop you.

B. There Are Many Different Motivations

1. Probably the strongest motivation is curiosity or natural interest. That is, if you have a curiosity about something, you will *want* to know more about this something; and with your own free will and with excitement and a natural interest, you will get yourself going to find out

*See diagram on page 119, to see how English words come from the ancient Latin language.

more about this something. (Flip back to page 5 and reread the second and third paragraphs of Section B, part 4, about "Q." Also flip back to the last section of Chapter 1. Can you find there other references to the power of curiosity?)

For example, let's suppose your father owns an accounting firm. He has told you that if you get a degree in accounting he will take you into the firm and some day you will become a partner. Your future will be assured. So you go to college and major in accounting. But you discover that you have no curiosity about accounting. You find it hard to pay attention in class. You fall asleep while you are studying. You have to force yourself to go to school every day.

Then your advisor tells you that you have to take a science course as a requirement for graduation. Suppose you take an ecology course. Suppose you find yourself interested in the subject. Suppose you start feeling excited and curious about it. You find the lectures interesting. You are eager to sit down and read your homework assignments. You even feel like going to the library and doing some extra reading. You have to do a research paper and you really want to know the answer to your research question.

Obviously accounting is the wrong field for you. What should you do?

2. Suppose you also have the motivation of ambition. That is, you have a powerful motivation to be rich and to own your father's accounting firm. You like the life style that will be possible if you do this. You have a strong desire to own a big house and an expensive car. You like to buy good clothes in the best stores, and if you become an accountant and go into your father's firm you will be able to have all these things. In this case, you will probably have a strong enough motivation (ambition) to force yourself to get through the accounting program and graduate. You will probably have a strong

15

enough motivation to spend your life as an accountant and as an accounting firm executive. But how will you spend your weekends and vacations? What will you run to do with your free time? Obviously, your love for the study of ecology will continue to interest you. It can become a hobby which you will take very seriously.

3. On the other hand, if you do *not* have a strong motivation of financial ambition and would be content to work as an ecologist (perhaps never making a fantastic salary), then you would be wise to give up the idea of being an accountant and, instead, major in ecology. If you are not ambitious for wealth and a high standard of living then you can decide to follow your curiosity and interest. You will be content with a lower income because you will be happy in your field.

4. Another motivation is a sense of responsibility. Suppose your parents have scrimped and scraped for many years to put you through school so that you can have a better chance in life than they had. Or suppose you are married and must increase your earning power to help support your family. If you have a strong sense of responsibility you will be able to keep going in school and do a good job despite lack of great interest or curiosity. A strong sense of responsibility will be a powerful driving force; and though you may get exhausted and be overworked, you will keep plugging away until you finish your schooling. (If this is your situation, you will need to schedule your time very carefully in order to have time for school, study, the other job, your family. The next chapter will help you make a schedule so that you can do everything you have to do in the most efficient and effective way.)

If, on the other hand, you do have a responsibility to others but not a strong sense of responsibility, you may let people down. You may feel it just isn't worth it, and you may end up neglecting those responsibilities.

People with responsibilities who have a strong sense of responsibility to motivate them are often willing to sacrifice for the sake of those to whom they feel responsible. Clearly, such a person is determined to succeed. This type of person is hard working and usually can be counted on to be successful.

5. Competition is another motivation. If you are a person who wishes to be the best, to do better than others, to beat your own past performance, then you will have a driving force that will help you achieve the success you desire.

6. Some people love a good challenge. They are motivated to achieve something that others believed couldn't be done. If the task is difficult, they are motivated to roll up their sleeves and jump in to accomplish the task. People with the motivation to take up a challenge will work long and hard to win success.

7. For some people the desire to do an excellent job, just because they love to do a job well, is a strong motivation. They will not stop until every detail is correct, until everything has been accomplished, and accomplished in a polished and excellent way.

8. There are other motivations as well. For example, some people are motivated to improve their values, to learn new skills, to learn about the world, etc. You can also have several motivations at the same time. You can love a good challenge and also be competitive and also have a natural interest in the subject. Imagine the great job you'd do if you had all these motivations!

C. When You Have No Motivation

On the other hand, imagine yourself without *any* of these motivations. You are not curious or interested; you are not ambitious; you have no responsibility to others; challenges and competition don't excite you; you have no desire for excellence. What's going to keep you going, then? What happens when the sun comes out and you feel like going to the lake? Or when you wake up in the morning and feel a little tired? It's obvious, you are going to cut school. You are not going to study. You may even end up dropping out.

You need a motivation. You need a strong motivation. You need as many motivations as you can get. Your success depends on it.

D. Increasing Your Motivation

Are you motivated? What are your motivations? Think about it. I hope, for your sake, that you have at least one good motivation. If you don't have one, try to get one.

Do **For Practice** on page 18.

After you have completed the **For Practice,** compare your lists with your classmates' lists. Do you have enough motivation? Do you need more? If you do, how will you get it?

First, you might try taking different courses until you find a subject that interests you. This sort of shopping around is what the first two years of college and your distribution requirements allow you to do. Make good use of this opportunity by consciously looking for a subject that interests you. Once you find a subject you like, you will be more motivated to get the other requirements out of the way so that you can concentrate on your area of interest.

Second, see whether you can stir up a sense of competition with yourself. Can you do better on the second test than you did on the first? Can you do the next paper better than you did the previous one?

Or try this: do you or your friends have the belief that you are a poor student? Perhaps you can rise to that challenge and prove to them and to yourself that you *can* be a good student. You might try making a secret pact with yourself to improve. And imagine how proud you and your friends or family will be when you do come through with better grades and more knowledge.

Or perhaps you can start thinking about where you are going to be in five years. Will you be working for the minimum wage in a dead-end, boring job? Or will you be making a good salary and looking forward to promotions and even better salaries? Maybe you will be making a contribution to some group of people or in a certain area of life.

E. Your Own Efforts
Can and Will Make a Difference!

Studying takes time and effort. Without motivation, without a driving force, you will not stick to your schedule; you will not get the work done; you will cut class; you will not learn. But with a driving force, with a good motivation keeping you going, you can do anything!

If you are doing poorly, face it squarely. Don't fool yourself by blaming others. Scold yourself by saying to yourself, "I'm not taking this seriously enough." Or, "My motivation is weak." Or, "I am responsible for my own success or failure. I'm as good as anyone else and it is up to me not to let myself down."

Be proud of what you know—use your new knowledge in your own thinking and in your conversations and actually impress people with what you know. This can also be a motivation.

Set your goal and stick to it. You are responsible for your own life and what you do with it. (Do you remember the remarks above on your control over your own life? Do you see the connection between those remarks and *this* section? Flip back if your memory is not *fully* clear about the earlier remarks.)

F. Motivational Pep Talk

Yes, this *may* be difficult. It may be difficult going back to school or just being in school.

It may be difficult disciplining yourself and paying attention and working hard.

But don't we all know that anything that is worth anything takes effort to get? What sense of accomplishment or achievement would you have if you didn't have to work for it?

If it's *too* hard, then you need to slow down, go back, catch up, or maybe get some special, extra help. Does your college have a Counseling Department? A Women's Center? A Veteran's Center? A Tutoring Service? They are all there to help you. That is their reason for existing! Look for them in the college phone directory or ask any teacher. Most of these extra services are offered free to students, whether they are taking one hour of class a week or a full load.

But if it's just plain *hard*—well, keep at it! You'll get it! Hard work never hurt anyone. And think of the rewards when you finally succeed (which you will).

And it will be worth more to you when you do succeed if you know it was a struggle and that you worked hard for it. Then you'll have something you can really be proud of—*something you made for yourself with your own effort.* (Look back to the last paragraph of Section E above.)

For Practice

List here all your motivations for being in school and also for taking this course:

For Being in School   *For Taking This Study Skills Course*

Your Summary

List here the most interesting, helpful things you learned in this chapter. Compare your list with your classmates' lists:

Items   *Page Number(s)*

CHAPTER 3

Scheduling

A. Finding the Time

1. All right, you have motivation. You have the driving force to go to classes, to study. But you also have a family, friends, other interests, perhaps another job. How are you going to attend to all these areas of your life and be sure you spend enough time on each? You wake up one morning in a panic. You have a test in two days, yet you can't see how you can find the time to do extra cramming because you have to work at your job every afternoon after classes. Your spouse or friends have plans for that evening and you have committed yourself to joining in with them. The next few days loom as days of anxiety, unhappiness.

And, worse, you seem to find yourself getting into this kind of mess a lot of the time. Although you are motivated to study, you find it difficult to arrange enough time to sit down and do the amount of studying you want and need to do. There are so many other tasks and responsibilities to take care of. You have to drive your children to school. You can't completely neglect your friends. You have to shop, clean, do the laundry, and run errands for your elderly parents. And so on and so forth.

The answer is to schedule your time. That is, you need to decide when you are going to do what and for how long. Then if you stick to your schedule, you will have time to do everything you want to do. You will be in control of your life and your time. That is, by thinking carefully and planning ahead, you can make the best use of your time and energy and eliminate a lot of needless anxiety about getting everything done. With a well-thought-out schedule, you *will* be better able to do everything you have to do.

2. Students have seven or eight activities in their lives: (a) class; (b) studying; (c) eating; (d) sleeping; (e) traveling; (f) relaxing; (g) other tasks and responsibilities (including family, home, etc.); (h) other job (if there is one).

Every one of these seven or eight activities is important enough to provide adequate time for. It is obvious that a student must schedule time for class, for study, for travel to and from school, for another job if there is one, for other tasks and responsibilities (family, home, etc.). Perhaps it is not so obvious why you need to schedule time for eating, for sleeping, for relaxing.

About eating: unless you eat properly and regularly you are not going to have the energy to keep up with all that you have to do. You probably have the belief that eating is important—but do you pay attention? Do you grab a quick-eat, take-out lunch on the run? Do you have three cups of coffee for breakfast? This is not going to provide you with the physical well-being you need to do well. You will feel better and function better if you make sure you have time to eat and if you eat sensibly.

About sleeping: not everyone needs eight hours of sleep, but this is approximately the amount of sleep most people need. Perhaps you are an exception. Perhaps you have been sleeping for six or even four hours a night for the last ten years and always feel well rested. However, if you are like most people, if you get less than eight hours of sleep you are fatigued, unable to do what you have to do. Students often cut back on their sleep when work begins to pile up. A test the next day and you haven't studied? Should you stay up all night? A paper due and you don't have it done? Should you go to bed later and get up earlier? No, don't solve your poor scheduling by cutting down on your sleep. Good scheduling will help you to do all your work and also get your proper amount of sleep.

About relaxation: not only does all work and no play make you dull, it also depresses you, wears down your morale, depletes your energy,

19

makes you feel sluggish, restless, sorry for yourself. Is it really important not to be depressed, to have good morale, to be full of energy, to feel refreshed? You can answer that question yourself. Schedule time to take care of your need to refresh yourself. You need it!

3. How much time should a person spend on these different activities? Specifically, how much time should be spent on studying? If you intend to do a good job with your courses, you need at least one or two hours *every* day to study for *each* class. When you get into the later chapters and see more specifically what studying involves, you will understand that a lot of time *is* needed if you are to do justice to yourself, if you are to get the most out of your educational opportunity and do your best as a student.

If you spend less than this amount of time you will be just touching your subject lightly and will do either a poor or mediocre job. You will not be able to learn your subject thoroughly.

4. If you are a full-time student, you must think of school *as a regular full-time job* requiring at least eight hours a day, just as any full-time job requires. You will be in class approximately three hours a day. Then you will need three to six hours a day out of class to study. Sometimes you may need more or less, but this is the average. Full-time students also often need to study several hours on the weekend.

If you are a full-time student and have a full-time job outside of school besides, it is just the same as having two regular full-time jobs. You are going to run yourself ragged if you try to put in the effort to do well at both jobs. I always advise full-time students with a full-time outside job to cut down on their course load and take only one course a quarter, two at the most. Some students, nevertheless, insist on continuing with these two full-time jobs, and they manage to survive. But it is always at a cost to their family or personal life or health.

I have never yet met such a person who was not tired most of the time, running on little sleep, with almost no family life or relaxation, and under heavy tension. If you have to live this way, then of course you must. But if you can find a way to make one of your full-time jobs a part-time job, you will be better off.

5. What would a typical, good schedule look like? It would look like Schedule I.

But what if you also have a part-time job for four hours every day? How would you fit this into your schedule? What activities would you cut down on to make room for these four hours? What if you have a full-time job for eight hours every day? When will you study? When will you relax or get to spend time with your friends and family? When will you eat? How much time will you be able to sleep? See Schedule II for an example of a schedule for a person with a part-time job.

This person with a part-time job has no time for relaxation and only 1 hour a day for other tasks, including spending time with the family, except for eating breakfast and dinner with them. This person can spend only 4½ hours a day for study. If extra study is required this person will have to do something like cut down on sleep and/or eating time or else not do the extra, needed study.

The first two schedules help those people arrange and control their time. By having a schedule they can make the best use of their day so they can be sure to get as much as possible done. Unfortunately, many students do not schedule their time. As a result, their day can typically go like Schedule III.

Which of the three schedules reflects the student's understanding that being a full-time student is indeed a full-time job in itself and needs to be taken seriously as such? Which schedule(s) make(s) the most efficient and effective use of time?

Do **For Practice** on page 22.

6. Of course there can be many variations in scheduling. No two people's schedules need to be the same. Each person has his or her own class schedule, family obligations, travel time, etc. Everyone does not have to take classes in the morning and study in the afternoon. In Schedule I, for example, the student arranged for study at 11:00; this gave the student only three hours to study in the afternoon. This student thought it best to break up her study time in this way. Another student might want to study at 9:00, go to class at 10:00, study at 11:00, go to class at 12:00, etc. Each person has to work out a

Schedule I

7:30– 8:00	Get up and get ready
8:00– 8:30	Eat
8:30– 9:00	Travel to school (park and get to class)
9:00–10:00	Class
10:00–11:00	Class
11:00–12:00	Study in Library
12:00– 1:00	Eat
1:00– 2:00	Class
2:00– 5:00	Study in school library
5:00– 5:30	Travel home
5:30– 9:00	Other tasks at home, dinner, relaxing with family
9:00–11:00	Extra study if needed or relaxing or other tasks
11:00–11:30	Get ready for bed
11:30– 7:30	Sleep

This is a 9-5 job. There may even be some work that has to be taken home.

What you do at this time can be decided on a daily basis, according to need. If extra study is needed, that will have first priority.

Time Spent Chart

Sleep:	8 hours
Eat:	2½ hours
Travel:	1 hour
Class:	3 hours
Study:	4–6 hours, as needed
Other tasks or relaxation:	4–6 hours, depending on study needs
	24 hours

Schedule II

7:30– 8:00	Get up and get ready (other tasks)
8:00– 8:30	Eat
8:30– 9:00	Travel to school
9:00–10:00	Class
10:00–11:00	Class
11:00–12:00	Class
12:00–12:30	Eat
12:30– 1:00	Travel to work
1:00– 5:00	Work at other job
5:00– 5:30	Travel home
5:30– 6:30	Dinner
6:30–11:00	Study
11:00–11:30	Get ready for bed (other tasks)
11:30– 7:30	Sleep

Time Spent Chart

Work:	4 hours
Sleep:	8 hours
Eat:	2 hours
Travel:	1½ hours
Class:	3 hours
Study:	4½ hours
Other tasks:	1 hour
Relaxation:	0 hours
	24 hours

Schedule III

7:30– 8:00	Get up and get ready (other tasks)
8:00– 8:30	Eat
8:30– 9:00	Travel to school
9:00–10:00	Class
10:00–11:00	Class
11:00–12:00	Relax
12:00– 1:00	Eat
1:00– 2:00	Class
2:00– 6:00	Other tasks, relaxing, traveling
6:00– 7:00	Eat
7:00– 9:00	Study
9:00–11:00	Relax
11:00–11:30	Get ready for bed (other tasks)
11:30– 7:30	Sleep

Time Spent Chart

Sleep:	8 hours
Eat:	2½ hours
Travel:	1 hour
Class:	3 hours
Study:	2 hours
Other tasks or relaxation:	7½ hours
	24 hours

For Practice

What do your days look like? Using the format of the above schedules, write down what you did yesterday. Then add up the hours in a *Time Spent Chart*. Do this to see how you use or misuse your own time.

Your Schedule Yesterday:

Hours   *Activities*

Got up and got ready (other tasks)

Time Spent Chart

Sleep:	____hours
Eat:	____hours
Travel:	____hours
Class:	____hours
Study:	____hours
Relax:	____hours
Work:	____hours
Other tasks:	____hours
	24 hours

Now compare this schedule with your classmates' schedules.

schedule according to his or her own preferences, needs, and situation.

Remember, a schedule should not be an inflexible straitjacket. It should only be a guideline for you so that you can better control your life.

What courses are available at what hours will also help determine when the student will have classes. Then, if a student has children coming home from school at 3:00, that student may have to do all his studying in the early afternoon and later in the evening so that he can be home attending to the children from 3:00–9:00.

Yet, again, some students may have only fifteen minutes of travel to school. Others may have to travel for an hour. Each student has to create a schedule that is *realistic* for him or her, depending on his or her own particular situation and needs.

It does no good to sit down and make up a beautiful schedule if it is not *realistic* for you. *You* are going to have to follow *your* schedule to get the good out of it. Therefore, you have to think carefully of what you can realistically do at what time and for how long. Take into consideration all the seven or eight activities listed above. Taking time to plan out a *realistic* schedule will repay you with increased efficient use of your time.

It will also cut down on your anxiety and that horrible feeling that your time is slipping away and you aren't getting everything done.

7. There is another important consideration to take into account when you build your schedule so that it is realistic for you. That is, are you a day person or a night person? Most people are either day people (functioning best early in the morning and needing to go to bed early) or night people (functioning best late at night and needing to sleep late in the morning).

What kind of person are you? When are you at your *peak energy level?* Do you like to go to sleep at 10:00 P.M. and get up at 6:00 A.M.? Or maybe, if you had your druthers, you'd even prefer to go to bed at 9:00 P.M. and get up at 5:00 A.M. Are you full of energy and ready to do some work, with good concentration, at 5:00 or 6:00 A.M.? Then, you are a day person and should build your schedule accordingly.

For an example, see Schedule IV.

Schedule IV (for a day person)

5:00–5:30	Get up and get ready (other tasks)
5:30–8:00	Study
8:00–8:30	Eat
	etc.

Or, are you a night person who just starts getting your highest energy up after midnight? Schedule V is an example of a schedule which would let you make the best use of your own natural inner clock or peak energy level if you are a night person.

Schedule V (for a night person)

11:30–noon	Get up and get ready (other tasks)
12:00–12:30	Eat
12:30– 1:00	Travel to school
1:00– 2:00	Class
2:00– 3:00	Class
3:00– 6:30	Travel home, other tasks, relax, eat
6:30– 7:00	Travel to school (two nights a week)
7:00– 9:30	Class (two nights a week)
9:30–10:00	Travel home
10:00–10:30	Eat
10:30–12:00	Other tasks, relax, extra study if needed
12:00– 3:00	Study
3:00– 3:30	Ready for bed (other tasks)
3:30–11:30	Sleep

This schedule shows you how a night person might organize his or her time for maximum efficiency, effectiveness, and realism.

Of course you may not be able to go this far because you may have to accommodate yourself realistically to your family, other job (if you have one), and the scheduled course offerings at your college. But what could be more self-defeating than for a morning person to try to study at night or for a night person to try to take classes at 8:00 or 9:00 in the morning? You probably know your own time clock, your own energy peak times. Build your schedule as realistically as you can so that you, as you individually are, can follow it with as much natural ease as possible. In this way you will be able to make the best

of the kind of person you are. It will make life a lot easier for you.

If it is impossible for you to go as far as Schedules IV and V suggest (because of family responsibilities or another job or scheduled course offerings at your college), then at least be aware of what kind of person you are. Try to build your schedule, if not perfectly, then as compatibly as possible with your own peak energy level.

Schedules can and should be as individual as the people using them, within the bounds of each person's own life situation.

Within these bounds, however, you can find ways to arrange your time so that you can realistically function to your own best advantage.

8. Research suggests that reviewing or looking over your work just before you go to sleep helps you remember it better. You might want to schedule time for this study activity before you go to bed. Perhaps in the one-half hour you schedule to "get ready for bed" you can go over once more the material you studied that day.

9. Schedules I and V provide for an activity called "extra study if needed." Schedules I, III, and V have a certain amount of time scheduled for "other tasks" and "relaxing." This is the time that you can use for studying if you get off schedule for some reason during the day or have to do some extra studying. In other words, schedules should have a certain amount of *flexibility* built into them. (If you have another job, however, your schedule will not be very flexible. This will be unfortunate should you get off schedule.)

For example, suppose you usually study for one hour after you come home from school before dinner. You schedule one-half hour for driving home. Then on a particular day you get a flat tire and it takes you two hours to get home. As a result you miss that hour of study before dinner. But you have "extra study if needed" scheduled in for later that evening. This is when you can catch up on the study you missed earlier in the evening when you got off schedule.

Thus, instead of losing that hour and worrying, you can easily fit an hour in later into your *flexible* schedule.

Do **For Practice** on page 24.

For Practice

Keeping all the above in mind, now make up a schedule for tomorrow. Then, tomorrow, try to follow your schedule as exactly as you can.

Your Schedule for Tomorrow:

Hours (to ½ hour)   *Activities*

Get up and get ready (other tasks)

Time Spent Chart (to ½ hour)

Sleep:	____hours
Eat:	____hours
Travel:	____hours
Class:	____hours
Study:	____hours
Relax:	____hours
Work:	____hours
Other tasks:	____hours
	24 hours

Now compare this schedule with the one you made on page 22 and with your classmates' schedules.

You will discover for yourself that you *can* be in control of your own life and time. If you have never made and used a realistic schedule then you will be impressed with the value of one. It may be hard at first to follow it, but if you keep working at it, the rewards will be great. Once you determine to be self-disciplined in order to make the most efficient and effective use of your time you will find yourself feeling more relaxed, more in control, and doing better in school.

10. So far we have been talking only about *daily* schedules. Now we are going to talk about *weekly* schedules. A weekly schedule is more useful than a daily schedule because it allows you to have a larger overview of your time. In the previous sections you have learned how to create a *realistic, flexible* daily schedule. You can now use what you have learned to create a more useful *weekly* schedule.

A weekly schedule does not have to have every minute accounted for. You basically need to fill in only time for class, studying, eating, sleeping, and other jobs or special activities, if any. If you want to you may, of course, fill in specific times for travel, relaxation, and other tasks. This is going to be your own schedule and you should create it in a way that will make it the most useful for *you*. Schedule VI is an example of what one person's weekly schedule might look like.

The blank spaces in Schedule VI are for "other tasks and responsibilities" or "relaxing."

There are some problems with this schedule. How would you advise this person in order to help her improve the schedule? Come up with one piece of advice for improving this schedule before you read on.

Do you notice, for example, that on Wednesday and Friday this person studies and reviews only one and one-half hours (8:30–9:00 A.M. and 11:00–12:00)? Wednesday's schedule could be improved if she changed the bowling to another night.

This person, also, has not scheduled any time for studying on the weekend. In order to provide for a realistically flexible schedule, she ought to write in "extra study if needed" for at least two hours on both Saturday and Sunday.

Schedule VI

Hour	Monday	Tuesday	Wednesday	Thursday	Friday	Saturday	Sunday
7:00	Get up Eat	Get up Eat	Get up Eat	Get up Eat	Get up Eat		
8:00	Travel Review	Children's Carpool	Travel Review	Children's Carpool	Travel Review		
9:00	English	English	English	English	English		
10:00	Math	Math	Math	Math	Math		Church
11:00	Study	math lab	Study	Study	Study		↓
12:00	Eat	Eat	Eat	Eat	Eat		
1:00	Biology	Study	Biology	Study	Biology		
2:00	↓	↓	↓	↓	↓		
3:00	Children's Carpool	↓	Children's Carpool	↓	Children's Carpool		
4:00		Travel		Travel			
5:00							
6:00	Eat	Eat	Eat	Eat	Eat		
7:00							
8:00			Bowling				
9:00	Study	Study	↓	Study			
10:00	↓	↓		↓			
11:00	Sleep	Sleep	Sleep	Sleep			

But the worst thing about this schedule is that this student doesn't have enough time scheduled for study. On only two days are there more than four hours of study. Count up the hours for study each day. Can you see that she is not spending enough time during the week on studying?

Clearly this student is a responsible parent and is spending time with the children. She is also trying to live a well-rounded life, setting aside time for bowling and for relaxing and doing other tasks during the week and on the weekend. Obviously, she has not fully understood that being a full-time student is a full-time job. She probably would not have wanted to take a regular full-time job because she knew she didn't have eight hours to devote to a full-time job Monday through Friday because of the responsibilities at home with the children.

Yet she is trying to be a full-time student. She is probably not going to do very well in school with this schedule. But if this person has a strong motivation to succeed then she will have to revise this schedule or, if that is impossible, plan a better schedule for the next quarter. Her next quarter's schedule might look like Schedule VII. Identify the improvements that have been made from Schedule VI.

This student has improved her scheduling in several ways. For one thing, she has scheduled all the classes in the morning which allows for more *regular* study time in the middle of the day. Perhaps that is when she has a lot of energy and can study well. This person has also eased the carpool problem by doing the driving every morning, leaving more free time in the afternoon. As a result, there is a *regular* time for study every afternoon instead of carpooling the children three afternoons a week. This person has also decided to study while eating, thus providing four to five hours of study every day at school. She has changed bowling to a day in which there has been sufficient time scheduled for studying. She has also scheduled in time for "extra study if needed" during the time that otherwise would be spent with the family. Thus, sometimes one has to be prepared to make some sacrifices in order to get a job done. In the first schedule, studying was sacrificed a great deal to family responsibilities. Here, family time is slightly sacrificed for study. Another alternative would have been to drop a course and become a part-time student.

These are the sorts of decisions a person has to make when trying to do two jobs well. In this person's case, she is trying to do the jobs of full-time parent and full-time student. Some painful and difficult decisions have to be made, and compromises are often the only way to solve such a problem.

In other words, this person is demonstrating a more serious commitment to being a successful student. Her schedule is getting more full, more *regular,* more disciplined. With this new schedule, this person has significantly increased her chances of being a success as a college student.

Do **For Practice** on page 28.

11. There are many advantages to a *weekly* schedule. One major advantage of having a *weekly* schedule is that everything is all laid out for you so that, at a glance, you can see what you are doing, what needs to be done, and when. This kind of long-range schedule also allows you to accommodate yourself to a time-consuming emergency or unexpected change of plans. With a *flexible* daily schedule you can often find another place *in the day* to fit in at least one extra hour of study. But what if the emergency took

up your whole evening? A *daily* schedule could not absorb that much missed time.

For example, your friend is in a serious accident and you have to take him to the hospital and wait there with him. By doing this you lose three hours that you had scheduled and definitely need for study so that you can keep up with your classes. You get back home at 12:00, which is after your scheduled bedtime. There is no way to fit in those three hours of needed study. There is a test coming up in a few days and a paper due in another class. You sit down on your bed and put your head in your hands and feel anxiety. You had counted on those three hours that evening to write the first draft of your paper. You wanted to get it out of the way so that you could have time clear to study for the test in the next few days. Now all those carefully made plans have been ruined.

But instead of panicking, you go over to your desk and look at your *weekly* schedule. You see that on the following day there are two hours scheduled in as "extra study if needed," and two more hours on the day after that are also scheduled in as "extra study if needed." You breathe a sigh of relief as you see that you can make up the lost three hours in the next two days. You get into bed, turn off your light, and sleep easy.

If you hadn't had a weekly schedule, you would not have been able to solve the problem of the lost hours so quickly and easily.

12. Another advantage of a weekly schedule is that you can fit in an unexpected assignment. Your teacher unexpectedly announces that you have a ten-page paper due in two weeks. If you did not have a weekly schedule, you would perhaps wait until two days before the paper was due, rush to the library, rush the paper, then cancel all appointments and stay up until 3:00 A.M. to finish it. You would have finished it, but you would know that you had not done as good a job as you could have done.

But with a weekly schedule, you know there is time that you have scheduled as "extra study if needed." You will be able to work on your research paper during those hours for the next two weeks. You will be able to do an excellent job. And you will not have to cancel any appointments or neglect your other interests or stay up all night trying to finish it on time.

Schedule VII

HOUR	MONDAY	TUESDAY	WEDNESDAY	THURSDAY	FRIDAY	SATURDAY	SUNDAY
7:00	Get up Eat	Get up Eat	Get up Eat	Get up Eat	Get up Eat		
8:00	Carpool	Carpool	Carpool	Carpool	Carpool		
9:00	History	History	History	History	History	Extra study if necessary	
10:00	French	French	French	French	French	↓	Church
11:00	Biology 2	Study	Biology 2	Study	Biology 2		↓
12:00	↓	↓	↓	↓	↓		
1:00	Eat and Study	Eat and Study	Eat and Study	Eat and Study	Eat and Study		
2:00							
3:00	↓	↓	↓	↓	↓		
4:00	Travel	Travel	Travel	Travel	Travel		
5:00							
6:00							
7:00							
8:00	Extra Study if necessary	Bowling	Extra Study if necessary	Extra Study if necessary			
9:00	Study	↓	Study	Study			Study
10:00	↓	Extra Study if necessary	↓	↓			↓
11:00	Sleep	Sleep	Sleep	Sleep			Sleep

13. With a weekly schedule you can also provide for a *regular* study time every day of the week. Studying regularly at the same time every day increases your ability to get into a routine that you will find easier and easier to follow. If you have scheduled study for every afternoon from 1:00 to 5:00, then after awhile you will have the mental attitude that afternoons are for study. Once you become used to this regular study time, you will find it quite normal and natural to study at this time every afternoon. Once you get used to studying at a regular time each day, it gets easier to resist the temptation to goof off.

14. In general, then, a weekly schedule that is *regular*, *flexible*, and *realistic* will help you use your time in the most efficient and effective way, giving you control over your life and reducing your anxieties and increasing your chances of success.

15. Your weekly schedule will be your master plan. You should tack it up on your wall and also have a copy in your notebook. The master plan weekly schedule, however, does not include all the specific tasks you have to accomplish each day. Therefore, you might also want to make yourself a little *list each day* of what you

For Practice

Below is a schedule for you to fill out. It should be your schedule for the rest of the quarter. Then, if you choose to follow it, you will surely increase your own chances of success. Do some very careful thinking and planning and reassessing before you fill it in. You might want to use some scrap paper to try a few different arrangements before you decide on the one that will be the best for you. When you are finished, compare your schedule with your classmates'.

Of course this schedule will not be written in concrete, never to be revised. No schedule is. You can always keep improving on it if necessary.

Remember that you don't want your schedule to be so strict that you get frustrated when you can't follow it exactly, minute by minute. *It is only a tool for you so that you can help yourself in your desire to make the best use of your time.*

Experience will teach you the best kind of schedule to make for yourself. For now, however, you should do these scheduling exercises so that you will know what schedules are and how to make them. Only after you have a clear and firm idea about scheduling will you be able to develop your own, individual scheduling technique.

specifically need to do. For example, you could list the specific course material, the number of the chapter, the exercise you need to do during the scheduled study hours. You could also include the doctor's appointment or the phone call to your friend about Friday night, etc. Here is an example of a student's *daily list:*

Need to study:
Chap. 9 in English (1:00–2:00)
Do exercises 12–20 in Math,
*   p.58 (2:00–3:00)*
Call Edith about Friday—
*   at 12:00 when I get*
*   out of class*
Pick up clothes at cleaners
*   on way home*
Work on first draft of
*   paper tonight*

This list could be made up the night before or in the morning. This list can be revised as the day goes on. For example, suppose you sit down to study at 1:00 and you feel an urge to do your math, even though your list suggested you might do it at 2:00. But the list is not written in concrete. The daily list is the most flexible of all the schedules.

Suppose after class at 12:00 you start talking with a friend and go have lunch and then go to study, and it isn't until 4:00 that you check your list and see that you forgot to call Edith. So call her then.

16. The *daily* schedule discussed early in this chapter was only to help you understand what a schedule is. You will have no need for such a daily schedule. It served its purpose as a learning tool and now we can forget about it.

What you do need is a *weekly* schedule. You should spend time and thought on creating your weekly schedule. And once you have made it, you should try to stick to it because it represents your best intentions and plans for yourself.

You can revise it, of course, if you can see a way to improve it as you try to follow it.

You may also find *daily lists* of specific tasks a useful aid along with your weekly schedule.

Now that you have learned about scheduling and how to make your own *realistic, flexible, regular* weekly schedule, no one can make you follow it. Only you can decide whether you will or not. It will be to your advantage to do so. (Look back to Section 14 above.)

B. What to Do with the Time

1. So far we have talked about two kinds of study: (a) regular study, (b) unexpected or long-range assignments. Regular study is scheduled to be done in the time called "study." The unexpected or long-range assignments can be done during the time scheduled as "extra study if needed." You want to use the "extra study" time for these extra assignments because your regular "study" time will be needed to keep up with the daily, regular assignments.

2. There is also a third kind of study to do. You do not have to schedule this type of study because it takes only a few minutes. This study is a quick review or read-over of the notes you take in class. You should *read over the notes right after you take them.* Stay in class for a few minutes and quickly read over the notes from that class. Also, when you go to class, get there early enough to spend a few minutes *reading over the notes you took the day before* in that class. If you do this review studying you are helping yourself remember the material better.

3. What about breaks? You are *not* expected to study for one or two hours straight without a break! But you do not have to schedule your breaks. You should take them as needed.

The reason for taking a break is to refresh yourself when you are getting restless, bored, tired, and are losing your concentration. When you feel this happening to you, say to yourself, "Guess I need a break." Take a break for no more than ten minutes. Get up and walk around. Relax. Do *not* get involved in some other activity. Do *not* go out and find some friends to sit down and chat with. You are taking a break but it is still study time.

Perhaps your break will consist of just turning and looking out the window for three or four minutes.

If you are going strong and are absorbed in your work you may find, to your surprise, that an hour has gone by and you never even thought of taking a break. Well, that means that you didn't need a break. Your concentration was strong. You did not need to refresh yourself.

When you study with that kind of concentration and absorption, you may find that you are exhilarated and refreshed by the very studying itself!

On the other hand, some people feel a need to take a break every ten or fifteen minutes. If you feel restless and are losing your concentration that frequently, then you ought to work on improving this because you are losing too much study time in breaks. One method is to schedule studying for only one-hour stretches. If you are this type of student then you should try to do it this way: go to class at 9:00, study at 10:00, go to class at 11:00, have lunch at 12:00, go to class at 1:00, study at 2:00, etc.

Taking breaks too frequently uses up your precious study time. It is also not helping you to increase and improve your concentration. Therefore, besides studying for only an hour at a time, you might also want to work more specifically and directly on learning how to take less frequent breaks. One way to do that is to say to yourself whenever you feel restless and want to take a break, "Let me study a few more minutes before I take my break." If you do try to study a few more minutes but are too restless to get anything out of it, then go ahead and take your break anyway. You do not want to force yourself because if you aren't getting anything out of your attempt to study then you are wasting that time. You might as well be taking the break. What you might do, though, in this case, is try to take shorter breaks.

The goal is to take fewer and shorter breaks. You want to strive toward the goal of being able to study with concentration for longer and longer periods of time, taking shorter and less frequent breaks. If you achieve this goal, then you will be using your study time to its maximum. (Page-flip to Chapter 1, Section H.)

Some people say that every student should study for about fifty minutes and then take a ten-minute break. But people are different from each other; people have different energy levels and attention spans. Moreover, the same person can work better on one day than on another or better with one subject than with another. Therefore, it is probably more realistic to say that each person should follow this direction: study as long as you can, then take a break if you feel the need to refresh yourself. But strive to take as few and as short breaks as possible. Do the best you can, trying not to waste your valuable study time. (Flip back to page 17 and reread Section E of Chapter 2.)

Of course, if you are not highly motivated and are taking courses that don't interest you, you may find yourself taking longer and more frequent breaks until you aren't studying at all. (Flip back to remarks on this same point in an earlier chapter. Find it before you read on—page-flipping is an extremely important skill to learn and practice.)

But if you are highly motivated and are taking courses that interest you, you will find it easy to take less frequent and shorter breaks, using your study time to its greatest effect.

4. What subject should you study first? Should you start your study with the hardest subject? The easiest? The one you like the best? The one you like the least? The shortest one? The longest one? The first one in the day? The last one?

No one can help you find the answer to these questions. Each person has to experiment and find his or her own best method. Some people sit down and just have a feeling of wanting to study a particular subject. Some people sigh and drag out the hardest one first—to get it out of the way. Some people prefer to breeze through the easy ones, leaving the harder ones for later—then they can settle down and spend all the rest of the study time on them.

The only rule here is to be sure you spend sufficient time on each assignment in order to do it completely and do it well. If you can't get all your work done in the allotted time for "study" then you may need to dip into your "extra study if needed" time. That is exactly what that extra time is for.

In later chapters you will learn what it specifically is that you should be doing during this study time. You will see then that you have a lot to do and need a lot of time to do it in!

C. Where Will You Study?

1. It is essential, first of all, to find *enough* time and the *best* time to study, as discussed above. But you also need to consider *where* you will do this studying.

What if your energy level is high early in the morning and you, therefore, realistically build a schedule that has you studying from 6:30 to 8:30 every morning? Except you forgot that your children are also up at that time talking, playing the radio, banging around in the kitchen. If you don't have your own study or a desk in your bedroom then you will be trying to study while they are interrupting you and breaking your concentration with their activity.

In this case, you need to schedule your study time either for when you are home alone or for when you can use the school or local public library or other quiet place where you can work undisturbed. You may be able to have a good place available only late in the afternoon, when your energy level is not high. That's life! Nothing's perfect. You will need to juggle the time and the place in order to try to find the best compromise you can. Maybe you will want to get up at 4:30 in the morning and study until 6:30. Maybe you will clean out a corner in your attic and put in a desk and lamp for yourself. There are all kinds of ways to solve these problems if you put your mind to it.

The major point is that there be as good a study place as possible at the best study time possible. Both the time and the place are important considerations for you to deal with when you build your schedule.

2. What makes a place good for studying? It is (a) available when needed; (b) convenient (you don't have to drive one-half hour to get there); (c) regular (same place every day); (d) quiet (recent research suggests that certain kinds of music may have a positive effect on studying—music you are familiar with and baroque music by such composers as Vivaldi and Bach; needless to say, music should not be blaring if you do play it while studying); (e) well lighted (not glaring, not

dim); (f) undisturbed; (g) comfortable (but not so comfortable that you are tempted to fall asleep!).

You may not be able to find the perfect place, the place that fulfills all these requirements. But find a place as close to the requirements as possible. If you can find such a place available at the times that are best for you to study, you are going to be able to study more effectively than if you can't fit the time and place together.

Go back to page 28 to your weekly schedule. Consider, now, where you will do the studying you have scheduled. Get a specific place in mind. Think about its availability at that time. Do you need to revise your schedule? If you do, carefully think of where you will study and when. Having provided for the best possible place at the best possible time, your schedule will be a good one for you. (Don't forget the desirability of as much *regularity* as possible in the time and place for study.)

D. Getting Ready to Study

1. All right, you have realistic time scheduled and you have a fairly good place. But before you sit down to get to work you had better be prepared so that you don't have to jump up every few minutes to do one thing or another.

a. Attend to your physical needs. (Bathroom? If you have just finished work, do you need a shower? Change of clothes? Something to eat? Nap?)

b. Psych your attitude up. ("Oh, great! In a few minutes I'm going to be able to study! I'm very eager to get my teeth into that subject!" You'll be surprised at the power of positive thinking. Brainwashing yourself is a good habit to get into for studying.)

c. Have your materials at hand. (Pen? Dictionary? Paper? Text? Notes?)

d. Warn your friends to keep away. (Your friends may be your worst problem. They may not be used to your being a serious student. They may feel threatened by it, be jealous of it, or just miss your good company. But you must tell them seriously that doing a good job in school is very important to you. Sincere friends will try to help you by keeping away when you are studying. A friend of mine who is a very serious student once showed me his schedule. I was scheduled in for 7:30 Friday night! It helped me see just how serious he was about keeping his life in order so he could succeed in school.)

2. You have the freedom to make a success of yourself. But in order to do this you need to put some order and organization into your own life. If you find yourself unable to accept the fact that you ought to have a schedule, then think very carefully about whether or not you are really ready to make a successful student of yourself. Perhaps the motivation isn't there.

If the motivation is there and you are filled with determination, then you will make the schedule and stick to it. Maybe you will not be able to do it very well at first, but as the quarters and years go by, you will do it better and better.

I'm not saying it's easy; I'm only saying it's necessary. The choice is yours.

E. Suggested Menu Items for Students in a Hurry

Breakfast:
1. Juice or fruit (keep a bag of oranges, bag of apples, bunch of bananas, canned or frozen fruit juice on hand)
2. 100% whole wheat or grain bread (a few slices of this kind of real wheat or grain bread is nutritious)
3. Eggs (boil a dozen and keep them in the refrigerator; they will last a week and are handy)
4. Coffee (if you must, but milk or herb tea is better—peppermint tea is good for the digestion; licorice spice tea is heavenly)

Lunch:
1. Sandwiches (as long as they are on your good bread)
2. Salad (this may have to be bought in the school cafeteria)
3. Fruit

Snacks:
1. Fruits, carrots, nuts, seeds, carob
2. A tasty concoction can be made by mixing peanuts, raisins, and carob drops together (make a big batch and keep at home in an air-tight container; then take baggiesful to school to munch on)
3. Health food type of candies (almost every store that sells candies now sells this type of goodie—look for ones without sugar)

Dinner:
1. Try to have at least one big meal each day. If you buy a canned ham you can eat slices and chunks of it hot or cold for a week. Buy a quantity of hamburger and make patties. Wrap each one separately and store in freezer for future use. These can be fried or broiled without defrosting. Also buy a pound of hamburger or a piece of beef (any cut) or a whole chicken (take out the bag of giblets). Wrap and freeze whole. Then, when you want to make dinner, take out one of the frozen items, unwrap and place in a shallow pan (with no salt, no spices, no butter or oil), and bake at 350° for 1½ to 2 hours, depending on size. The result will be delicious, and what could be easier?
2. An hour before the frozen roast is done, pop potatoes in the same oven. Be sure to pierce the skin with a fork so that the potato won't explode in the oven. (Yams and sweet potatoes are among the healthiest of foods!)
3. Vegetables or salad

Special Suggestions:
1. If you can acquire a taste for yogurt, it will do you a lot of good. It is nutritious and excellent for the digestion; if you have knots in your stomach and other uncomfortable feelings in your digestive tract, yogurt is soothing. Plain yogurt with cut-up fruit in it (canned or fresh) is a delicious treat. Many school cafeterias have yogurt and fruit so that you can prepare this for yourself at school.
2. Another health snack to have at home is a bowl of cereal. Put in a few tablespoons of unprocessed bran and/or wheat germ and raisins or cut-up fruit (with fruit you won't need sugar). Add some cream, if you like it, for a special treat.

F. Suggested Shopping List for Students in a Hurry

This shopping list should hold you for one or two weeks:

100% whole wheat bread (buy extra loaves and keep in refrigerator)
One to two dozen eggs (boil a dozen to eat during the week—keep in refrigerator)
Bag of apples
Bag of oranges
Bunch of bananas (you can also, if you have a blender, make milkshakes with bananas, milk, orange juice)
Raisins
Dry cereal (with little or no sugar and no additives or preservatives)

Unprocessed bran and wheat germ
Canned ham
Several pounds of hamburger (some you can make into patties to freeze and some you can freeze in chunks for "hamburger roast")
Different cuts of meat (even the cheap cuts will be good if you bake them frozen, as described above), whole chickens. If you are a vegetarian, buy tofu instead and cut it up in salads, put it in omelets, fry it in oil, cook it with vegetables, etc.
Bag of potatoes (white, sweet and/or yams)
Carrots, cucumbers, green peppers, lettuce, tomatoes, whatever salad makings you like
Peanut butter
Jelly
Salad dressing
Tuna fish
Mayonnaise
Butter or margarine
Can of peanuts or other nuts
Milk
Cream
Peppermint or other herbal tea
Carob drops
Seeds (sunflower, pumpkin, etc.)

In later chapters you will be learning about memorizing material. For example, if you had to remember this shopping list, how would you do it?

Do **For Practice** in next column.

How did you do? What method of memorizing did you use? Did you just try to repeat the items over and over until you thought you had stored them in your memory? If you used that method, how well did it work?

A better, more effective method for memorizing is to arrange the items into a certain order or pattern. After you have decided which new, different arrangement to use, and after you have written the items down in that new order or arrangement, you will find it easier to remember the items.

Suggestions: Put all the items in alphabetical order and try to remember them in that order.

Or put all the soft items in one list and the hard ones in another list. Then put all the ones on the soft list in alphabetical order and the same for the items on the hard list.

Or put them in the order in which you would place them in your kitchen, starting at the northeast corner of your kitchen and going

For Practice

Memorize the shopping list in a five-minute period. Use any method you wish for memorizing. After the five minutes are finished, put the list aside and see how many items on the list you can recall. Write them down; take two minutes for recalling and writing down the words. Then go back and look at the original list.

from top cabinets to floor cabinets, from the front of the cabinet to the rear, etc.

Or put them in the order in which you would eat them from the start of breakfast to the end of bedtime snack.

Compare your method of memorizing with your classmates' methods. Were any methods more effective than others?

All these different orders and arrangements are called "mnemonic devices" or memory tricks. ("Mnemonic" comes from the Greek word for "memory.") Each of the suggestions above is a different memory trick or mnemonic device.

Other mnemonic devices or memory tricks are famous ones, like "Thirty days hath September, April, June, and November; all the rest have thirty-one, except February, which has twenty-eight and in Leap Year twenty-nine."

You probably have some mnemonic devices of your own: Do you have a favorite recipe or do you have a certain way to change the oil in your car? Do you have a list in your head of the tools and materials you need and the order in which you use the tools or materials and the steps of the procedure? If you have such a list in your head, then that list is the mnemonic device you made up to help you remember how to do that procedure. The trick in studying is to *consciously* make up memory tricks to help you put facts, information, material in a certain order that, *because* it is tricky or orderly, makes it easy for you to remember the material. How would you memorize the recipe for making a "hamburger roast" (see "Dinner" in Section E, above)?

More about this in the next chapter.

Your Summary

List here the most helpful things you learned from this chapter. Then compare with your classmates' lists.

Items   *Page Number(s)*

CHAPTER 4

Your Memory

Proper Storage, Firm Storage, and the Copy, Check, Correct Method

A. Proper Storage

1. First of all, your memory always works perfectly. There is only one exception. Namely, there are some serious illnesses which can prevent the memory from working. But if you are in school, functioning, and are not under a doctor's care for some sort of serious illness, then your memory is probably in perfect condition.

But, you may ask, if my memory works perfectly then why can't I remember well?

Yes, it may seem to you that your memory is at fault. But here is good news. Your memory is not at fault. You yourself are at fault because you did not store material away in your memory *properly* and *firmly* in the first place.

2. The memory is like a bank vault or a library. It stores material until you want to retrieve it.

Let's say you have a bank vault. You want to store some material there for safekeeping. You have a thousand old photographs, some baby teeth, several diamond rings, a dozen gold coins, a hundred love letters from a number of different people, the mortgage of your house, and ten different insurance policies as well as term papers from all your high school and college courses. You go to your bank vault, open the door, and toss everything in at once and then slam the door.

Next month you want to retrieve one of the photographs. You return to the vault, open the door, and look inside. It is a big mess. In order to find the picture you want you will have to rummage through all the other stuff. You will probably have to give up.

You go home and your friend asks you where the picture is. You say, "I couldn't find it. I have a very bad vault."

But really, what you should have said was, "I couldn't find it. I didn't put all my things away in order and now I can't find anything anymore!"

This is how it is with your memory.

Or let's say you have a library. New books are arriving every day. Each day you take the new books and put them on the shelves in no particular order. In a week someone asks you for a specific book. You look at the shelves and scratch your head. You haven't the slightest idea where that particular book is. You know you had it. You know you put it on a shelf. But you can't remember where.

Do you say to the person, "I can't find it. These are very bad shelves"? Or do you say, "I can't find it. I didn't store these books in an orderly way. Now I can't find where I put anything"?

This is how it is with your memory. If you can't find something in your memory then it is your own fault because you did not store it away properly.

3. How do you store material *properly* in your memory? You do it in the same way you would store material properly in a bank vault or a library. You must figure out some orderly procedure and then file things away in categories or batches, putting like with like. In the vault, for example, you would put all the baby teeth in one place, all the letters in another, all the photographs in another, and so on.

Just as in a library you would put all the history books together, all the novels together, all the chemistry books together, etc.

Better yet, you could file things away even more carefully and precisely than that. You could put the photographs in some kind of order. For example, you could put all of Mary's

35

pictures in one pile, all of your parents' pictures in another pile, etc. Or you could file them by year, putting the oldest ones on the bottom and the newer ones, year by year, on top of them, with the newest ones on top.

And in the library, to make your books even more easy to find, you could arrange all the history books alphabetically by their titles or, if you preferred, by their authors' last names.

This is also what you must do with material you wish to store for safekeeping in your memory vault. You must arrange the material in some logical order. If you do this then the material will be stored *properly* in your memory and you will, later, be able to find material in your memory when you want it.

Then you will say, "I have a good memory." Actually, the truth will be that you have stored material *properly* in your memory so that you can retrieve it when you want it. The memory holds material for you. It can hold all the material you put into it but only in the form in which you put it in. If you add material in a helter skelter, disarranged, disorderly way, your memory will be containing a mess. The material may be there in your memory, but it will be unrememberable, unretrievable. You will try to remember it but you will find only confusion.

For example, you want to store in your memory the seven or eight items to include on a schedule. You want to store this material so that you will be able to remember it later for a test. What should you do in order to store this material properly so that you can remember it later? Yes, you need to put it in some sort of logical or orderly form.

4. What about arranging those eight items in chronological order (in time sequence from the first item you do to the last item you do)? That is, first you eat, then you travel, then you go to class, then you relax, and finally you sleep. This is a logical and orderly way to arrange those eight items. When you want to remember the eight items all you need to do is remember they are stored in chronological order. Then think of the first thing you do and you will remember "eat." And so on down the list.

We have just made a *mnemonic device*. As noted at the end of the previous chapter, "mnemonic" comes from the Greek word for "memory." A

"device" is a tool or mechanism. In other words, by arranging those eight items in a logical and orderly way we have made a memory tool. This arrangement or mnemonic device or memory tool is a way to prepare the material for proper storage. By doing this we can remember it later. (Flip back to page 33 for the first remarks on this topic.)

You will want to make up a mnemonic device (memory tool) for everything you want to remember. This means making up a logical and orderly arrangement for your material. This is the way to prepare material for *proper* storage. There will be more on this in future chapters.

5. If you can't think of any logical way to organize or arrange the material to prepare it for proper storage, then think of something tricky or funny or weird. For example, in Seattle there is a funny mnemonic device for remembering the streets downtown. The streets, from south to north, are: Jefferson, James, Cherry, Columbia, Marion, Madison, Spring, Seneca, University, Union, Pike, Pine.

How could anyone ever remember all those streets and in their proper south to north order? What mnemonic device could we use to arrange all these names in a proper way for storage?

Here is the funny mnemonic device: Jesus Christ Made Seattle Under Pressure.

The first letter of each of these words corresponds to the first letter of each pair of streets. It is easy to remember this funny mnemonic device. It is much easier to remember the mnemonic device than it is to remember the twelve streets in order. Once you remember the mnemonic device, you will have a handle on remembering the twelve streets in order. You have now prepared this material for proper storage. Material that is properly stored can be easily retrieved later.

Remember the mnemonic device mentioned on page 33: "Thirty days hath September, April, June, and November; all the rest have thirty-one, except February, which has twenty-eight and in Leap Year twenty-nine." It would be hard to remember how many days there are in July. But by remembering the mnemonic device, one can quickly figure out that there are thirty-one days in July. That informtion, because properly stored, is easy to retrieve.

Music students have two well-known mnemonic devices. One is for remembering the name of each space on the musical scale: FACE. Remember this mnemonic word ("face") and

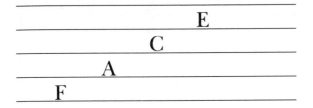

you will know the notes. There is another, different kind of mnemonic device for remembering the name of each *line* on the scale: <u>E</u>very <u>G</u>ood <u>B</u>oy <u>D</u>oes <u>F</u>ine. One can easily remember this funny mnemonic device. Once you remember that mnemonic sentence you will have the notes: e, g, b, d, f.

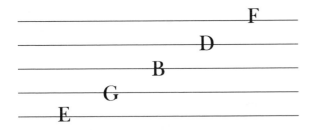

6. There are all different kinds of mnemonic devices. They can be logical or they can be funny or weird, as long as they put the material in some sort of order that will make it easy for you to remember it later.

You want a handle on the material. With a handle (i.e., mnemonic device) you know how the material is stored in your memory. Then when you want to retrieve the material from your memory, all you have to do is remember the mnemonic device; that will help you remember the material itself. For example, it is easier to remember Every Good Boy Does Fine than the mere letters: e, g, b, d, f. It is easy to remember that you have the eight items for a schedule in a chronological order. Once you remember that the mnemonic device for the material is chronological order, you can recall the actual items themselves. You have stored them in a logical way. As a result it is easy to retrieve the material from your memory. For example, when trying to retrieve books from a library you know the arrangement (mnemonic device) is that the

books are stored by topic and then, within each topic, alphabetically by authors' last names.

It doesn't matter what mnemonic device you make up. You may be the only one in the world to have a particular tricky or logical device. But that is fine. Because you are the only one in the world who is going to use your device! If it works for you, if it gives you a handle on your material, if it helps you store the material properly, then it works for you. That's the important thing.

7. For each batch or chunk of material that you want to prepare for proper storage, you have to decide what mnemonic device is going to be most appropriate and useful for you. Should you store this particular batch of material in a chronological way? Or should you have an alphabetical mnemonic device? Or should you make up a mnemonic device that is a funny sentence made up of words using the first letter of each word on the list you want to store in your memory? If you are a musician, you might want to identify the composer's theory or the patterns in the phrases of music you want to memorize.*

8. Are all these questions and decisions wasting your time? Is trying to find the most appropriate and useful arrangement (mnemonic device) for each piece of material wasting your time? *Of course not.* The more time you spend *processing* the material in your mind (i.e., thinking about it, creating mnemonic devices for it, working on it, going over it), the more familiar you are getting with it. *You want to get very familiar with the material because this helps you store it in your memory even better,* and *processing* the material is how you become familiar with it.

Do **For Practice** on page 38.

9. These mnemonic devices are for memorizing lists, terms, formulas, etc. Some material, however, cannot be put into these types of devices. Chapters 14, 15, 16, 18, and 19 will show you how to memorize that other type of material. The rest of this chapter, though, relates to *both* types.

* Jeanne Boardman, my piano teacher, introduced this musician's mnemonic device to me.

For Practice

Make a mnemonic device for memorizing the first ten items on the shopping list on pages 32 and 33. First you have to decide what each item is; for example, is 100% going to be the first word of the first item, or will you call it whole wheat bread, or will you call it bread? Will you call that item "bread, whole wheat" or "whole wheat bread"? This will make a difference if your mnemonic device is going to be alphabetical. When you are done, compare your device with your classmates' devices. Is yours the best for you? Does a classmate have one that you like even better than your own? Get ideas from your classmates for future use. The more kinds of devices you have to choose from, the better chance you have of finding a device that is just right for the material you want to store in your memory.

B. Firm Storage

1. Yes, you have to prepare your material so that you can store it *properly,* that is, in a logical and orderly way or in a tricky, unusual way (according to some mnemonic device) so that you can retrieve it later. But to store it *properly* is not enough. You also have to store it *firmly.*

For example, you have stored all your books properly on the shelves. They are all in an orderly, logical system (by topic and, within each topic, alphabetically). But suppose you have placed them carelessly on the shelves? You have not pushed them in firmly up against the back of the shelf. Some of the books are sticking half out over the front edge. It won't take long before those books are falling on the floor. Or you have them standing up without book ends to hold them firmly in place. Before long, they will be falling over to the side, some piling up on top of others.

Thus, even though they were originally put into a proper system or order for good storage, they were not *firmly* placed. As a result, there is a mess. Some of your books get lost, others get mixed up.

The same is true of your memory.

2. You have to put your properly stored material *firmly* into your memory vault or memory library. There are two main methods for firmly storing material in your memory.

The first and more well-known method is repetition. Just repeat the material over and over and it will become firmly stored in your memory. This is how performers firmly memorize a piece of music or a part in a play. (Later in this chapter you will learn the *Copy, Check, Correct* method of repetition for firm storage.)

3. Another method of repetition is discussed in Chapter 6. It is cross-referencing. Here is a brief introduction to cross-referencing for firm storage of material in your memory.

Cross-referencing is like the page-flipping I have been asking you to do when I have asked you to flip back to a certain page and reread a certain section. Your memory is like the part of the book already finished. It is already there, back aways. When you look back at what is already there, you strengthen your memory of it. You look at it again; you think about it again; you review it. This makes it a stronger memory. This sets it more firmly in your memory. Next time you will find it more quickly and easily.

Or think of your memory nerves as metal cables, smooth, hard surfaced. If you want to remember something you have to make a strong, deep groove in the surface of that nerve cable. The stronger and deeper the groove, the longer it will last. If you want a strong groove that will not disappear or get worn away in time, then you have to go over and over that groove strongly and many times.

This is why the process of repetition is needed. Repeating the material over and over is the way you etch or engrain a strong, deep groove in your memory nerves. This will help keep older memories alive and help store new material firmly in your memory.

4. Therefore, to be sure the material already stored in your memory is strongly and firmly set, look back at (review) what is in your memory whenever you can. An excellent time to do this is when you are trying to memorize something new. Look back in your memory for some other, already stored material that is similar to the new material. (The new material may remind you of something you already know.) Well, stop and try to recall that other material from your memory.

For example, suppose when you were memorizing the shopping list above you came to "raisins" and suddenly remembered that you used to make a special kind of raisin cookie. If you had stopped and gone back into your memory for that recipe, you would have, in a sense, brushed off and shined up that memory, making it strong and firm.

But something else would also have happened. You would have increased your ability to memorize "raisins"! In other words, by dipping back into your memory to find a connection with something new you are trying to memorize, you can memorize the *new* material better!

Thus, an excellent way to store material firmly in your memory is to make as many connections as possible between the new material you are trying to remember and the old material already stored in your memory.

Whenever your teacher brings up material in class, whenever you read material in a book, try to think of something in your own life, your own experience, your own memory that relates to the new material. This is cross-referencing.

Again, this will have two good results: (1) it will help keep the older memories sharp and clear; (2) it will increase your ability to memorize the new material.

A third benefit of making this kind of connection or association between the old and new is that the new material might shed a new light on the old material. It might help you see the old material in a deeper or clearer way. More on this in Chapters 5 and 6.

5. Here is an example of how making connections works: in a psychology class you are learning about fear of tests. The instructor tells you that the symptoms of test-anxiety are sweating palms, increased heart rate, queasy stomach. Should you just write these words down in your notebook and then when you go home to study just try to memorize these words by repeating them over and over? Or should you, when you settle down to study, look back into your own memory for your own experiences with test-anxiety? Should you try to remember any time when you felt this? What did it feel like? If you ever had test-anxiety, that memory will pop up for you. You will then review what it was like. Did you have sweaty palms, increased heart rate, queasy stomach? Yes, indeed. It was awful. Now you are ready to memorize the material you learned in class. You can now repeat the words over and over—but now they will get stored very quickly, easily, firmly, because these memories are like hooks that grab onto the material and hold it for you.

6. The second method—which is, in a way, a variation of the repetition methods—for firmly storing material in your memory is *using* the material a lot. This method is helpful for memorizing a formula in science or math: use the formula on many problems, in many different equations. You will know that deep memory grooves are being made when the formula

springs more and more readily to mind as you work on one problem after another. (This method may have the added advantage of improving your *understanding* of the formula and its use.)

7. When you want to store new material firmly in your memory you should be sure to have it written down first. You want to memorize the shopping list: all those words are written down. You want to memorize the symptoms of test-anxiety: those symptoms are written down. You will then have something that can't be lost as you try to develop your mnemonic devices and do your repetitions. They will not get lost as you go back into your memory to make the connections and brush off your older memories.

But what happens when you don't have the new material in writing? You can lose it before you memorize it.

Suppose you are sitting in class listening to a lecture. You are not taking notes.

You think you will be able to remember the material just from listening because it is well organized by the teacher and you feel you understand it very well. You do not think of the lecture again. A month later on the test you wonder why you can't remember the material in the lecture. You think you have a terrible memory. (Flip back to Section B.3 before you read further.)

However, it is not the fault of your memory. The problem is that you did not make a nerve groove or memory trace. You didn't *process* the material at all. The material was like a feather whisking lightly over a piece of steel cable. No trace was left. (Flip back to earlier remarks on *processing* and *memory grooves* before you continue. Find the first remarks made in this chapter about these ideas.)

But what if you had been in class and taken notes? What if you had reviewed your notes after class? What if, later, you had worked on your notes, correcting them as a result of readings in your textbook? What if you had made connections between the new material and any memories you might have already stored on the topic? What if you had arranged the material into a mnemonic device? Would there have been a nerve groove then? Yes, of course. All that processing would have been like a share in-

strument tracing a groove over and over, leaving a strong, deep trace on the cable. Thus, you would have been able to remember the material. It would have been *firmly* stored.

Stop and remember: all the methods given in this paragraph have been previously discussed. Do you have a firm, strong memory of having read about them already? If not, page-flip until you find the material before you continue. *This* is how you learn; *this* is how you remember!

It is not your memory's fault that there was no trace of the material. It is your own fault for not repeating the material enough to make a strong memory trace or nerve groove. It is your own fault for not *processing* the material in your mind, for not making connections.

For example, if you had ridden a bicycle five times when you were ten years old how well would you remember how to ride it today? But if you had ridden a bike every day for ten years and then didn't ride one again for five years, would you remember how to ride it today? The principle is the same for anything you learn: repetition is essential for firm storage over a period of time. And if you can relate the new to the old, all the better.

8. Moreover, it is the *physical* activity of repetition that is most effective for making nerve grooves or memory traces. If you simply repeat the material over in your mind you are not *physically* repeating it. To physically repeat it you would have to say it out loud. But even better, to get the full benefit of physical repetition, you should *write* it over (or, if you are a musician, *play* it over). The physical activity of actually *writing* material over helps make that nerve groove or memory trace stronger, deeper, more long lasting.

Of course, when you say or write material over, you must do so *with thought and concentration*. It will not help if you repeat merely by rote, simply mouthing words or making words on paper. *You must repeat the material with understanding.* (Making memory connections between the new and the old also helps you to do this.)

9. Thus, in order to remember something you must *process* it: you must try to connect it with what is already in your memory. You must also arrange the new material into some logical or funny order (mnemonic device). You must then repeat this device over and over. You must do this repetition physically (reciting it out loud or writing it down).

If you do all this, the material you wish to remember will enter your memory *properly* and *firmly*. You will have made deep nerve grooves or strong memory traces.

Then when you need that material later, as for a test, you will look to your memory and the information will appear.

Your memory simply holds in safekeeping whatever you put in it. If you store material *properly* and *firmly* then your memory will prove that it is a perfect vault or library for you. Remember, your memory works perfectly; *and it is you yourself who must do the proper and firm storage.*

10. All right, you have just stored some new material properly and firmly in your memory. Now you must be sure to review it periodically so that the groove remains deep, so that the memory won't get weak and fade away. (Making connections between the old and new material is one way to review and has already been discussed above.)

Perhaps you will be interested to know what scientists have discovered about how quickly newly learned (newly stored) material fades from the memory if review doesn't occur right away and regularly. They have discovered you can't afford to wait until some future time to review the material. You need to review the just-learned material right away and periodically thereafter or you will lose it.

The "Forgetting Curve" in the next column shows that you can lose as much as 30 percent of your just-learned material in one day if you have not done enough repetition when originally memorizing, i.e., storing, it. And if you do not periodically review the just-learned material, you can lose 90 percent of it in less than a month! Bad news for students who think they just have to listen once to a lecture or write class notes and go over them a few times to be able to remember the materials for a test at the end of the quarter. (Flip back to page 38 and reread Section B, parts 1 and 2. These paragraphs indicate when you should do the reviewing necessary to keep your material fresh, strong, and secure in your memory.)

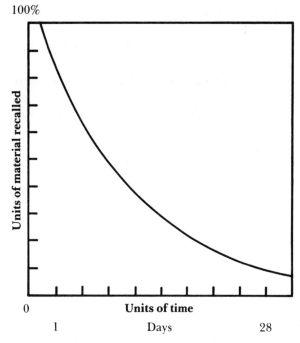

A characteristic forgetting curve
(adapted from Walter Pauk, *How to Study in College,* 2nd ed.; Boston: Houghton Mifflin Company, 1974, p. 55)

C. Trying to Remember Something: A Real Life Story

Last week I was driving in my car. I heard a beautiful piece of music on the car radio. Not able to write and drive at the same time, but wanting to catch and remember the name so I could buy the record, I listened very carefully when the piece ended. The announcer came on and said, "David Montgomery at the piano, playing Schubert . . . opus 171. . . ." He said more about the name and date, but I can't remember it. In fact, I forgot it almost as soon as he said it. The only reason I remember the pianist's and composer's names and the number of the opus is that I worked hard at storing that information. This is how I did it as I was driving:

I knew I probably couldn't hold all the announcer's information in my *short term memory* for very long. (The *short term memory* keeps material that isn't written down for only a few seconds and then, if you haven't found a way to hang on to it—pft—it's gone!)

So I quickly decided what the key words were and I repeated them over several times to get them solid in my short term memory. (Repetition will keep unwritten material in the short term memory for a few hours, a few days at the most.)

I said out loud: "David Montgomery at piano (I knew I needed the performer's name). Schubert opus 171 (I needed the composer and something for the title—I had aleady lost the actual name of the piece and the date). David Montgomery Schubert 171 David Montgomery Schubert 171. . . ."

After repeating this over and over, I felt I had it solidly enough in my short term memory so that I wouldn't lose it right away. Then I began to try to transfer it to my *long term memory* where it could be stored safely for a longer time (the *long term memory* is our regular memory that we have been talking about).

To transfer the information over to my long term memory I had to do more than repeat it over and over. I knew I should make connections between old memories and the new information. I also knew that without being able to write it down I would have to make some sort of mental image or picture as my mnemonic device. So I made a mnemonic device of those words as rounded stones and, in my mind, I carved them and then laid them down side by side. This took some time, but I could see the letters and words very clearly and *the longer it took the more processing I was doing. We all know that the more processing the mind does on material, the more firmly it will be stored!* The illustration at the bottom of the page shows what my mental picture mnemonic device looked like.

The reason I used stones for my letters was because of the connection I made with the name "David" and my own feelings and memories. To me, David is a strong name (like a rock). Also "Montgomery" reminded me of a mountain ("mont" is the French word for "mountain"), which is made out of stone. "Schubert" has, to me, a soft, round sound, so my imagined stones had round, smooth edges. The "171" was diffi-

cult to connect, but I saw them as tall, like a mountain. Thus, I had made associations between the new words and the feelings or information (like the French word) already stored in my memory.

This information was now firmly in my long term memory, thanks to the connections and mnemonic device. Then, to be sure I would keep this newly stored material in my long term memory until I could get to a record store, I kept reviewing (recalling) it from time to time; this was my repetition activity. And it worked. When I got to the record store, I could easily retreive this information from my memory.

D. Sabotaging Your Own Memory

There is a way, unfortunately, by which you can sabotage your retrieving the properly and firmly stored material from your memory. The way you can sabotage yourself is to lack confidence in your memory's ability to hold material for you and to lack confidence in your own ability to retrieve material from your memory.

If you strongly believe that you have a poor memory and that you are unable to remember material, then you can sabotage yourself.

How can you overcome this problem? Reread this chapter, Sections A and B. Try to believe what is said in those sections—they tell the truth. Then you must practice it. Follow the directions given in those sections and in the following section. You *can* succeed at this! It is up to you—because you alone have the power to choose what you will do with your own mind and your own life. I'm not saying it's easy, only that if you *will* it and if you *work* at it, you *can*.

E. The Copy, Check, Correct Method

1. In Section A you learned how to prepare certain kinds of material for proper storage. You learned about placing these kinds of material in a logical, orderly, and/or tricky mne-

DAVID MONTGOMERY
SCHUBERT 171

monic device (remember, you will learn how to arrange other kinds of material in later chapters).

In Section B you learned that physical repetition is necessary to make the nerve grooves for firm storage. The present section will show you exactly how to do the physical repetition so that you can firmly store your properly ordered material.

2. Let's say you have worked on the initial processing of your material and now you have that material ordered in a mnemonic device. For example, you want to store in your memory the eight items to be included in a schedule. You place them in a chronological mnemonic device because that seems a logical order to you. On your paper you have written:

Eat
Travel
Class
Study
Other job
Other tasks + responsibilities
Relax
Sleep

Now you need to physically repeat this mnemonic device so that you can store it firmly. This is how you do it.

a. After you have thought about the material and found the mnemonic device that seems the most logical order to you, you should write it over neatly on a piece of paper and put it aside. Now *copy* it over from memory. Actually write the mnemonic device down on another piece of paper without looking at the original.

b. When you have copied it to your best ability, look at the original and *check* your copy against it.

c. If you have not copied it exactly, then *correct* your copy. Actually write in the corrections. If you have left some things out, write them in. If you have them out of order, cross out the items incorrectly placed and put them where they belong.

d. Repeat steps a, b, and c. Continue to repeat the *copy, check, correct* method until you can copy the material in its mnemonic arrangement perfectly. As you begin to feel that you can copy it perfectly, you can try saying it out loud instead of writing it down. But be sure that you write it down in the first stages, because writing it down will make the strongest, firmest nerve grooves.

3. For some kinds of material, for example a list or a definition or dates or a formula, you can use *flash cards*, if you think it appropriate or useful. This is how a flash card works: you write your mnemonic device on one side of the card (the "card" can be a piece of paper or an actual card, of any size). On the back of the card write the identification of the material. Type your flashcards if you can. See examples on page 44.

Now put your cards in a pile. To start with, you can have them so that the identification sides are facing up. Look at the first card. Write down (*copy*) on a piece of paper the information that is on the back. Then look at (*check*) the back. Did you get it right? If not, *correct* your copy. Try again (be sure not to look at the information on the card while you are writing your copy). Check again. Correct again if necessary. If not, go on to the next card.

When you have gone through the whole pile, go through it again. After you can do the whole pile correctly, shuffle the cards so they are in a different order. Go through them again. By this time you can say the information out loud and perhaps even paraphrase before you check. By this time you have the material pretty well stored in your memory.

Finally, turn the cards over and say (or write, if you feel insecure at first) the identification on the other side. Go through the pile. Copy, check, and correct all the cards, as described above. Shuffle to put them in a different order and repeat until you know that you know the material.

When you can go through the pile with either side up, then mix up the cards so that some have the identification side up and some have the information side up. Go through the copy, check, correct process again.

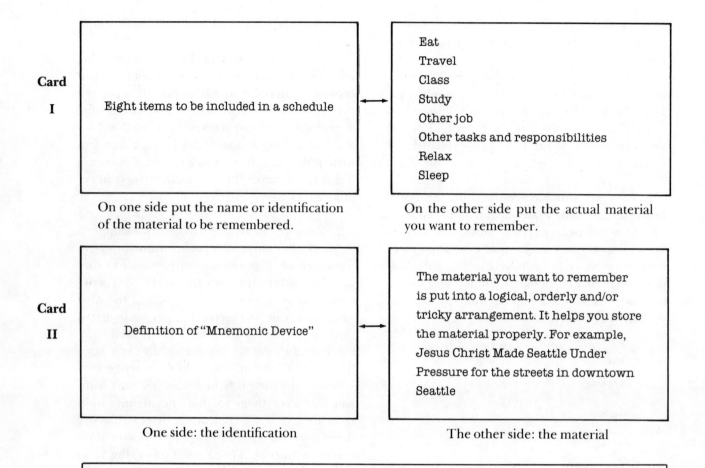

Card I

Eight items to be included in a schedule

⟷

Eat
Travel
Class
Study
Other job
Other tasks and responsibilities
Relax
Sleep

On one side put the name or identification of the material to be remembered.

On the other side put the actual material you want to remember.

Card II

Definition of "Mnemonic Device"

⟷

The material you want to remember is put into a logical, orderly and/or tricky arrangement. It helps you store the material properly. For example, Jesus Christ Made Seattle Under Pressure for the streets in downtown Seattle

One side: the identification

The other side: the material

For Practice

Take a card (a 3 × 5 card is a typical-sized card for this purpose) or cut a piece of paper into a small square or rectangle. Then make this into a flash card for the mnemonic device you made for the practice exercise above on page 38 for the first ten items in the shopping list.

Now make three more flash cards based on information on page 32. Identify one card for the chunk of material on breakfast, one for lunch, and one for dinner.

But what must you do before you can complete the flash card?

Yes, first you must prepare the material for *proper* storage (as in Section A of this chapter). But how do you do this?

Yes, you must rearrange, reorder, the items in each chunk according to what you think is the most logical arrangement. Or you can, instead, choose to arrange the items in a tricky or funny mnemonic device. Then, when you are satisfied that you have a good logical order or suitable clever mnemonic device, write the device or logically ordered list on the other side (see example of Card I above).

Now make three more cards, one for the definition of "proper storage" (see example of Card II above) and one for the definition of "firm storage." Make the last card for the definition of "the copy, check, correct method." Compare all your cards with your classmates' cards.

Now follow the directions above in part 3. Do what that section tells you to do and you will learn how to use flash cards.

In the process you will also learn what to eat and the definitions of "proper storage," "firm storage," and "the copy, check, correct method"! Perhaps you and your classmates can now test each other to see how well you have used this method.

When you review your flashcards on following days, you will find that you can go through the cards more and more correctly and easily and quickly. This will mean that the nerve grooves are deep and clear, that the material is firmly stored, and that you will have nothing to worry about when you are tested on this information.

Do **For Practice** on page 44.

4. Remember, you must concentrate while you are doing this studying. Rearranging material, developing mnemonic devices, doing the copy, check, correct method *is* studying.

Focus all your attention on your work. Certain thoughts and concerns may keep floating into your mind to distract you from your concentration on studying. You need to push those distracting thoughts away forcefully. Say to yourself, "I'm studying now. I'll think about this other stuff later." (Page-flip back to pages 29 and 30 and reread part 3. Also flip to page 12 and reread Section H, especially part 3.)

5. In the case of a definition (as in some of the examples above), when you copy you can paraphrase the definition if you like. Just be sure that you include everything from the original in your paraphrase. Remember that your original definition was worked out by you to be the best definition possible. That is your mnemonic device and you want either to copy it exactly or to remember the exact meaning so that if you paraphrase it you will not leave anything out. (Do you remember reading earlier about paraphrasing? Can you find where? Try to page-flip back to that other information. *Take a few minutes to do this now.)*

Finally, keep always in mind that *when you copy, check, correct you must do it with understanding and concentration.* It will be a waste of time simply to copy words down or recite them without understanding.

6. It is possible that when you are copying over your mnemonic device you may hit upon improvements. Perhaps as you copy over the material without looking at the original you will get an idea of a clearer, more logical way to organize the material. If this happens, good! Replace the original mnemonic device with your new, improved version and then use that new better version as the mnemonic device (arrangement) to copy, and make an improved flash card (if you are using flash cards).

7. In some subjects, such as math or chemistry, there are many formulas to remember. Students often find it difficult to store this kind of material. First, it is hard to find a mnemonic device for a formula like $E = mc^2$. In these cases, it is often a matter of simply remembering the formula itself.

But there is one method, which was mentioned earlier (can you find it?), that you can use to help yourself store this type of material, namely: use the formula you want to remember on many problems. This will give you *familiarity* with the formula. The more you use the formula on problems, the more you understand how it works, the more familiar you become with it, the more times you are physically repeating it, making deeper nerve grooves for firm storage.

8. To sum up, the activities you will be doing during your study time will include (a) figuring out the best mnemonic order you can find for your material to assure *proper* storage; (b) making flash cards if appropriate; (c) using the copy, check, correct method and/or using formulas on many problems to assure *firm* storage; (d) making as many connections as you can between the new material you are trying to learn and old material you already have stored in your memory.

9. Once you have *properly and firmly stored* some material in your memory, you should *review* the material at least once a week to keep the nerve groove in good shape. That is, at least once a week, copy, check, and correct all your mnemonic devices from the first day of class. If you firmly stored the material when you originally studied it, then you can do the review mentally. Once it is already stored and you are just reviewing it, you don't need to physically copy it anymore. At this point simply repeating it over in your mind is enough to make sure the nerve groove is still there, as deep and strong as ever.

On the other hand, if you do not periodically review the stored material, the nerve grooves can begin to fade. Then a month or two later when the mid-term or final comes, you will look into your memory and not be able to find some of the material you stored there. You will have to go back and re-store the material. *This will waste more time than if you had done periodic reviews throughout the quarter.* Periodic reviews will ensure that once material is properly and firmly stored it will remain that way. (Page-flip to the "Forgetting Curve." *Page-flipping is an important storing, processing, and reviewing activity. Do it now.*)

10. Research shows that we remember most easily, quickly, and firmly those things that are of special interest to us and those things that we learn during shocking or outstanding experiences, e.g.: "I will always remember every detail of the day my dog died," or "I can describe every problem in the first car engine I ever rebuilt all by myself," or "I remember a lot about Keats' poetry because I got very exciting insights into poetry in that class, thanks to my teacher, whom I also will never forget—she was great!"

To remember things that are of special interest or importance to us, we do not need the copy, check, correct method; we remember these things almost automatically and perhaps for life. But for school work, even in courses which are of special interest and importance to us, we *should* use the copy, check, correct method—just to be sure!

11. Do experienced and good students have to process material this way too, that is, arrange and repeat it? Yes, that is what makes them good students! However, as a student gains more experience, he or she will find his or her own most efficient and effective personal way to process the material, that is, *(1) arrange it into mnemonic devices; (2) copy, check, and correct; and (3) review. As you gain experience, you too will find your own best way to use these study skills as you process the material, trying to store it properly and firmly.*

Your Summary

Items   *Page Number(s)*

Answer this question: Is it a useful activity or a waste of time for you to fill in the *Page Number(s)* column above? Why?

CHAPTER 5

The Reality Check

A. Is It True or False?

A teacher tells you in class, "It very rarely rains in New York City." Do you, as a student who lives in New York City, just lift up your pen and, without bothering yourself, simply write it down in your notebook? Or do you say, either out loud or to yourself, "Hey! Just a minute. That isn't true!"

What if you were a student in Peru who has never been to New York City? What if you heard your teacher say, as you sat in class in Lima, "It very rarely rains in New York City."

You would probably nod your head and write the information down in your notebook.

In order to be able to make sense out of what you hear in class and read in your textbook you need to be able to decide whether what you are hearing and reading is true or not.

What was the reason the student in the first example could tell whether the statement given in the lecture was true or false? The reason is that the student could give the statement a *reality check*.

B. How to Make a Reality Check

A reality check is when you check what you hear or read against your own experience, your own knowledge, your own sense of reality, against what you have stored in your memory. You hear or read something. You think about what you know of the subject referred to. You check or measure what you hear or read against what you yourself know, what is in your memory. Then you can make a judgment: "That statement is wrong. It does rain quite a bit in New York City. I know because I have experienced it myself in real life." (Yes, reality checking is also cross-referencing or making connections between new material and the old, already stored material.)

The student in Lima, Peru, cannot make his own instant reality check about the rain in New York City. Should a person who has no experience with something, who has nothing stored on that topic, just accept whatever someone else says about it? If you want to take the chance of learning false ideas, then you can.

What should the Peruvian student do in order to be sure that he is getting true information? The student has several choices: (a) he can simply believe the teacher as an authority. This would be reasonable if the teacher has lived in New York City or is usually accurate and truthful. Then that teacher could realistically be considered an authority, a resource person, and could reasonably be believed. (b) The student, who may have reason to doubt the judgment of the teacher, can ask other persons in Lima who have lived in New York City. They would be persons who the student believes are reliable authorities or resource people on this subject. (c) Or the student can go to the library and look up statistics about New York City's rainfall. (d) Finally, and most fun of all, the student could hop on a plane and fly to New York, staying for a few months or a year to find out first hand, by direct experience, what rain in New York is really like.

All of these ways will help the student give a reality check to the information he heard in class. The direct experience method is not always the most convenient method—unless you have lots of time and money. Researching in the library or asking reliable resource people is more practical in most cases.

Of course I am not suggesting that you run to the library every time you hear a statement about something you have not directly experienced. But when you are a student—and when you are a citizen in a democracy—it is important to give a reality check to any statement about a topic that is of a *serious* or *important* nature.

47

C. The Words We Use and the Real Things in the World

1. A statement is a group of words that tells about something out there in the real world. You are sitting at a desk reading these statements that are printed on this page. Here, give this next statement a reality check: "There is a big gorilla right behind you. It is going to eat you up if you look around." Will you look around? Are you afraid to look around?

If you are sitting at a desk in a room in Houston, then you know that statement is false. You give it a reality check by checking that statement against what you know of reality. You know that there are (probably) no gorillas running around Houston. Consequently, after this reality check, you can say, "That statement is ridiculous."

However, if you were studying in a forest in Africa, you might very well be careful not to turn around. That is, until you gave the statement an even closer reality check. You know from direct personal experience and perhaps also from research you have done that gorillas are vegetarians. Therefore, from your reality check you know the gorilla will not eat you up, even if it *is* standing right behind your chair. It might take you away to its home in the trees, or it might throw you on the ground and jump up and down on you. But it won't eat you up.

2. Here is a statement: "Below these sentences there is a box with a circle in it." What does this statement refer to? Give this statement a reality check. Is it true or false?

It is true.

3. Here is another statement: "Here is a picture of a tree." Give this statement a reality check. Is the statement true or false?

It is true.

4. Here is another one: "Outside my window is a balcony." Is this statement true or false? Give it a reality check.

The only way you can give this statement a foolproof reality check is to come over and look out my window. Or you could ask me whether it is really true that there is a balcony outside my window. Then, according to whether you think I tell the truth or not, you will or will not believe me. (There really is a balcony outside my window.)

5. What about all the information you have read in this book so far? Do you think it is true or false? Can you give a reality check to everything in this book? Perhaps you have not had any direct, personal experience with some of the material in this book so you cannot give it a direct reality check. But perhaps you have had experience with other material in the book and so you have already determined whether what the book says about the material is true or false.

For example, if you have frozen up when taking a test, then you will know, from your own reality check, that the material later on in Chapter 7 has truth in it. You know that some people really do in the real world freeze up when taking tests. But you may not have had any experience doing the activities which Chapter 7 says will help you. Therefore, you cannot tell whether that part of the book is true or not; you don't know whether doing these activities will truly help you or not. How will you become able to give that material a reality check so that you can judge whether what it tells you will work or not, is true or not?

You can ask someone who has tried those activities. You can do research on methods scientists have come up with for helping people overcome this freezing-up problem. Or you can actually do those activities yourself. All these methods will help you give the material a reality check so that you can determine whether what the book says is true or false. In this case, doing the activities yourself is probably the best method. Try it yourself. After you have tried doing the activities that the book says will help you, you will be able to say, "Hey, that book is right. Those activities really help," or "No, the book is wrong. Those activities don't help. At least they didn't help me."

D. Familiar and Unfamiliar Information

1. As in the case given just above, you often will hear or read statements that contain some material that is familiar to you and also some material that is unfamiliar to you. In the example given above, the material about freezing was *familiar* to you. The material about the activities to stop freezing was *unfamiliar* to you. Thus, part of what you read above you could give an immediate reality check to and part of it you could not give an immediate reality check to but would have to investigate further.

Whenever this situation occurs, you should distinguish what is familiar to you and what is *un*familiar to you in the new material that you are hearing or reading. The part that is familiar you can give an immediate reality check to. If you judge it to be false, you can put it aside. If you judge it to be true (that is, if it checks or associates with what you already have stored in your memory), then it will simply be another repetition of already stored material. Giving it a reality check will have the effect of reinforcing its nerve groove and, thus, storing it more firmly. (Page-flip to page 38, Chapter 4, Section B, part 3. Do this before you read further.)

2. For example, someone tells you that Anton Chekhov was a Russian writer who wrote four major plays and that the last one was written in 1905. You have studied Chekhov a lot. You quickly, almost instantaneously, give this *familiar* information a reality check. You know (it is stored in your memory from your earlier studies) that he was a great Russian writer. You know he wrote four major plays. And you know . . . (let's check that date again) that he died in 1904! Therefore, the person who said the last play was written in 1905 is wrong. That information is false. You had other information stored in the library of your memory. The topic was familiar to you and so you could quickly judge the truth or falseness of statements about this topic. But just to be 100 percent sure you might want to look the date up in an encyclopedia. *You never want to miss a chance to correct any mistakes you may have stored away earlier.*

3. If you hear something strange on a familiar topic, listen very carefully. You may learn something new about that topic or be able to correct a mistaken idea you had about it. (It is important, here, to page-flip to page 39 and re-read the last paragraph of part 4. Do this before you go on.)

For example, the Peruvian student may have believed his teacher was a reliable source and as a result stored away the false information given by that teacher. Then one day that student hears someone who lived in New York for many years say that it rains a lot in New York. What should the student do? A close-minded student would say the new information on that familiar topic is false because he has other information stored away. But an open-minded student would say, "Wait a minute. I have other information stored away in my memory. But this person seems like an excellent source. I had better investigate further, just to be sure. I certainly don't want any false information stored in my memory!" And this open-minded student might then decide to go to the library and check New York's rainfall statistics. He would then be able to correct false information stored away, replacing it with correct information. This student is keeping his memory library up-to-date and as accurate as possible. By being open-minded and willing to investigate further, you can do the same with your own memory library.

Investigation and re-investigation and checking new information against information already stored in your memory allows you, more reasonably, to reject false information and gain true information. If you had true information stored away, all these activities will reinforce the nerve grooves of that information, causing it to be even more firmly stored than before.

4. But what do you do when you read or hear something that is *unfamiliar* to you? You cannot associate or check it with what you already have in your memory—remember this is *unfamiliar* new material. You've never learned it before. You are like the student in Peru hearing for the first time about the rain in New York. It is unfamiliar. Your memory is blank on this topic. For example, I tell you, "At the rate we are going, in five years air pollution will be so bad seven out of ten Americans will have lung cancer." Is this true?

Well, like the student in Peru, to discover the

truth you have to find a way to give this unfamiliar information a reality check. *You will have to investigate the topic.* What are your options? Which ones are appropriate for your present investigation?

You can ask a reliable resource person or authority (appropriate). See Section B (a), (b).

You can do research on it in the library, etc. (appropriate). See Section B (c).

You can re-evaluate and assess your already stored knowledge (somewhat appropriate). See Section D.2.

If it is possible and convenient, you can have new direct, personal experience of it (not appropriate and, hopefully, *won't* occur!). See Section B (d).

As you do one or more of the above methods of investigation you are gaining your own understanding of this topic. You are deciding for yourself (possibly with the help of your resource people and research) whether that unfamiliar statement is true or false.

You won't be able to give your final answer on whether you agree with a particular statement or not until you have looked at, studied, heard more about, and possibly experienced the reality yourself. Then you are able to give the statement you heard or read a reality check. You can then say, "From my research and personal experience, I can tell you that your statement is false" (or true or partially false and partially true, whatever the case may be, as you have discovered it).

By the time you have learned enough about the new unfamiliar material to give the statement you heard or read a reality check, you have made it *familiar* material! By this time you have got it stored away firmly in your memory. It is now something more that you know.

In the future, when you hear statements about that topic you will find them familiar to you and will be able to give them a reality check more quickly and easily.

E. Reality Checks Are Important for Learning

This is how people learn. They start out, as a baby does, with nothing familiar to them. Their memory is empty. Then, a certain chain of events is experienced repeatedly. (I have a pain. I cry. Someone makes me feel better.) After this

happens a few times it becomes familiar. It is grooved into the baby's memory nerves. Then, one day, after this chain of events has become familiar to the baby, she feels a pain. The baby then more or less says to herself, "If I cry now, someone is sure to make me feel better. It is true that this is how it always is." So the baby cries in order to make the third step happen.

The baby has learned to associate or check new familiar happenings with already known, stored happenings. As a result, when the baby feels a familiar painful feeling, she can associate or check that feeling with something she already knows from experience. Then the baby knows that it is true that if she cries someone will come to help. (If, after all this learning, no one comes, the baby will be confused.)

Slowly, bit by bit, we build up experience with the real world. We build up a stock of stored knowledge. With this knowledge we can make reality checks on new information. (Remember, making connections between the new and the old information, cross-referencing, is making reality checks.)

If we read or hear something new that is *unfamiliar*, on the other hand, we have to begin to learn about it so that we can decide whether what people say about it is true or false. Then we can start to store the new experience, new knowledge. With this newly stored knowledge we can then make even more reality checks more quickly and easily about even more new statements in the future. And so it goes.

F. Checking Reality Makes Life More Interesting

Don't take any wooden nickels and don't automatically believe any new unfamiliar information. Before you accept the new unfamiliar information as true, go out and gain more knowledge from resource persons and/or research and/or gain personal experience concerning the topic. And if you *have* had experience but haven't *thought about* the experience before, do so now. Then you will be able to give the new information a reality check based on your own knowledge and/or experience. Then you will be able to judge reasonably for yourself whether that information is true or false.

If you approach your studies with this attitude, you will find your studies more interesting and yourself more excited and involved.

You are an authority and expert on reality, just as much as anyone else with the same amount of knowledge and experience. And if you don't have enough knowledge and experi-ence on a specific topic to judge whether what you hear or read about it is true or false, then you can, by golly, go out and gain the knowl-edge and/or experience necessary to make your own reasonable reality check.

Do **For Practice.**

For Practice

Make up three statements that are true or false about topics you are familiar with. Exchange with a classmate and try to say whether each other's statements are true or false. How could you find out if you don't know? Then tell each other which are the true and false statements and how you learned that they are true or false.

Your Summary

Items   *Page Number(s)*

Remember to compare your list with your classmates'.

CHAPTER 6

Making the Most of Your Memory

Cross-Referencing and Page-Flipping

A. Cross-Referencing

1. When you give new material a reality check, you check or measure the new material against what you have already experienced or already know. That is, you check the new material against what is already stored in your memory. You learned this in previous chapters. Here we will go even further.

In order to give the most complete and effective reality check possible you need to remember *everything* you have learned or experienced about that topic. This means searching your memory for every experience, every piece of information or knowledge you have stored there. The more you can recall, the better your reality check.

As you recall information from your memory for the reality check, you are repeating that material one more time, thus reinforcing that nerve groove. (Reinforce your nerve groove on this by page-flipping to page 39, last paragraph of part 3. You've done this before? Good!)

The most successful students and researchers and conversationalists make these thorough reality checks, searching their memory for *all* related knowledge and information.

We can call this kind of search, as one scans over his or her entire memory bank or library, *cross-referencing*. You *cross-reference* the new information with all the other material stored in your memory vault or memory library, making sure to make comparisons and contrasts with old information.

If a person is not used to doing this cross-referencing, it may seem like a lot of trouble, and it may seem to take too much time. But it is well worth the effort because the result is (a) you reinforce what you already have stored, (b) you understand the new information better, and (c) you respond with more depth and completeness

to a test question or to a comment made in discussion or to your own self-question (if you are working on your own research).

2. The first and easiest kind of cross-referencing is checking to see what is missing in your own memory on a specific topic. For example, someone says something and you check your memory to see whether you know anything about that topic. If you don't, or if you know something but not much, then *you must fill in the gaps*. You need to complete, as much as possible, your store of information on a topic. Always be trying to fill in, complete, correct any store of information you have. This is how you can do it:

Imagine the ideal classroom. The instructor is presenting a lecture with material that is unfamiliar to you. You must make sure that this new, unfamiliar information is cross-referenced to information you already have stored in your memory. How? Ask questions, as below:

TEACHER: We are going to talk today about the cause of the fear and anxiety students can feel when taking exams. First, environmental factors are perceived by the organism and at the same time . . .

STUDENT: Wait! What do you mean by "the organism?"

TEACHER: I mean a person, an individual human being, a student.

STUDENT: And what are "environmental factors"?

TEACHER: An environmental factor is something that exists in the world; for example, that you have a test coming up the next day. That is an environmental factor. It is a real fact or factor that exists in the environment or in the world around you, in the world in which you live.

STUDENT: Okay, thank you.

TEACHER: . . . at the same time, your cognitive processes make you aware of expectations. Then . . .

STUDENT: Excuse me, what do you mean by "cognitive processes"?

TEACHER: In this connection they are your mental activities that give you knowledge of the world and of yourself in it. In other words, your mind is constantly, throughout your life, observing events and remembering what you have already observed and learned. Your cognitive processes are your mind's doing this so that you can know what the world is like and how you fit into it.

STUDENT: How do these cognitive processes make me aware of expectations?

TEACHER: Your cognitive processes, that is, your mental activities, put your memories of your past behavior together with your knowledge of the world. This adds up to what you can expect of yourself in a certain situation.

STUDENT: What kind of situation? How does this work specifically?

TEACHER: Oh, like you are sure you are going to fail the test because you have failed tests before (this is your memory), and you believe you are not a good student and perhaps not even a smart person (whether it is true or not, this is your own personal understanding of reality). The result is that your cognitive processes make you aware of the expectation that you are going to fail the test coming up the next day.

STUDENT: Okay, thank you.

TEACHER: . . . then you compare the environmental factors and the expectations and if there is an undesirable mismatch, you will have a biochemical reaction and . . .

STUDENT: What is an "undesirable mismatch"? Give me an example.

TEACHER: You compare the environmental factor that a test is coming up with the expectation that you are going to fail. This is undesirable. A desirable match, on the other hand, is that you have a test coming up and you expect to pass it.

STUDENT: Then what about the "biochemical reaction"?

TEACHER: When you become aware of an undesirable match between environmental factors and your expectations, chemicals are released into your body and they cause reactions such as shaking hands, increased heartbeat, etc. Your cognitive processes will then interpret these biochemical body reactions as fear and . . .

STUDENT: Why will I interpret these reactions as fear?

TEACHER: Because you have learned to identify these cues (shaking hands, faster heartbeats, etc.) as fear. Rightly or wrongly, this is what you have learned and this information is stored in your memory. Or you might interpret these same cues as anxiety or panic, however you have learned to name these biochemical body cues.

STUDENT: Okay, thank you.

TEACHER: . . . and you will then behave fearfully or in panic and, in fear or panic, you may give up, freeze up, or run away.

STUDENT: How can I change this?

TEACHER: You can work on changing your expectations by becoming a person who can pass tests.

STUDENT: How?

TEACHER: By learning and using study skills. Then you will know how to study, how to understand and remember your material, how to take tests. How to succeed as a student.

On the next page is a diagram of what just happened as you related and associated the new information with what you already know as you took the teacher's store of information (expressed in his or her own words) and made it fit your *own* understanding. You cross-referenced the teacher's new ideas to your own memory stores, which are structured in your own way, in your own words.

3. This student has already begun to change the words provided by the teacher. So far so good. But now the student must go home and, during study, proceed to the next stage of more completely cross-referencing or making connections. This means the student must, more thoroughly, search her stores of memory for what is already known (learned, experienced) about this topic.

The lecture was about fear during tests. The student, yes, has experienced it and knows what it is! The student, while reading and thinking

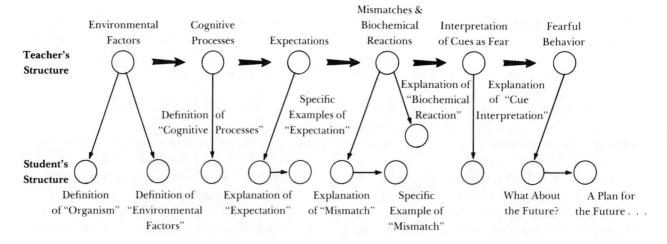

about the notes from the lecture, should stop and recall her own test-fearful experiences. Perhaps the student will talk to herself this way while reflecting: "The teacher said this is caused by having expectations of failure. Is this true? Well . . . I do expect to do a poor job because I have not done very well on tests in the past. Hmm. The teacher said this expectation, when matched up with a test coming the next day, will make my body produce certain chemicals that will cause my heart rate to increase and my hands to shake. Do I have these experiences? Yes! Before a test I get butterflies in my stomach, my hands get cold and shaky, I get . . . nervous, afraid. Isn't that what the teacher said happens? Hmm. That's right! I get these physical cues and I call it fear. Then I tell myself I'm afraid . . . and when I'm afraid I want to run away and not take the doggone test! Okay, I think I understand this now."

This student has *consciously cross-referenced* (given a personal reality check to) the new information the teacher presented. The student has related (reality checked) this unfamiliar information with familiar information she already possesses from prior learning and experience. Now the new unfamiliar material is all related to the older familiar information and is well understood; and in the future *this* will be familiar material, too!

4. The next step is to take the new-information-connected-with-the-older-information and reorganize, restructure, rearrange all this combined information into a mnemonic device. This will prepare the material for *proper storage*. Once you have this new logical rearrangement (mne-

monic device), you can start to *store it firmly*. How? Yes, through the copy, check, correct method. You will copy, check, and correct the properly restructured, rearranged material.

Here is an example of how one student might begin to restructure the above combined (new and old) material to make her own structure (arrangement, mnemonic device) for proper storage:

a. I fear exams because I have failed them in the past and expect to in the future.

b. Whenever I see a test coming up, I expect to fail again, and chemicals are sent into my body that make me feel I am afraid.

c. The way to get over this is to learn how to be a good student and how to take tests successfully.

d. When I learn this, my cognitive processes will tell me I can expect to pass future exams that come up.

e. Then when my cognitive processes match up the environmental factor (the test) with my expectations, I will have a good match (my expectations will be that I will pass) instead of the old undesirable mismatch (that I will fail).

f. Then chemicals will not be released into my body to create fear cues such as shaking hands and increased heart rate.

g. I won't feel fear.

h. I will actually pass the test.

Now this student fully understands, grasps, and has made this material her own! This material, *because it was so well cross-referenced (reality checked), is well understood*, is structured in a way that makes sense to this student, is stored securely in her memory. Then, when the student needs to remember (retrieve) this information, the material will come right up. For example, on the next test, the teacher asks:

"What causes a student to feel fear when taking a test?"

Our student will answer: "The student will have an expectation of failure based on the student's memory of past experiences. This expectation is an undesirable mismatch with the test coming up. Such a mismatch causes chemicals to go into the body to cause physical cues, such as shaking hands and increased heart rate. The student interprets these cues as fear and, because of this, is feeling fear."

This is an excellent answer and shows the student fully understands the concept.

The student *processed* (that is, cross-referenced, reality checked, restructured, copied, checked, and corrected) the information the teacher presented. In other words, the student *thought about* the information, *asked questions, related (cross-referenced)* it to her own life. The student *rearranged* the material and then worked on *storing (remembering)* it firmly. Processing would also include *reviewing* the material periodically, after the initial study of it.

It is all these mental activities (all this *processing*) that makes it possible for you to grasp, understand, and store material for easy retrieval later. *The more actively you process (work on) material, the more firmly and properly it is stored and the more easily you can recall (retrieve, remember) it later* when you need it for a test or to participate in a discussion or even an informal conversation with your friends.

Do **For Practice** on page 56.

5. Here is another example of how to cross-reference material. In high school, in your senior civics course, you learned that even with an increasing population the percentage of people voting is decreasing.

Then, in college, you take an American history course. In this course you learn about education in the United States. In a lecture, your teacher gives you information about the desire of the people after the Revolutionary War to have free public education so that we can have citizens able to be a responsible electorate.

If you do not cross-reference this material with what you already have stored in your memory, you are not making the most of your mental library and your past education.

But if you *do* cross reference the new material, you will find that you have knowledge stored away in your memory that can add depth to what you have just learned in the lecture. You can add to your notes or contribute to the class discussion or include on a test the information that the hopes of the early United States citizens have apparently not been fulfilled because today fewer and fewer people are voting. This interesting piece of relevant information will add dimension, scope, depth, and interest to the topic for you.

Here is another example. In an English history class you learn that in 1588, England, under Queen Elizabeth, defeated the powerful Spanish navy and became the master of the seas and the greatest world power. Then, in a following quarter, you take a literature course on Shakespeare. In that course you learn that Shakespeare lived in what was called a "golden age" of English culture and that Shakespeare wrote with admiration and love about his queen, Queen Elizabeth. By mental cross-referencing you come across information you stored earlier about England's history in the time of Queen Elizabeth. You put that information together with what you are learning about England's golden age and Shakespeare's admiration of Queen Elizabeth. "Ah ha!" you say. "Sure! England had just become the greatest world power. No wonder there was a golden age. No wonder Shakespeare admired the queen so much. This makes a lot of sense!"

Now you are better able to understand and appreciate the relevance of Shakespeare's themes about the power of royalty. You can understand and appreciate that he was living in a time when his country was the greatest world power and his queen was the most powerful sovereign in the world. Thus, cross-referencing has added richness and depth to your studying and understanding.

For Practice

You should now take the information in the above question-and-answer section on pages 52–53 (fear and exams) and process it yourself. How?

Yes, first cross-reference the information with *your own* knowledge and experiences that are already in your memory. *Relate the new information to what you already know.* Reflect, think, remember, put two and two together. Then reorder the information according to *your own* best sense of logic.

It may look something like the other student's structure (page 54). But it will probably also have something special or different of your own in the arrangement you make for yourself.

Exchange with a classmate and compare your arrangements. Are they different? In what ways?

6. At first, if you are not used to cross-referencing, to scanning your memory for related information, it may take some effort and concentration to do it. However, as you gain experience and practice, you will not only find it easier and quicker to do than at first, but you will also begin to enjoy pulling together pieces of information stored away in your memory and thereby giving a fuller, richer dimension of understanding to the topic under study or discussion.

This is part of what learning, thinking, and being an intelligent, educated human being is all about. And you do these activities during your study time. These activities are part of studying!

B. Page-Flipping

1. Have you ever had the experience of reading something and saying to yourself, "That reminds me of something I read earlier. I have a vague recollection of it"?

What do you do when this happens? Do you flip the pages back until you find that other, previous mention or discussion of the idea? Or do you just shrug your shoulders and go on reading, forgetting about that vague recollection? (You have already been asked to page-flip, so you already have stored experience on this activity—if you have been doing the page-flipping as asked.)

If you forget about it then you are, unfortunately, missing an opportunity to increase your understanding and strengthen a nerve groove.

2. *You should page-flip as you read.* Page-flipping is *cross-referencing one part of your reading with another part of your reading.*

This is how it works: you are reading along and you come across a phrase or idea that you vaguely remember you had read before in that book or in another recently read book. What should you do? Forget it and go on? No. You should try to recall it clearly and strongly. If you can't, then you should flip back through the pages of the book until you find what you had vaguely remembered reading before. (I won't be around to tell you when and where to page-flip. You have to learn how to do it by yourself!)

Thanks to your memory, there was a trace stored away from your earlier reading. Thanks

to your memory, that idea was given back to you when you came across it again in your later reading.

That memory may have come back to you weakly or vaguely. But the important thing is that it came back to you.

Why is it important that it came back, even as a vague recollection? It is important because *now you have the opportunity to go back and find that other, first mention of the idea.* Why is this important? It is important because (a) it will give you the opportunity to reinforce the idea so that it will be stored more firmly, (b) it will add completeness to the idea because you will now include in your understanding of it what was previously said about it, and (c) it will allow you to exercise and strengthen your memory and thinking processes through this cross-referencing practice.

3. You may ask, "But what if my memory doesn't give me back any vague recollections of ideas that I read earlier?"

There are two main reasons why your memory would not do that. (a) You did not understand the idea when you first read it; you did not give that idea a reality check but just let the words slip past your eyes. If this happened, then, of course, there would be no trace of that idea in your memory, so how could your memory remind you of it? (b) You are not sensitive to the vague reminders given to you by your memory; your memory may start to give you a recollection but you are in a hurry or are not aware of the importance of paying attention to these vague recollections. If this happens, then it is not your memory's fault but your own, for not paying attention.

How can you correct these problems so that your memory *will* give you these important recollections and so that you *will* pay attention to them?

Simple: give all ideas a reality check as you read them. This will ensure that a nerve groove or memory trace is being made so that the material will be stored for you; also, whenever you feel a little niggling feeling that you already have read a certain idea, stop and think. That little niggle is your memory trying to give you the recollection. Then you will be able to try to conjure up a stronger memory of that idea or, if you can't, you can page-flip until you find it. This may take some time, but it is well worth it.

4. Try to become familiar with how your memory works. It can do a lot for you if you know how to help it do its work.
Do **For Practice.**

Did you page-flip in all the cases indicated above in your list? You should always do so.

Equally important, you should page-flip on your own whenever you yourself pick up or sense or remember a previous reference to the material you are presently reading. *It will increase the time it takes to read through an assignment—but it is well worth it because it will help you understand the material more completely and thoroughly.*

Page-flipping makes your mind sharper, clearer. Become a good page-flipper and you will become an excellent student!

For Practice

This textbook asks you to do page-flipping as you read it. Look back over this chapter and find places where you are asked to page-flip.

List the page-flipping directions found in this chapter.

Your Summary

Items   *Page Number(s)*

Remember to compare your list with your classmates'.

CHAPTER 7

Taking Tests

A. Yes, You Can Learn How to Take Tests Well

When you get your first test back from your teacher, you will experience the "Moment of Truth." This is the moment when you see whether your notes were any good, whether you had studied enough or correctly or the right things, whether you forgot material during the test, whether you understood and remembered the material but didn't say it well on the test.

Before the first test in a course you are flying blind, so to speak. You do not know what kinds of questions this particular teacher is going to ask. You don't know what this teacher is looking for or expects. Before the first test you have to be ready for anything and hope for the best.

This chapter will help you prepare for several different kinds of questions that you might find on a test. It will also try to give you some insight into what teachers are generally looking for and expecting.

B. Why Tests Are Useful

Please do not think that passing tests is the ultimate goal and purpose of going to school! The truly important things are understanding, learning (gaining knowledge and skill), and improving yourself.

Tests, however, are an important part of the learning process. For one thing, a test will let a teacher know how much his or her students know or don't know. Then the teacher has an understanding of how much help the students need, how quickly or slowly they should progress. Often, a teacher will use the results of a test to improve his or her own teaching methods. For example, if everyone on a test gets a failing grade, the teacher can do several things: (a) go more slowly and carefully to be sure the students are understanding everything at every step; (b) try to motivate the students so they will study more and as a result be better prepared; (c) arrange special sessions to help students catch up; (d) prepare more teaching aid materials to help get the ideas across; (e) reassess his or her teaching techniques and, if necessary, change them.

If, on the other hand, most students do well but a few students fail, the teacher can arrange special meetings with these failing students to help them or can, in some other way, provide or suggest extra assistance for these students. Thus, tests can be used by teachers in the same way that doctors use tests: to diagnose the situation so they can help cure any problems that might exist.

Tests are also useful for another reason: students can use the test score to find out how they stand. Students lacking in confidence sometimes find that good grades on tests can help them to relax and feel more confident. On the other side of the coin, an overconfident student may have his or her attitude corrected by a low grade on a test. In other words, test scores can often give students a realistic picture of how they are doing and whether their studying techniques are effective or ineffective.

There is yet another good reason for tests. This may, in fact, be the most important reason. Namely, in studying for a test a student reprocesses the already studied material. That is, the student, by reviewing, makes sure he or she understands the material, has it arranged by the best mnemonic device, and has it firmly stored. Also, a student who has not yet processed the material will do it on the days before the test, making the mnemonic devices and using the copy, check, correct method. In this way the student will actually learn the material *because* of a test.

To say it another way, the pressure of a test causes a student to make sure the material is processed (understood and properly and firmly stored). Without this pressure, some students might simply take lecture notes and read the textbook assignment but never process the material in order to understand it and store it properly and firmly in their memory. We can say about these students, "They took the course but they didn't learn the material."

There are even some students who do not feel that tests are a painful pressure. They enjoy processing the material, understanding it, and storing it in their memory—in other words, learning. A test, for them, is just a deadline for when they should have finished processing the material.

C. The Different Kinds of Test Questions

1. There are basically only two kinds of test questions: (a) fact questions; (b) thought questions, which are a combination of fact and opinion. (Pure opinion questions are rare.)

2. For fact questions you will have to know a specific date, a specific name, a specific list, a specific event, etc. The answer will usually be short. Only one answer is correct. You either know the answer or you don't. For example, "Who was the president of the United States in 1900?" "When was the U.S. Constitution ratified?" "What eight activities are included on a schedule?" Can you answer this last question without looking back? Try it in **For Practice**.

Either you knew the answer or you didn't. Often this type of question is of the multiple-choice or fill-in-the-blank or some other short answer variety.

There are two parts to a multiple-choice question. First, there is the question. Second, there is a list of possible answers; you are supposed to *recognize* and select the correct answer or answers from this list. However, when you answer a multiple-choice question, follow this method:

a. Read the question.

b. Do *not* immediately read the list of possible answers to try to *recognize* the correct answer or answers.

c. Instead, *without looking at the list of possible answers,* try to *recall* from your memory (remember on your own), the correct answer to the question.

d. Then, only *after* you have recalled (remembered) the answer *on your own,* you can look at the list of possible answers. Now you will be looking to find the answer *you already remember as the correct answer.*

You should use this method because research has shown that *recalling* (remembering on your own) is more accurate, more effective, and easier than trying to *recognize* an answer included in a list of possible answers.

For example, here is a multiple-choice question: "A good schedule will have several quali-

For Practice

Answer the question in Section C, part 2, from memory. The eight activities are:

1.   5.

2.   6.

3.   7.

4.   8.

Now check your answers with your notes or this textbook.

ties. Select the correct qualities from the following. Underline all correct answers." Now stop and try to recall the qualities a good schedule should have. Have you *remembered (recalled)* those qualities? If you have, now you can continue with the test and read the list of possible answers: "(a) realism; (b) regularity; (c) motivation; (d) flexibility; (e) sleeping." Do you see the answers you have recalled? (You should have underlined *realism, regularity,* and *flexibility.* Motivation is not a quality of a schedule. Motivation is a quality the person or student, you, should have. And sleeping is not a quality; it is an activity.) How did you do? If you had first looked at the list trying to *recognize* the correct answer, *without first trying to recall,* you could have been confused. *Recalling* helps you answer multiple-choice questions.

3. For thought questions, on the other hand, you have to understand a concept, an idea, a body of information, etc. The answer will tend to be long and in your own words. Often you will have to rearrange the ideas and pieces of information you studied in order to come up with an answer that puts them together in a different way. For example: "Of all the results of the United States Civil War, which one result has had, in your opinion, the greatest impact on the women's liberation movement? Why?" Another question might be: "In building a schedule for studying, what problems will a full-time student with two children and a full-time job encounter? Can these problems be solved? If they can be solved, *how* can they be solved?"

4. For that latter question, you would have to combine both your own thoughts and also facts. You would have to think about several different ideas you learned about scheduling. You would also have to remember the eight items to be included on a schedule (which are facts); you would have to remember how much time is needed for studying and for other important activities (like sleeping, etc.). Then you would have to put all of these different facts and ideas together in order to answer the question. Can you answer this question without looking back at your notes or this text? Try it in **For Practice** on page 62. Then check to see how you did.

5. Usually more points are given to a thought question than to a straight fact question. That is, the question, "What should a student do to make sure he or she succeeds in school?" is obviously going to take more time and effort to answer than the question, "What is the mnemonic device for the spaces on the musical scale?" The thought question might be a 10–15 point question whereas the fact question might be a 1- or 2-point question.

6. You must figure out before you answer a question whether it is a fact or a thought question or a combination. Then you will be able to answer it better.

Remember, the main difference between a thought question and a fact question is that with a fact question, the answer is usually short and you either know it or you don't. "Who is the President of the United States?" "Which generals during the Revolutionary War fought in the Battle of White Plains?" "What is the name of Shakespeare's first produced play?" "What is the formula for water?" There is no place for opinion. You just write down the exact fact being asked for.

In a thought question you need to do more figuring and thinking and evaluating and judging. "Compare the themes of the novels *The Idiot* and *The Magic Mountain.*" "Which accounting system would be most efficient for a company with a $100,000,000 a year profit? Why?" "Do you agree that the Treaty of Versailles helped cause World War II? What are your reasons?" Obviously these thought questions all require that you also know some solid facts. Mainly, you have to scratch your head and try to put different facts (pieces of information) together and also have an opinion of your own. *But always try to give facts to support your answers on a thought question.* It will make your answer better.

D. Several Questions at One Time

A thought question will often be made up of several questions. You must identify all the questions and you must answer every single one of them! In the thought questions given in the last paragraph, can you see how many questions are in each one of them? In the first question

For Practice

Answer the question in Section C, part 4, from memory.

Compare your answers with your classmates' answers.

there is only one openly asked question: How are the two themes familiar? However, there are two other *hidden* questions that you must answer first: What is the theme of *The Idiot*? What is the theme of *The Magic Mountain*? But in the second question, clearly, openly, there are two questions: *What* is the best system for the company *and why*? You must answer *both* those questions. You must say what the best system would be and then you must *also* tell why. How many questions are included in the third question? See whether you can tell how many there are. Answer before you go on.

There are two questions in it: did the Treaty of Versailles help cause the war? Then, whether you agree or disagree, you *also* have to give the *reasons* for your answer.

Sometimes a student will answer only one part of a thought question. It is very unfortunate when she or he answers that one part perfectly—but neglects to answer the other part of the question. In such cases the teacher has no other choice but to give the student only one-half the credit. After the test is handed back, those students, who knew the answer but just didn't pick up on its being part of that question, will feel like kicking themselves.

How can you avoid making this mistake? Read over the test questions very carefully. As you answer each question, keep looking back at the question to see whether you are covering every aspect. You need, mainly, to be *careful*. Better to be overly careful and safe than quick and sorry.

Read over each question very carefully and pick out how many questions are really in it. Some questions can have even three or more questions in them.

E. You, the Test, the Teacher, and the Grade

1. So you plan to throw the bull on a thought question? Don't do it. Your teacher will know you are trying to avoid answering the question and will have a negative impression of your ability and intentions and may look with an unfriendly eye upon the rest of your work. Say as much as you know and leave it at that. At least your credibility as a sincere student will not be harmed.

2. Does it ever happen that you understand the question and know the answer the teacher is looking for but you disagree with the teacher? Or do you have special information that was not in the lecture or text? For example, you have always had a special interest in World War II and know more about D-Day than you learned in class. Should you give your special, better information or should you give only the limited information the teacher is looking for?

Always, always, always *first* give the answer the teacher is looking for, the answer that was included in the text and class lectures. Give this answer *first. Then*, and only then, can you add your own special information. You need to add it with a clear introduction. For example, you can add: "While the above answer is what we learned in class, I would like to add some further information." And then go ahead and write down what you know.

You should do it this way because in order to get full credit for your answer you need to let the teacher know you have been to class, paid attention, and learned the required information. Any extra or special information you have, any disagreements (and they must be backed up with facts, of course) you have, can be added to the end of your answer—and always with an introduction to let the teacher know what you are doing. Often a teacher will be very pleased to see your extra information or your disagreement. It will show that you are not only a fine student (because you first answered in terms of the class requirements) but that you are also an independent thinker. Instead of an A, you might get A + + for that answer!

3. *Remember, teachers are not mind-readers!* Remember that the teacher will be correcting twenty to thirty or more tests and will be looking for certain answers to the questions. You have to keep in mind that your teacher is human and needs you to spell out what you are doing if you are going beyond the limits of the question.

4. For thought questions, always give as generous an answer as you can, especially if the question carries a lot of credit. For example, on a 10-point thought question you should write at least a few paragraphs, not just one sentence. For a 25-point question, however, you should write one or several pages. Give definitions, facts, examples, causes, effects, or whatever else might be appropriate. This is especially true for take-home tests.

Take the thought question mentioned above about the scheduling problem for the full-time student with the full-time job and two children. "In building a schedule for studying, what problems will a full-time student with two children and a full-time job encounter? Can these problems be solved? If so, how can they be solved?"

Suppose this is a 25-point question. Suppose you answer: "She will have a problem finding enough time to study and also spend enough time with her children. This problem can be solved by her quitting her job."

I would give this answer about 3 of the 25 points. This answer is not generous enough. It does not go into 25 points' worth of information and discussion. Also, while the answer is correct about *part* of what the problem is, the proposed solution is not well thought out or thoroughly discussed. You may have known more than you wrote, but I would never know just from reading your answer. (How many points should you get for your answer in the **For Practice** exercise in Section C, part 4, above?)

Here is an answer that would get all 25 points:

A full-time student with two children and a full-time job will encounter time problems when building a schedule for studying. These time problems will cause morale problems because she will find she cannot do a good job at school and also as a parent, which is really also a full-time job. First of all, there will be time problems because being a full-time student is just like having a full-time job (15 hours a week minimum in class and, thus, 30 hours a week for study, for a 45-hour week). This student will have the equivalent of three full-time jobs: regular job, student, and parent. For the student and regular jobs alone, the person will have to schedule 80–85 hours a week (if he or she wants to do an excellent job as a student). However, since the student has two children, it is not very likely that he or she will be able to schedule a full 45 hours for school work and, thus, will probably not do an excellent job as a student. This may cause the person to feel unhappy and to have poor morale as a student. But if the student sacrifices family for studying, he or she will probably feel guilty and lose morale as a parent. Second, there will be time problems because besides the three full-time jobs that must be scheduled, there are also other activities, like sleep-

ing, eating, traveling, house duties (like shopping, cleaning, cooking, laundry), and recreation. No doubt there will be little or no time for recreation. Loss of morale can also be expected if a person has to spend day after day and week after week and month after month with a heavy load of work and responsibility with little or no recreation.

Daily, during the work week, the student will have to schedule approximately 16 hours for school and work. This leaves very little time for the other activities and the children. If the student works on weekends, then there is some time during the work week to spend with the children, but then on the weekends the parent will be working—and possibly studying.

With this kind of schedule, which probably won't provide for 8 hours of sleep a night, how can the student schedule study for peak energy times? Will this student, with all these burdens, *have* any peak energy times? If he or she does, it will not be very likely that he or she will have the luxury of scheduling for them.

This student's problems can be kept under control by very careful and exact scheduling and by accepting that it may not be possible to be an excellent student. But any crisis or unexpected change could wreck the schedule. Thus, the only real way to resolve this student's extreme time and morale problems is for this student either to take a part-time job or go to school part-time or live with his/her parents (or someone) who can take over basic care of the home and children.

5. Always answer exactly and precisely to the point of the question. To do this, of course, you need to understand the question and be clear about what it is asking. Read the question carefully and calmly. Try to understand the question exactly (also be sure to identify how many questions are included in it). Make notes, preferably an outline, before you write.

If you read a question a number of times and still can't clearly see what it is asking you, then ask the teacher to help you understand what it is asking. If the teacher refuses, leave that question until the end. Perhaps when you get back to it after answering the other questions, it will make more sense to you. It is always possible that the question is unclear. In this case, you will have to discuss the situation with your teacher, during the test or afterwards.

If you don't care to take it up with the teacher—even if you think the problem is the teacher's fault—then you will be stuck with the consequences. If you find yourself in this painful situation, you might want to reread in Chapter 1 the section called "Problems with a Teacher?"

After you have clearly understood what the question is asking for, then answer *directly and exactly to that point.* As you prepare your material and gather your ideas and/or facts, ask yourself whether this is really what the question is asking about, whether this answer is going to answer the question *precisely to the point.*

Before you write your answer, and also as you are writing it, check with the question to be sure you are on target. If you finish the test early, go back over the test and recheck just to make sure.

Sometimes a student who has thoroughly prepared for a test and has the material stored properly and firmly in his or her memory and understands the material perfectly will do poorly on a question because the student misreads or doesn't fully or clearly understand what the question wants. The student gives a generous, well-supported answer. But, heartbreakingly, it is not the answer asked for by the question. The teacher, probably understanding what has happened, would like to give the student credit for a full and well-written answer. But this is not possible because the student has really not answered the question.

Sometimes, if the teacher believes the student is sincere (i.e., the teacher knows the student does not throw the bull or try to wriggle out of a direct answer), the teacher will give the student partial credit. This is one situation in which a reputation for honesty and sincerity may make the difference between 0 points or 50 percent, or more, of the points. (Do you remember that you just recently read about this? Flip back and find the other place.)

6. Pay attention to the credits for each question. If no credits are actually written down for each question, then use your own judgment as to which are the heavy or important questions and which the lighter or simple questions. For the big credit or important questions, be *generous,* spill your guts, give all the relevant information and ideas you can.

If you have only an hour for the test and there are ten questions, you need carefully to allot your time to each question according to the importance of each question. You may not be able to be completely generous as a result. You

have to use your best judgment about this.

Experience taking tests will help you improve your judgment about which questions should be answered more fully. Experience will help you learn how to allot your time so that you can answer each question sufficiently, according to its weight. Making notes or outlines will help you give proper answers.

F. How to Overcome the Fear of Tests

What if you are a nervous wreck when it comes to taking a test? What if you freeze up and your mind stops working? What if you are convinced that you will do a poor job? (Stop and think of a page-flip you can do. Do it!)

Here is some advice to help you relax so that you can do your best.

1. First of all, be sure that you studied sufficiently. Did you study every day and review every week? Did you process the material by (a) reality checking to understand the meaning of lectures and text; (b) completing and correcting your lecture notes with the help of your text; (c) ordering your material into mnemonic devices; (d) making flash cards if appropriate; (e) using the copy, check, correct method; (f) reviewing before and after class and once a week? If you did all those activities, using all those study skills, then the material should be properly and firmly stored in your memory.

2. The night before the test, before you go to sleep, review your material, perhaps doing the copy, check, correct method in your mind. When you copy, check, correct in your mind, you can do it very quickly. Remember, this is just to review one more time, to give those nerve grooves a last touch.

I suggest doing this just before going to sleep because, as mentioned in Chapter 3, some researchers believe that if people study just before going to sleep, they will remember better. You can also do a quick review before you go into the test. It is impossible to study too much! In fact, *overstudy is recommended.*

3. When you get into the room, do not drive yourself crazy by trying to remember everything to make sure it is safe in your memory. If you stored it properly and firmly during all your study and review, then it is there. No doubt about it. Safe and secure, just like your money in the bank vault, all neatly stacked on shelves, ready to be retrieved when needed. Calm down. Relax. Have confidence in your perfect memory. You know you understand the material. You know you have stored it properly and firmly. If you didn't understand the material and didn't study and didn't store it properly and firmly, you are quite right to worry! Maybe next time you will be better prepared by doing all these activites during time scheduled for study.

A dress rehearsal or self-test before the test will help you practice recalling (remembering) your stored material. Chapter 8 gives a full account of how to do this.

4. *When you get the test, read all of it over before beginning to answer any of the questions.* An exception to this would be a short-answer test with many, many questions. In that case you should look at several questions here and there at random. You should look the test over before you start answering it because it will (a) remind you of the subject and get your mind working; (b) help you find the easy and hard questions. *You will want to answer the easiest questions first*; (c) let some questions help you with other questions. Sometimes a word or phrase in one question will remind you of something that will help you answer another question.

Before you begin, be sure you have determined which questions are the more important or weighty ones requiring more time. *Allot your time so that you have an approximate time table:* ten minutes for this question; five minutes for that one; thirty minutes for the other one.

Then begin, starting with an easy one first. This will help your self-confidence, get your mind working well, warm you up for the harder ones. *If, as you are answering one question, an idea for another question pops into your mind, write it down in the margin or on a piece of scrap paper so you don't lose it. Still tense? Take deep breaths.*

5. When you write answers to essay questions, the following information about the actual writing will be helpful.

First of all, you will need scrap paper!

On the scrap paper write down the informa-

tion and ideas that immediately come to mind as you read the question. Do not let these thoughts get away. Jot them down right away. Then, put your thoughts and information together into a logical form. An outline type of format is very useful here. (Chapter 14 will give you specific help on making outlines.)

Finally, write down your answer on the test paper. As mentioned above (Section E, part 5), be sure you are addressing the exact point or points of the question. Are you addressing *all* the aspects of the question?

Be sure to reread your answers before you hand in the exam. Perhaps yet another part of an answer will come forth at the last minute from your memory. Perhaps you will catch a mistake.

If you are unable to complete the exam in the allotted time, write down at least a bare outline of the answer and hand this in. If nothing else, your instructor will realize that you know the information. You may be able to get credit for the question with a good outline.

Remember, keep an eye on the clock to try to avoid not finishing in time.

Be as careful, precise, and accurate as you can; follow all the suggestions given earlier in this chapter.

G. Practice Your Test-taking Skills in This Course

Look at the tests in this course as experiments or practice sessions. Don't be afraid or nervous. The first tests will not be graded. After each test you will have the opportunity to check your answers against your notes. Then your teacher will go over the tests with you in class so that you can get the correct answers.

These tests are to give you the opportunity to judge your own notes and study methods and ability to answer correctly. Then you will be able to improve whatever it is that might be preventing you from doing well on tests. (Were your lecture notes complete? Did you fully understand the material? Were your mnemonic devices logical? Did you copy, check, correct enough? Etc.)

These tests will contain all the different kinds of questions that you will find on tests in your other courses. There will be all different types of long and short answer questions, fact and thought questions. This will let you become familiar with many kinds of questions and gain practice answering them.

As your experience grows, as you improve your note-taking and study habits and study skills, you will increase not only your ability but also your self-confidence.

Even if you get everything wrong on your first tests, don't worry. You have the ability to succeed. You may be sabotaging yourself with your lack of self-confidence and your past difficulties and fears. But if you keep plugging away, you will discover that you can do it. (Can you think of a page-flip to do? Do it.)

You have to start by getting your feet wet. Jump into the first tests and see how you do with the help you have had so far in this course.

Your Summary

Items   *Page Number(s)*

Compare your lists with your classmates'.

CHAPTER 8

Self-Testing: The Dress Rehearsal

A. Why You Need a Dress Rehearsal for a Test

There is a last step in the study process. After you have gone through all the steps outlined and discussed elsewhere in the book, you will be ready for the last step.

This last step is going through a dress rehearsal for the test you will have to take, just as a pianist who has been learning a concerto to play in a concert will have a dress rehearsal just before the actual concert. The pianist will pretend it is the real concert and will play the concerto as well as possible.

Actors also have dress rehearsals to prepare for the real performance. They spend weeks, sometimes months, memorizing their lines, improving their understanding of their role, repeating their parts over and over. Then, just before the actual performance, they have a dress rehearsal. In the dress rehearsal, they pretend it is the real thing and try to do it perfectly.

The purpose of a dress rehearsal is to see whether there are any little details that are not quite perfect. The performers run through the material and, if something is not quite perfect, they can clear up the problem before the real performance takes place.

Thus, students, too, should have dress rehearsals. Just before the test, the student should run through the material as though it were for the real test. In this way the student can see whether there is anything that is hard to recall or any confusion or lack of understanding. Then the student can correct that problem during the dress rehearsal. As a result, the real test itself should go very successfully indeed!

B. How to Have a Dress Rehearsal: Give Yourself a Test

But how can a student have a dress rehearsal? The teacher has the test. The student can't get hold of the test to go through it for practice beforehand!

But there is a way. It is not as perfect as for the musician or actor, who can actually do the real thing without the audience's being there. But it is better than nothing and does help polish up any rough edges and make sure that recall is quick and easy.

The method is for the student to give himself or herself a test. Yes, you will make up a self-test. You will try to make up a test that you think your teacher might give you on the material. You give yourself broad thought questions that put the material together in different, unusual ways. You also give yourself specific fact questions. You give yourself hard questions, questions that cover all the material you have studied. You give yourself questions that will allow you to practice, as if in a dress rehearsal, the test that your teacher will soon be giving you.

This is how you do it:

1. Put your flash cards and copying paper and notes away. Then think, think, think about the material and try to come up with hard, exacting questions that will test your overall understanding as well as your knowledge of specific facts.

2. If you can't think of questions, peek at your notes or the text to remind yourself of some of the topics. Give yourself one question at a time. Make up the question.

3. Then actually write out the answer as smoothly, clearly and completely as possible. *You are practicing recall when you answer your question.*

C. How to Answer and Correct Your Self-Test Questions

1. After you have answered a question to the best of your ability, as if it were on the real test, look back at your notes to check and correct your answer. If you have not recalled everything, then try to answer the question again—this will be another copy, check, and correct activity. Then, but only after you have got the first question in your dress rehearsal self-test straight, ask another question. Keep trying to recall and give clear, smooth, complete answers to these questions you give yourself. Answer as carefully and completely and well as you would for real on the actual test. You will be surprised how much help this will be!

Learning how to give yourself truly helpful self-tests requires practice and experience. As you progress in school, gaining experience and practice, you will increase your ability to self-test. I discovered the self-test dress rehearsal method in graduate school—my tests became all A's after that.

Do **For Practice** below.

For the last **For Practice** question you could have added some illustrations or diagrams (e.g., of flash cards or a mnemonic device). This question gives you the chance to pull together information from different parts of your notes. This kind of broad question is especially helpful in

For Practice

Here are some examples of some self-test questions. (Yes, they are exactly like questions on a real test. They *should* be!) After you answer each question, go back to the textbook and your notes to check your answer.

1. What are the activities that one must include in a schedule? (fact question)

2. Give an explanation of the SQ3R method. (fact and thought)

3. How would you make flash cards to remember (store properly and firmly) your explanation of the SQ3R method? (thought and fact)

Compare your answers with your classmates' answers.

your self-testing. As you try to recall everything and anything that might pertain to a question, as you try to combine one part of your knowledge with another, you are strengthening *both your understanding and your recall*.

2. And if, as you check back with your notes, you find that you have not recalled some material that *does* pertain to your question, you will be able to strengthen your recall of that material right then and there.

Then you might want to try to answer that question again, this time recalling and stating *all* the relevant material from your notes.

Imagine how primed you will be for your test (or a discussion or your own research) if you go through this kind of serious self-testing dress rehearsal.

D. When Should You Have Your Dress Rehearsal Self-Test?

Self-testing should occur only *after* you have completed and are satisfied with your copy, check, and correct work.

You can give yourself a self-test whenever you finish copying, checking, and correcting a set of notes. This can be part of your regular, daily study. You may not want to (or be able to) take the time to self-test regularly every day during each study session. If you can, it is better for you. If you can't, then you can't.

However, whether you have the time to self-test every day or not, you *must* be sure to self-test just before a real test. As you study for your test, going over all your flash cards and mnemonic devices, be sure you include a self-test at the end. Make sure you have time at the end of your study before your test to give yourself a complete and thorough self-test dress rehearsal.

E. Is All This Trouble Worth It?

Practicing to take a test by the means of self-testing is very important. Even if you don't anticipate the exact questions the teacher will ask, you will, nevertheless, be improving the strength and flexibility of your recall as well as your skill in stating answers. It will also help your self-confidence.

Self-testing dress rehearsals can sometimes mean the difference between a B and an A, or between an A − and an A +.

The above method for self-testing, like all the other methods taught in this course, are for you to use as you wish. If you want to be an A or A + student, you will practice all the methods until you are highly skillful. If you are content to be a C or B student you can put in less work and acquire less skill. It is up to you. This course provides you with tools for your toolbox. It is up to you whether you want to become an expert with these tools or whether it is enough for you to have only a medium or even lesser skill.

As with everything else in this course, to learn this skill completely you always have to be trying to improve the quality of your thinking; you have to be motivated, disciplined, willing to put in sufficient time and effort.

You can do it if you want to. But only you can decide how much effort your own educational plans and purposes are worth.

Your Summary

Items   *Page Number(s)*

Compare your list with your classmates'.

CHAPTER 9

Using the Material

A. On Tests

1. Here's some good news. You already know how to use the material on a test! Chapter 7 discussed the need to answer fact and thought questions, to give full, generous answers, to give general answers with specific details to back them up, to allot your time and answer according to the weight and importance of the questions, to add extra information that you know from outside the class. You also know how to give yourself a self-test as a dress rehearsal and how to answer those questions.

2. You have also been taking tests in this course and so you have some experience in using *on tests* the material you have studied.

B. For Other Purposes

1. Let us consider, now, how you can use *for other purposes* the material you have learned. What are these other purposes? These other purposes come up all the time in your life. Do you want to understand what is happening in the world? Do you want to improve your relationships with other people? Do you want to solve problems that occur in your family, friendships, work? These are all situations in which you will have a use for your knowledge.

For example, suppose a major industry intends to build a new plant and use the river near it for dumping wastes. Suppose that industry has been able to get governmental permission to use the river that way because the river is not being used for human consumption at this time. The river is also not generally used for fishing. You read this information in the newspaper.

Then you hear about an organizaton which is interested in fighting pollution and conserving our resources. This organization is going to try to reverse the government decision about letting the industry use this river for its wastes.

You discuss the situation with a friend. Your friend says, "So what? No one uses that river. It's not going to hurt anybody."

But you took an ecology course in which you learned that in the future water will be scarce. In fact it will be so scarce by 1990 that we will have to desalinize ocean water to provide water for drinking and cooking. You put two and two together and realize that even though that river isn't being used for human consumption now, it may be needed twenty years from now!

You tell this to your friend. Your friend also took the same ecology course you did. But your friend simply took it to get the credits in order to get the degree in order to get a job. Your friend was playing the "grade and degree game" in that course. Your friend simply took in the words and memorized them, but never *processed* the material, never really *learned* the material. Your friend did not give reality checks and did not really understand the material.

You look at your friend and realize that this person might as well not have taken the course. You realize that there are probably a lot of people who have heard about pollution and the scarcity of resources but who don't *really* understand, it, who haven't given that information a *serious* reality check.

You start to get worried because you *did* give the material a reality check. You really *did* learn and understand the material. You really *do* know that in twenty years that river might help ease the very *real* resource problem that we are going to have.

You join the organization and work to help conserve that river.

What you are doing is using what you learned. *You have converted school learning into action in the real world. And the world will be the better for it.*

Your friend, on the other hand, who thought the ideas and material in the class were all junk and just stuff to remember for a test, hasn't

71

really *learned* anything. Your friend, though a college student who has taken many courses, cannot use the course material for any other purpose than for taking a test in that course. Too bad.

2. My final words to you on this subject are that I hope you will make the effort to use what you are learning in this course to help you do well in school, and that you will use in your life what you learn in school.

School gives you the opportunity to learn and profit from the experiences, discoveries, ideas of others. Then add to this what you yourself have experienced and have already learned. If you approach your courses this way, also using the skills and thinking processes discussed in this book, then you will surely emerge from college a wiser person whose intelligence has been developed and strengthened and whose knowledge can be put to good use to enrich your own life and perhaps even others' lives as well.

Your Summary

Items   *Page Number(s)*

Compare your list with your classmates'.

CHAPTER 10

Checklist—Where You Are So Far

The Study Skills and Procedures You Should Now Be Practicing and Using

In Class

—*Pay attention—focus—concentrate!*
—Take complete notes of what is important—paraphrase if you want.
—Copy from blackboard exactly.

Review

—Before class, review the notes you took the day before.
—After class, review the notes you just took.
—Periodically review all material since the course began.

Deep Study

—Gain understanding of the material by giving reality checks and making connections between the new and the old material (by cross-referencing and page-flipping).
—If text coordinates with lecture notes, add to and correct notes as you read the textbook assignment.
—Make mnemonic devices of the material in your notes. This will prepare the material for *proper* storage.
—Make flash cards of these arrangements if appropriate.
—Copy, check, correct the mnemonic arrangements and flash cards (if you have any). *Write* your copies for most effective nerve grooving. This helps you store your material *firmly*.
—At least once a week review all your mnemonic arrangements and flash cards.
—*Pay attention—focus—concentrate!*

Study for a Test

—Review all mnemonic arrangements and flash cards.
—Copy, check, correct the above. You can do this orally or mentally if you have already, during deep study, made the firm nerve grooves by writing your copies as you copied, checked, and corrected. If you did not process the material during deep study, then you need to do it now by following the checklist of activities for deep study.
—Self-test dress rehearsal. Write and answer questions. Copy, check, and correct.

You have also learned the importance of motivation, how to schedule, and how to take tests.

You may have been using a dictionary already. However, as you begin to learn how to read your textbook in the following chapters, you will absolutely need a dictionary.

For general everyday use and convenience you can purchase and keep with you an inexpensive paperback dictionary. Some rare words, you will find, are not included in this kind of dictionary. For these words you can use the more complete, hardcover dictionary. If you can't afford this more expensive book, you can find one in your college or local public library.

What dictionary should you buy? In all the inexpensive paperbacks the words included are basically the same. To decide which dictionary is best for you, look through several of them.

Read the definitions of the same words in several dictionaries. Pick the dictionary whose definitions are easiest to read and most understandable to you. Also, look for the pronunciation guides (some are at the bottom of the page; some are on one page at the beginning or end of the book). Your dictionary's pronunciation guide ought to be one that you can understand.

CHAPTER 11

The Words and the Sentences

A. Understanding the Words

1. Here is a sentence in a philosophy textbook: "Every person who does not have a penchant for fun ought to excoriate himself or herself."

Do you understand this sentence? Is this sentence true or false when you give it a reality check? You can't tell, of course, unless you can understand every word in this sentence.

Look up the words you don't know. After you have looked up the words, you understand that, paraphrased, the sentence means: "Every person who does not have a strong liking for fun ought to severely criticize himself or herself."

Now you can give this statement a reality check. By checking with your own experience and your own moral and ethical values you can see that you either agree (think the statement is true) or disagree (think the statement is false). Or perhaps you will want to read on and see what the author of the book has to say. Perhaps you haven't thought about this idea before and are not very experienced in life. You want to have an open mind and see, by reading further and thinking more about it, whether you will agree or not.

Here is another sentence, this time from a history textbook: "King Henry V's hunting doublet had a guardant of a lion on it."

Do you understand this sentence? Again, if you do not understand all the words you will need to look them up.

You use your dictionary and then you can understand that the sentence means: "King Henry V's hunting jacket had a picture on it of a lion looking face out."

But do you know what a doublet looks like? Did your dictionary have a picture of it? If not, look up "doublet" in an encyclopedia or a history picture book or go to a museum. Try to *investigate* so that you can get a good understanding of what this word means.

2. For the abstract words in the sentence from the philosophy textbook, you cannot look up pictures. There are no pictures of "penchant" or "excoriate." To understand *abstract* words completely you need to *think* about what they mean. You may need to look the abstract word up in several different dictionaries to get a fuller, more complete definition so that you can understand it better.

3. But with words that refer to *things*, you can find out what the *thing* looks like and that will help you understand the word easily. You look up the word "guardant" and there in the dictionary is the picture of an animal staring face out at you. Now you know exactly what that word means. You look up "doublet" and see a picture of a tight-fitting jacket of a certain design. Now you know exactly what that word means. Then when you go back and reread the sentence "King Henry V's doublet had a guardant of a lion on it" you know exactly what that sentence means.

Do you agree or disagree with this sentence about the king's doublet as you give it a reality check? Well, with such a sentence as that, the author you are reading can probably be considered a good resource person and you can probably simply take his or her word for it.

B. Understanding the Sentences

1. Thus, it is clear from these examples that when you are reading *you first must understand the meaning of every word*. If you do not understand the words you cannot understand or give a reality check to the sentences. And in order to understand and make sense of what you are reading, you *must be able to understand every sentence and give a reality check to as many sentences as possible*.

For example, you read in your novel for a literature course: "When Clara went into the bedroom to see whether the jewels she had hidden were still safe, she almost fainted! The armoire was askew!" Do you understand this? Can you picture what these words are referring to?

a. Look up the words you don't know in a dictionary.

b. Find a picture of an armoire, since it is a thing. Think about what "askew" means, since it is not a thing, but is more abstract.

Now you can *fully* understand that second sentence, which, paraphrased, means: "The wardrobe (a large piece of furniture used to store clothes) was not squared up against the wall."

You can even picture what this looks like:

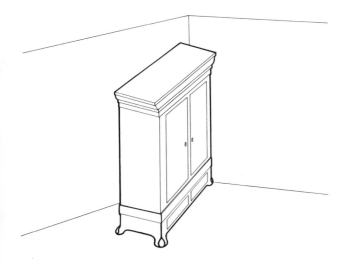

Now when you reread the paragraph you can picture and understand the entire meaning fully. "When Clara went into the bedroom to see whether the jewels she had hidden were still safe, she almost fainted! The armoire was askew!" Obviously she had hidden the jewels behind the armoire. The fact that it was askew meant someone had moved it away from the wall—probably to steal the jewels! (Reading is more exciting when you know what is going on.)

2. Of course if you have to stop and look up every word you don't know and then give every sentence a reality check by picturing the things and by thinking about the abstractions, it will make you read very slowly. Yes, to begin with. But as your vocabulary increases and as you get more practiced at these skills, you will find your-

self reading more quickly and with more understanding (and interest) than ever before.

Advanced students, students with a good vocabulary who are well practiced and experienced in this kind of reading, can read new material on *familiar* topics very quickly, making almost instantaneous reality checks, understanding the meaning and/or picturing as they read. They are almost seeing a series of pictures moving across their mind's eye rather than laboring over individual words and sentences.

This is the goal for which you are striving. It may take several quarters or even years. But when you get there, it will be well worth the effort!

But when even these advanced students come upon a subject with which they are *unfamiliar*, they have to slow down. With an unfamiliar topic they have to spend time on their reality checks. They may have to spend some time thinking over the new ideas, re-evaluating their own experience and philosophy, investigating with further research, trying to picture the new things. Only by doing these activities can a student, even a very experienced and advanced student, make unfamiliar material more familiar. Once the new material has been made familiar, however, the good student can then go quickly when reading more new material about this now familiar topic. (Page-flip to a previous section that tells how to learn familiar and unfamiliar material.)

3. In other words, *remember that you are reading in order to know more about reality.* The words were put on the page by some author who felt she or he knew something about reality and wanted to share this information with others. As you read, you need to keep trying to think about the reality out there in the real world referred to by the author's words. You need to think about whether what the author is saying about reality is true or false. If you have had your own experience with the topic, you can give your own reality check, based on your own personal understanding. You are then, probably, as much an expert on that topic as the author. If, on the other hand, you do not have experience with the topic, if it is unfamiliar to you, you have to investigate it so that you *can* decide whether what the author is saying is true or false. Of course in some cases you can assume the author is a reliable authority or resource person. In this case, you will believe that the author is telling the truth, and you will believe it and store that information away in your memory. But even in this case, you will still want to try to picture what the author is referring to in the real world. (Can you think of some page-flips? Do them.)

Do **For Practice.**

For Practice

What do these sentences mean? Use a dictionary, then paraphrase each sentence. Compare your answers with your classmates' answers.

a. The friable torte was in the shape of a terrapin.

b. She savored going into her boudoir and devising anonymous screeds.

c. Our peregrinations eventually took us to the nether parts of the globe.

d. The statue on the ersatz plinth was garbed in a plicated domino.

Yes, all these words are English words!

Your Summary

Items   *Page Number(s)*

Compare your list with your classmates' lists.

CHAPTER 12

The Paragraphs and Their Main Ideas

A. Understanding the Paragraphs

1. Now you will want to know how to understand a whole paragraph. You can't understand the book or article you are reading unless you understand every paragraph in it.

And you can't understand a paragraph unless you understand each sentence in the paragraph. As you learned in Chapter 11, if you have a problem understanding a sentence, first be sure you understand all the words. Then you need to give the sentence a reality check.

2. If you come across a sentence you still don't understand, even after understanding all the words and giving it a reality check, you should read ahead to the next sentences in the paragraph. Perhaps you will get a clue from the following sentences that will help you with the sentence you can't understand. Read to the end of the paragraph—perhaps even dip into the next paragraph looking for a clue, or go back and reread earlier sentences or paragraphs. If all this fails and you still can't understand the difficult sentence, you will need to ask someone (your teacher or a fellow student) what the sentence means.

Chapter 17 will give you some further suggestions about how to seek information.

3. If a particular paragraph still remains unclear or confusing to you, even after you understand all the sentences in it, you will need to reread that paragraph, giving more reality checks, making more connections with your stored memories. Perhaps paragraphs before or after the difficult one will shed a light. Go back and forth, trying to seek what the author is trying to tell you. You may begin to get a faint glimmer, then you may get a stronger light. Then, finally, the full meaning might dawn. Perhaps you can get a clue by page-flipping to earlier chapters or pages. Yes, all this may take time, but we all have to do this to understand difficult paragraphs.

You should try not to go on to the next paragraph until you understand the one you are reading. This is extremely important. If you cannot understand the meaning of a particular paragraph, you should stay with it until you understand it. Work at it until you get at least a vague glimmer of understanding. The meaning may then get clearer as you read ahead. But if you do go on, be sure you keep going back to see whether the difficult paragraph is clearing up.

If you don't do this, you can get lost; you will find the next paragraph hard to understand fully if you don't understand the one that came before it. Continuing to read when you don't understand the previous paragraphs is how you can finally get completely lost in your reading.

The time is well spent when you stop and try to understand a difficult paragraph. And, remember, you can always ask your teacher.

B. Finding the Main Idea

1. The problem is this: In order to understand a paragraph you have to know what the author is *trying to tell you* in the paragraph. (This will be its main idea.) And it is not always easy to know what the author wants to tell you in each paragraph. Sometimes an author doesn't write very clearly. Sometimes an author is writing nonsense. Sometimes the paragraph is just introducing or concluding an essay or article and doesn't really have a main idea (except to make an introduction or conclusion). All this can be confusing to the reader and can make it hard to understand what the author is trying to tell you in each paragraph.

But in every normal paragraph you need to know what the author is trying to tell you (its main idea). *A paragraph will have one and only one main point or idea that the author is trying to get across to you.* This is so because that is how authors write. They divide their writing into paragraphs, telling you one main idea or point in each paragraph. When they finish that one point or idea, they make a new paragraph and go on to their next idea. Remember, for each paragraph, an author sat down with one idea in mind and wrote a paragraph to tell that idea to you. Therefore, you need to be able to pick up on what that one main idea is. Otherwise, you will not be able to understand fully or completely the meaning of that paragraph. But how can you find a paragraph's main idea? How can you find out what the author is trying to tell you?

2. This chapter is going to teach you how to find the author's main idea in each paragraph. The method I am going to teach you is roundabout. It will show you how to find something else first, something that *is* easy to find. And when you find this other something, you will then, automatically, be able to find the main idea!

There are two exceptions to this:

a. As mentioned above, sometimes the writer doesn't write clearly. This is unfortunate for the poor reader. (Yes, if your textbook seems very unclear and hard to understand, discuss this with your instructor. Perhaps she or he will consider ordering a better-written textbook, if one is available.)

b. Also, as mentioned above, sometimes writers don't know what they are talking about! (They are only human and can make mistakes.) If you give thorough reality checks you may be able to find this out. If you come to the suspicion that the writer is wrong, is writing nonsense, then discuss it with your instructor. As you learned in Chapter 5, you are an expert on reality and can judge other people's ideas against your own sense of reality. Just be sure you always keep your mind open, ready to learn something new, because it may be that the writer is correct and you are wrong. Your teacher may be able to show you that your reality check was not correct. On the other hand, you may be able to point out to your teacher that the writer made a mistake.

3. This roundabout method is for the purpose of teaching you to find main ideas. However, once you have developed your ability to find main ideas, you won't have to use this method anymore. You won't need it anymore. It is just a method to get you started. It is a method that will help you increase your sensitivity and awareness about main ideas. (Of course, you can also use it if, for example, you run into a particularly hard-to-understand paragraph later on.)

C. The Three-Step Method for Finding Main Ideas

1. The first step of this roundabout method is to know there are six kinds of paragraphs, each one with its own one main *purpose:*

a. *Information* paragraphs (which give you different items of information about a subject).

b. *Thesis/Proof* paragraphs (which prove a point or convince you to believe an idea).

c. *How-To* paragraphs (which tell you step-by-step how something was or is made or done).

d. *Definition* paragraphs (which define the meaning of a word or phrase).

e. *Story* paragraphs (which tell you in a series of events what happened to someone).

f. *Problem* paragraphs (which discuss a problem, sometimes including its cause and/or its solution).

2. The second step is to learn how to ask six specific questions. The questions will help you find out which of the six kinds of paragraphs you are reading. It is not hard to answer these questions. (Some paragraphs are a combination of more than one kind, e.g., both *information* and *definition.* See Section F, below.) And once you find out what kind of paragraph you are reading, you can then easily find out what that paragraph's main idea is! Remember: *there are only six kinds of paragraphs and only the same six questions to ask for each paragraph:*

a. Is this paragraph giving me different items of information about a certain subject?

b. Is this paragraph trying with examples to convince me to believe a certain idea?

c. Is this paragraph showing me step-by-step how something is or was made or done?

d. Is this paragraph giving me the definition of a word or phrase?

e. Is this paragraph telling me in a series of events what happened to someone?

f. Is this paragraph talking about a problem and maybe its cause and solution?

Cross-reference these six questions with the six kinds of paragraphs listed above. Do you see the connection?

3. The third step is to ask "What subject?" or "What idea?" or "What something?" or "What word?" or "What happened?" or "What problem?" when you get a "yes" answer to the related question. (Before you go on, cross-reference these questions with the questions in Section B.2 above. Do you see the connection?) For example, if I get a "yes" answer to my question, "Is this paragraph giving me information about a certain subject?" then I ask, "*What* subject?" *The answer to that question is the main idea of that paragraph.* Automatically.

D. Examples of How to Use the Six-Question/Six-Paragraph Method

1. The *information* paragraph. Read the following paragraph and ask the *information* question: "Is this paragraph giving me different items of information about a certain subject?"

Our college is not very old. It was built in 1970. It is one of three campuses that make up one large college. Our campus is the most beautiful of the three and has won a prize for architectural design. There are both vocational and college transfer programs. The average age of our students is twenty-seven and there are many veterans and people returning to school after ten, twenty, or even thirty years. We believe most of our teachers are dedicated and truly want to help their students.

The answer is, "Yes." (The information includes date, number, beauty, students, programs, etc.) And then we ask, "*What* subject?" The answer is, "The author's college." So what is the main idea of this paragraph? The main idea is, "The author's college." *The main idea is the same as the answer to the question, "What subject?"*

(Did that paragraph give examples to try to prove a point? No. Did it tell step-by-step how something was made or done? No. Did it define a word? No. Did it tell in a series of events what happened to someone? No. Did it discuss a problem? No.)

2. The *thesis/proof* paragraph. Read the following paragraph and ask the *thesis/proof* question: "Is this paragraph trying with examples to convince me to believe a certain idea?"

I believe that astrology has some value—but only in a very limited way. The only part of astrology that I believe in at all is that a person's sun sign really does seem to influence a person's character. For example, my friend Jennifer is a typical Aquarius, idealistic and unconventional. Gene is the perfect Sagittarius: independent, outspoken, gregarious. James is quite clearly the intense, self-improving, private Scorpio. Not one of these people could fit under any other sun sign but the one he or she was born with!

The answer is, "Yes." (The examples: Jennifer, Gene, James.) Then we ask, "*What* idea or point?" The answer, and the main idea, is, "Sun signs and personalities are related." (Or one could say, "Sun signs seem to influence a person's character"; or "It seems a person's character is influenced by the sun sign"; or, "Sun signs and certain characters seem to go together." It doesn't matter how you say it, as long as the idea is captured in your paraphrase.) When you ask the other five questions, even if you get more than one "Yes," the main idea will still be the same! Don't worry about getting more than one "Yes." (Section F below will explain.).

3. The *how-to* paragraph. Read the following paragraph and ask the *how-to* question: "Is this paragraph showing me step-by-step how something is or was made or done?"

There are many ways to prepare a meal for friends. But I have my own personal method. First I spend days looking through all my cookbooks for a special dish that inspires me. Then I sit around thinking of what would go with the main dish. I think of the colors and textures. For a day or two I keep reviewing my menu, daydreaming about how it will all look and taste. Finally, on the day of the dinner party, I rush around like mad, cleaning, shopping, cooking, and, at the last minute, when the guests are actually arriving, I throw on something clean and hurry out to meet them, breathless and flushed. But they expect this of me and no one minds—because they always enjoy the delicious, artistic dinner.

The answer is, "Yes." (The steps: look at cookbooks, think of colors and textures, rush around, etc.) Then we ask, "*What* something?" The answer, and the main idea, is "How the author prepares a meal for company." Ask the other five questions. (Did you get more than one "Yes"? If so, you will see that the main idea is the same for all of them. See Section F, below.)

Do **For Practice** on the next page.

Don't read the following answers until you have discovered for yourself the main idea for each of the **For Practice** paragraphs.

Answers: **(a)** The author's intention is to prove a point. The point (main idea): *Treating children with respect is a good way to bring them up* (or use any paraphrase that captures the same idea). **(b)** The author's intention is to give information about the topic (main idea): *The new women students in community colleges.* **(c)** The intention is to tell how to do something (main idea): *How to have a true friendship.* (If you found other intentions, did you still come up with similar main ideas?)

Did paragraph **(a)** actually convince you? It tried to by giving several proofs of the good results of the author's method. Did paragraph **(b)** give you several pieces of information about the new women students? It told you who they are, what percentage of new students they are, what the colleges are doing for them, what educational experts are saying about this phenomenon. Did paragraph **(c)** tell you how to have a true friendship? It gave you several steps: be respecting and worthy of respect, have concern and be there to give help or ask for help, have trust in each other and talk over problems.

4. The *definition* paragraph. Ask the *definition* question of the following paragraph: "Is this paragraph giving me the definition of a word or phrase?"

People often wonder what we really mean when we say we are on strike. The dictionary says a strike is a work stoppage. Yes, it is that. But the word also means something more to us. When we hear that our brothers and sisters are on strike we understand it to mean that these people are suffering and they have taken the only, last way left to them to protect themselves from an unfair or cruel employer. Of course this was more true fifty years ago, but it still has the same meaning not only for the old-timers but also for some of the younger people who have had rough experiences in some industries.

The answer is, "Yes." And *what* is the word that is being defined? "Strike." This word, then, is the main idea of the paragraph (the word and its definition). Is this paragraph doing anything else? Is it giving you pieces of information about a subject? Well, yes, sort of. And what is that subject? Lo and behold! It is the same answer as we got above: a strike. So that is still the main idea. Is it also trying to give examples to prove a point? Not really. Is it telling, step-by-step, how something is done or made? Not really. Is it telling in a series of events what happened to someone? No. Is it discussing a problem? Maybe. And what is that problem? "The problem workers have that makes them go on strike." So "strike, the definition, and reasons people have them" is the main idea of this paragraph. You see, answer the "yes" answers and you automatically get the main idea of the paragraph (even if you get more than one "yes" answer).

5. The *story* paragraph. Ask the *story* question of the following paragraph: "Is this paragraph telling me in a series of events what happened to someone?"

We got as far as Crystal Lake. It was going to be a whole weekend away by ourselves. At Crystal Lake we stopped for late lunch. Fruit, bread, peanut butter, and wine. A lot of wine. We ate and drank and talked by the lake until it grew cool and the sun was disappearing. We decided it was too late to drive on, so we went back to the town we had seen just before Crystal Lake. The next day it rained. We packed up and drove home. We spent the day at a double feature. But since both of us love the movies, the weekend, though not as exciting as we had planned, was most wonderful anyway.

The answer is, "Yes." And then we must ask,

For Practice

Following are three paragraphs. Each of the paragraphs is an example of one of the three types discussed above. As you read these paragraphs, ask the three questions you have just learned. When you get a "Yes" answer to one of the three questions, *then ask the appropriate main idea question.* For example, if you get a "Yes" answer to the *information* question, ask: "What subject is this paragraph giving me different items of information about?" The answer will, *automatically,* be the main idea of that paragraph. (Do you see how this connects to Section C, above?)

If you get a "Yes" answer to the *thesis/proof* question, then ask: "*What is the point* that the paragraph is trying to prove to me with examples?" The answer will, *automatically,* be the main idea of that paragraph. (Cross-reference with Section C, above.)

And if you get a "Yes" answer to the *how-to* question, then ask: "What is the something this paragraph is telling me step-by-step how to make or do?" The answer will be the main idea. There is one paragraph for each of the three intentions. First read the three paragraphs through. Then go back and ask the three questions for each paragraph. (Don't worry if you can't decide on only one. Your main idea will still be correct. See Section F.)

a. The old-fashioned theory of child-rearing is that children should be seen and not heard. My own experience with my four children, however, tells me that hearing children, talking with them and respecting them as individuals and human beings, is a better approach. I have always treated my children this way and now all of them, from the youngest, who is twelve, to the oldest, who is twenty, are independent, self-confident, active, out-going people. My method of bringing them up was to believe they were capable of taking responsibility and of having good sense. That this approach was correct is shown by their now being able to do every household job, their being able to find and keep jobs (to make their own money). My approach included having them join in my conversations with my friends and contribute their own ideas. As a result, they are all interesting conversationalists and have a wide range of interests. Finally, because I treated them as friends, they all are able to make and keep good friends. Seeing how my children are growing up has persuaded me that my approach is better than the old-fashioned approach.
Main idea:

b. New women students account for about 75 percent of the increase in community college enrollment in the past few years. These women students are, in large part, older women returning to school after their children have grown up and left home. Some of these women are what are now called "displaced homemakers." They are women who are recently divorced, widowed, or otherwise "out of work" as mothers and homemakers. More and more community colleges are developing special programs or courses for these new women students, to help them get oriented to the world outside the home and to help them build their self-confidence. Educational experts are saying that women administrators are helpful to these new students because they act as role models, helping the students gain a more positive idea of what a woman can accomplish.
Main idea:

c. Do you want to be able to make and keep true friends? First of all, the friendship must be based on respect. You actually have to respect the way your friend thinks, feels, and behaves. You yourself will also have to be someone whose attitudes, behavior, and feelings are respect-worthy. In other words, you cannot think of your friend as one who should be at your disposal to do what you want when you want it. Second, a true friendship is based on a sincere concern for the other's well-being. You will actually be caring whether your friend is doing well, and you will want to be there to help if your friend needs you. You will also be able to ask your friend for help if you need it. Third, the friendship will be based on trust. That is, you both will be absolutely certain that the other one respects and cares for you, and you will know that if your friend seems cold or unfriendly to you or hurts your feelings, it is something you can talk over and that your friend will be sorry to have hurt you and will be glad of a chance to do better and be a better friend.
Main idea:

"*What* happened?" (The series of events: stopped for lunch, got late, stayed overnight, rained next day, went to movie.) What happened is, "The author and her friend had a good time on the weekend, even though the plans had to change because of rain." This is the main idea. Ask the other five questions. Is the paragraph giving pieces of information about a subject? Yes, *about the weekend.* Is it giving examples to prove anything? No. Is it showing step-by-step how something was done? Yes, sort of. What? *How the weekend was spent.* Is it talking about a problem? Sort of. What problem? *The rain made them change their plans.* Add all the "Yes" answers up and you get the same one main idea: "The author and her friend had a good weekend even though the rain made them change their plans."

You may want to paraphrase the main idea differently. That is fine. Each person may want to paraphrase it differently—just as long as the paraphrase captures the main thing the paragraph is doing or the main idea it is trying to get across.

6. The *problem* paragraph. Now ask the *problem* question of the following paragraph: "Is this paragraph talking about a problem and maybe its cause and solution?"

My house is often a big mess. My children are very busy with their projects and are always leaving the sewing machine, thread, half-sewn material, drawing pads, crayons, jigsaw puzzles, games lying around. Not to mention their coats, school books, sweaters, scarves, gloves, and boots. I think if I had the guts to throw out everything that they didn't put away they'd soon learn not to leave things lying around!

The answer is, "Yes." Now we need to ask, "*What* problem?" The answer is, "The author's children make the house a mess." Is the discussion of the problem including the cause? Yes, the children's busyness and leaving things out is the cause of the mess. Is a solution discussed? Yes, throw things away! Asking the other five questions gives us the same main idea: Information? Yes, *about the things lying around.* Trying to prove anything? Yes, that *there is indeed a mess.* Are we being told step-by-step how to do something? No. Is any word being defined? No. Add up all the answers to the "Yeses" and we get the

same one main idea: "The children make a mess by leaving things around, and throwing the things away might help cure them."

Do **For Practice** on page 83.

Answers: In **(a)** the author's intention is to tell you what it is that happened. And what happened? *The dreamer was chased by and finally escaped his father.* This, then, is that paragraph's main idea. Paragraph **(b)** has the intention of discussing a problem, explaining its cause, and giving a solution. What is the paragraph's main idea, then? It is: *Litter is caused by careless people but providing litter baskets and signs will help stop the problem.* The intention of paragraph **(c)** is to define a term. What is that term? It is "academic freedom." *This term's definition* is the main idea of that paragraph.

If you now feel pretty confident that you understand this method and you have got the main ideas of the practice paragraphs given in the preceding sections, then skip Section E. Go directly to Section F. If, however, you still feel somewhat confused and feel you need some more help understanding the method, read E; then, if you still do not feel confident, go back and reread parts 1 through 6 of Section D.

E. Main Ideas: Review

1. A main idea, then, is what a paragraph is all about. Does the author want *to inform you* about a topic? *Then that topic is the main idea.*

Does the author want *to give you a step-by-step rundown* of how something is or was made or done? *Then that product or process is the main idea.*

Does the author want *to give you a definition* of a word or term? *Then that definition is the main idea.*

Does the author want *to tell you what happened* in a series of events? If so, *then "what happened" is the main idea.*

Does the author want *to discuss a problem,* its cause and/or solution? If so, *then that problem, its cause and/or solution is/are the main idea.*

2. This, again, is the process for finding the main idea:

Ask the six questions to find out what kind of paragraph it is, to find out what the author's in-

For Practice

Following are three paragraphs; each one is an example of one of the three types just explained above. Ask the three questions you have just learned and, for each "Yes" answer, ask the *appropriate main idea question.* That is, if you get "Yes" for the *definition* question, ask, *"What is the word or term* that is being defined?" The answer is the main idea of that paragraph.

If your "Yes" is to the *story* question, ask, *"What is it, in a series of events, that happened?"* The answer is your main idea. If the *problem/cause/solution* question results in a "Yes," ask, *"What is the problem, cause and/or solution* the paragraph is discussing or explaining?" The answer, of course, will be the paragraph's main idea.

a. Last night my friend had an interesting dream. In his dream his father was chasing him. Every time my friend began to hop on one leg his father almost grabbed him. Then my friend would begin to run in a normal way and he would pull out far ahead of his father. Then my friend jumped over a fence and escaped altogether.
Main idea:

b. There is a lot of litter on campus. People do not pay attention and drop trash all over the place. One can find candy and gum wrappers and cigarette butts on the floors and on the outside walks. On the tables in the lounge and lunchroom are used coffee cups, overflowing ashtrays, discarded papers, and heaven knows what all! We need to put litter baskets and signs everywhere to try to get everyone on campus to improve these careless habits.
Main idea:

c. Academic freedom is an important concept, in higher education especially. Academic freedom means that a teacher can put forth any ideas he or she wishes. It should also mean that students have the freedom to disagree with the teacher and that students also have the right to express their views. Academic freedom means that the classroom should be a place for the free exchange of ideas. Academic freedom means that teachers and students have the right to seek the truth without fear of a higher authority saying, "You are forbidden to question and criticize." In short, academic freedom means freedom of thought, which is essential in a democracy.
Main idea:

Discuss answers with your classmates.

tention or purpose is. When you find out what kind of paragraph it is, then you can ask the appropriate *main idea question.*

a. If it is an *information* paragraph, the appropriate main idea question is: "What *topic* is the information about?" *The answer to this question is automatically the main idea.*

b. If it is a *thesis/proof* paragraph, the appropriate main idea question is: "What *point* or thesis is the author trying to prove to me?" *The answer is automatically the main idea.*

c. If it is a *how-to* paragraph, the question is:

"What is the *product or process* that this step-by-step procedure makes or does?" *The answer is the main idea.*

d. If it is a *definition* paragraph, the question is: "What *word or term* is being defined?" *The answer is the main idea.*

e. If it is a *story* paragraph, the appropriate main idea question is: "What *happened?*" *The answer is the main idea.*

f. If it is a *problem/cause/solution* paragraph, the question is: "What *problem, cause, and/or solution* is the author discussing?" *The answer is the main idea.*

F. Paragraphs with More Than One Purpose (Which Are Two or More of the Six Types)

1. In some paragraphs, as we have already seen, the author has more than one purpose or intention. She may want to talk about a *problem* and also give *information* about it. But even in this case, there is still only one main idea. We can say, in these cases, that the one main idea is complicated or complex. Fortunately, as we have discussed in the previous section, the method for finding a *complex* main idea is the same as the method for finding a *simple* main idea (only one purpose in the paragraph).

a. For example, read the following paragraph:

In a word, a dictionary is a wordbook. With the aid of a good dictionary you can get the word or give the word, pass the word or spread the word, have words with someone or find words for what you want to say.

Did the author intend *to give us some information* on a particular subject? (What is your answer? I'll tell you at the end of this part what my answer is. Don't read ahead!) Did the author want the paragraph *to prove a certain point* to us by giving us examples to persuade or convince us? Did she intend *to tell us,* step-by-step, *how a process or product is done or made?* (Is there a one-two-three step approach, to show us how to do something?) Did she want the paragraph *to give us a definition* of a word or phrase? Did the author want *to tell us,* in a series of events, *what happened* to someone? Finally, did she use the paragraph *to discuss a problem?* Be sure you have your own answers before you read on.

My answer is that yes, she did want to give us information. About what topic? "What a dictionary is and what it helps us do with words." (She wrote: "With the aid of a good dictionary you can get the word or give the word," etc.) And no, she didn't give any examples to convince me of anything (well, maybe she did give examples of things dictionaries can help us do—this does convince me that a good dictionary is useful). Okay, what about her defining anything? Yes, she is telling us, in a way, what a dictionary is: she says it's a "wordbook." But did she give a series of events to tell us what happened to some-

one? Definitely not. Did she discuss a problem? Not at all. Did she give us a step-by-step procedure for how to do something? Not really. She did tell us *what* dictionaries do, and she did tell us what we can do with words. But she didn't give us a step-by-step procedure for how to use the words. She only told us we could use them, but not exactly how, step by step. I don't believe the author intended to give us instructions or teach us how to use words. I think she just wanted to tell us that "dictionaries are full of words and are useful to us because of all the uses that words have." And that is my paraphrase of her main idea. I only need to reduce it down to a shorter form for more convenience. Maybe I can paraphrase it this way: "What a dictionary is and what it helps us do with the words in it"; or, "Dictionaries—they help us use words"; or, "Dictionaries help us use words"; or, "Dictionaries are books about words"; etc. There are many ways to say the same complex main idea; each person can paraphrase it differently, as long as the author's purpose for the paragraph is captured. Reread the paragraph. Did your paraphrase of the main idea capture what the author wanted to get across?

Remember, *there is no one perfect way to paraphrase a main idea.* Just be sure you see what the author is driving at, what he or she is trying to do in the paragraph.

b. Here is another example:

A child in elementary school may lose self-confidence if she or he can't learn to read in the first grade. The child's peers will call the one who is not yet ready to read "stupid." The child will feel stupid. This will cause suffering. An adult who went through this as a child may still have the scars, may still feel stupid as a student.

Do **For Practice** on page 85.

c. Here is another example:

By 1990 more and more apartments will be outfitted with devices for circulating filtered air. The old-fashioned phrase "fresh air" will be replaced, perhaps by the phrase "raw air," and this will be considered increasingly unsuitable for delicate lungs, especially in urban areas.

Do the first **For Practice** on page 86.

For Practice

Answer the following questions about paragraph **b**:

Is the author trying to give you different items of information about a certain topic?
If so, what topic?

Is the author giving you examples in order to prove something to you?
If so, what point?

Is the author defining a word or phrase for you?
If so, which one?

Is the author telling you, step-by-step, how something is made or done?
If so, what is that something?

Is the author telling you the series of events concerning something that happened to someone?
If so, what happened?

Is the author discussing a problem, possibly including the cause and solution?
If so, what is the problem (and cause and/or solution)?

Compare your answers with your classmates' answers. Remember, there can be many different correct ways to paraphrase the same idea.

---

d. And yet another example:

There are now rather more than three billion people on earth. For the three leading nations of the world, the population figures are now roughly 700 million for China, 250 million for the USSR, and 200 million for the United States.

Do the second **For Practice** on page 86.

e. Finally, find the main idea for the following paragraph:

In 1904, a time when psychology was just getting started, school authorities in Paris approached Alfred Binet and asked him to develop an objective method for detecting mental retardation in children. In effect, they requested that he devise a simple, workable test of intelligence. Before he could devise such a test, of course, Binet first faced the task of deciding exactly what it should measure—that is, what would be meant by the term intelligence. . . . He finally settled on the view that intelligence refers primarily to the ability to judge, comprehend, and reason well. It is interesting to note that today, more than 70 years later, modern definitions of intelligence retain much of the same flavor, often relating this characteristic to the abilities to adapt to new circumstances, deal with complex or abstract materials, and solve intellectual problems.

Do **For Practice** on page 87.

For Practice

What is the main idea of paragraph **c**? (Remember to ask all the questions as in **For Practice** on page 85.) Compare your answer with your classmates'.

For Practice

What is the main idea of paragraph **d**? (Remember to ask all the questions as in **For Practice** on page 85.) Compare your answers with your classmates'.

---

2. If you had tried to find the main idea of these paragraphs without first finding out what kind of paragraphs they are, you might have had some trouble. But when you start with finding out the kind of paragraph each one is, you can automatically end up with its main idea.

As you practice and gain experience using the six *what-kind-of-paragraph questions,* and then the appropriate *main idea questions,* you will increase your ability to see the main idea right away. When this happens, you can stop consciously going through all the questions. Remember, they were taught to you just to train you to find main ideas. Once you have developed your ability to find main ideas, you can do the questions less and less.

3. At the stage at which you feel you can do without the exact procedures, your inner mind will actually be rapidly, subconsciously, running through the steps and procedures. You won't even know it. You will read a paragraph, think about it, trying to see what the author wanted to get across to you; your inner mind will be rapidly going through all the questions, and, then, the main idea will strike you. And when that happens (but only after sufficient exercising and practicing), you will find you have become an efficient main idea spotter.

If, however, you should come across a partic-ularly hard paragraph, you can always pull out all the questions and go through them consciously and carefully until you find the main idea.

G. Some Problems with Finding the Main Idea

One reason why finding the main idea is difficult is that it is not always actually written down in the paragraph. Sometimes you have to read between the lines to figure out what the main idea in the paragraph is.

Another reason is that sometimes the first sentence of a paragraph is there to draw you into the subject, but it is not the main idea. For example, read the following paragraph:

Let us now contrast the life experiences of children, adolescents, and adults. A child's environment can significantly affect his or her intellectual growth. If, for example, a child's first school experience is in a hostile environment, the child will not be able to learn well. A hostile environment may be one that is sexist (hostile for girls), elitist (hostile for blue collar workers' children), racist (hostile for minority children).

The first sentence says the author is going to be discussing the differences between children's, adolescents', and adults' life experiences ("Let us now contrast the life experiences of children, adolescents, and adults"). But is this

For Practice

Find paragraph **e**'s main idea.

Be careful not to stop with the "Yes" answer to the *definition* question. This is a complex paragraph. The author wanted to get across the idea that . . . oh, but you figure it out! Then compare your results with your classmates'. If you go through the six questions and ask all the questions exactly as shown before, you will be able, quite easily, to come up with the main idea. But be sure you do *exactly* as shown. *Follow the procedures through all the steps.* Otherwise you may get off the track. Later, when you have had more experience, you can stop following the procedures with exactness. But for now, do it as shown. You won't be sorry!

Is the author trying to give you different items of information about a certain topic?
If so, what topic?

Is the author giving you examples in order to prove something to you?
If so, what point?

Is the author defining a word or phrase for you?
If so, which one?

Is the author telling you, step-by-step, how something is made or done?
If so, what is that something?

Is the author telling you the series of events concerning something that happened to some-one?
If so, what happened?

Is the author discussing a problem, possibly including the cause and solution?
If so, what is the problem (and cause and/or solution)?

Compare your answers with your classmates' answers. Remember, there can be many different correct ways to paraphrase the same idea.

the main idea of the paragraph? Does the paragraph actually contrast these three different groups? Let's see.

Does the paragraph give you information? No, there is really no factual information here. Does it try to prove a point? No, there is no evidence or proof presented. Does it define a word or phrase? Yes, it does define what "hostile envi-ronment" may mean. Does it tell how something was or is made or done? No. Does it tell you the events in a story of what happened? No, there is no character and there are no events that oc-curred. Does it discuss a problem, cause, and/or solution? Yes, it does discuss the problem of a school's hostile environment and the harmful effect it can have on a child's ability to learn. (It

For Practice

Now find the main ideas for all the paragraphs of the essay "Life in 1990" on pages 154-55. Stop after each paragraph and compare your main idea paraphrase of that paragraph with your classmates'. Discuss the type of paragraph it is. Together go through the answers to all the questions of the procedure. Only after this has been done, go on to the following paragraph. Your instructor may want to do this practice with you over a period of several days. It may take a long time to do your own work, compare and discuss with your classmates, correct mistakes (if any). But you will learn a lot!

MAIN IDEAS:

Paragraph 1:

Paragraph 2:

Paragraph 3:

Paragraph 4:

Paragraph 5:

Paragraph 6:

Paragraph 7:

Paragraph 8:

Paragraph 9:

Paragraph 10:

Paragraph 11:

Paragraph 12:

Paragraph 13:

Paragraph 14:

Paragraph 15:

Read page 156 for some clues about the main ideas of some of these paragraphs. Do this only after you have found your own main idea for these paragraphs.

tells the problem—the harmful effect—and gives the cause—a hostile environment of sexism, elitism, and/or racism. It does not, though, give the solution.) Even if you answered "Yes" to the other questions, the main ideas will all be the same anyway. That is the wonderful thing about this method!

By now answering the two intention questions for which there was a yes answer we can find the main idea: "A hostile environment, which may be racist, sexist, or elitist, can harm a child's ability to learn." There is nothing here about the adolescent or adult.

Thus, we can see that the first sentence just gave you a general overview of perhaps an entire article. It is an *introduction* to a general subject but is *not* the main idea of a particular paragraph.

Likewise, sometimes the last sentence of an article or chapter will be a conclusion for the whole article and *not* the main idea of the particular paragraph.

Do **For Practice** on page 88.

H. Where to Write Down Your Main Idea Statements When You Are Reading an Assignment

When you find the main idea, write it in the outside margin of the book next to the paragraph. This is where main ideas should be written down. They are like the title or name of the paragraph. It will tell you what the paragraph is all about. As you look in the left-hand margin of each paragraph you will see what the main idea of that paragraph is and you will immediately know what that paragraph is all about. By reading all the main ideas in the margin you will be able to have an overview of your reading. This will be helpful for review. More on this later.

Your Summary

Items   *Page Number(s)*

Compare your list with your classmates'.

CHAPTER 13

Underlining the Supporting Material

A. What Is in a Paragraph?

1. As you have just learned, every paragraph has one main idea that the paragraph is all about. Okay, so what are all those other words and sentences doing in that paragraph? Why not just state the main idea and go on to the next main idea?

An author adds all those other words and sentences in order to give the reader a *fuller understanding* of the main idea. An author knows that the readers will need some details or examples or further explanation in order to understand completely the main idea.

A paragraph, then, is most usually made up of a main idea and all the supporting material (details, examples, etc.) needed to back up or fill out that main idea.

There is also a third unrelated type of sentence you can find in a paragraph: a *transition.* Chapter 17, Section K, part 2.g, explains what transitions are. Briefly, they are a "bridge" that leads you from one idea or part to another. "Next" is a transition. So is "first," "second," "finally," "as a result," "for example," "therefore," etc. When you find a sentence or paragraph which really just leads you from one thought to another it is probably a transition and not related directly to the main idea.

In terms of meaning, a paragraph will have only two kinds of things making it up: the one main idea plus all the material to support (or back up or fill out) that one main idea. This is all that a paragraph basically is. (There are also words put in to give the writing personality.)

2. You have learned how to find a paragraph's main idea. You have learned that you should write the main idea in the left-hand margin beside the paragraph. Now you will learn how to underline. *You should underline the supporting material* (that is, the backup or fill-in material).

Then, the main idea (in the margin) and the supporting material (underlined) is what you will want to store in your memory. Once you select these two parts out of the paragraph, you can ignore and forget about the rest of the paragraph (all those extra words put in for smoothness and personality).

B. How to Underline

1. Underlining a paragraph is *streamlining* it so that when you read just the underlined words they read like a telegram.

Imagine that every word is a dollar and you want to keep the price down. For example, here is a letter you are going to send your friend:

Dear Irene,

My vacation starts next Wednesday and I can hardly wait. As soon as I get off work I'm jumping into my car and coming to see you. I should arrive in San Francisco around noon on Friday. But just in case, let's plan to meet at 3:00. Just for fun, let's meet at our favorite place, the snake house at the zoo. I can hardly wait to see you after all these months.

Let's say that you forget to mail this letter. On Wednesday you realize that the letter is still in your pocket. You are frantic! It will take too long for a letter to get to her. You must send a telegram. You take your letter out and plan a telegram based on the most important information you had written in the letter. You underline that important information so that you can read it over the phone to the telegraph office. You are poor, so you have to keep the words to a minimum.

Do **For Practice** on page 91.

For Practice

Go back and underline the necessary words in the letter to Irene. Compare your underlining with your classmates'.

Here is one way to do it:

Dear Irene,

My vacation starts next Wednesday and I can hardly wait. As soon as I get off work I'm jumping into my car and coming to see you. I should <u>arrive</u> in <u>San Francisco</u> around noon on <u>Friday</u>. But just in case, let's plan to <u>meet</u> at <u>3:00</u>. Just for fun, let's meet at our favorite place, the <u>snake house</u> at the <u>zoo</u>. I can hardly wait to see you after all these months.

Or: "Arrive San Francisco Friday. Meet 3:00. Snake house. Zoo."

When Irene gets this telegram she will know everything she needs to know in order to meet you, which was your *main idea* in sending the telegram. That was also your *main idea* in writing the letter. In the letter, however, since words didn't cost a dollar each, you were able to throw in a lot of words just for friendship and self-expression. As a result, the *main idea* may not have been so clear in the letter. But in the telegram, in which you included only the most vital information, the *main idea* was crystal clear. You had the main idea of wanting to arrange a meeting with Irene. You backed up this main idea with the supporting material of the day, time, place.

2. Let's say that you *did* remember to mail the letter on time. Irene got the letter and saw from the return address that it was from you. She was so excited that she tore open the envelope and *skimmed* the letter breathlessly, trying to get the main idea, trying to see as quickly as possible

what the message was mainly all about. Most of the words were not read; her eyes picked out only the words which informed her of the main idea—that you were coming Friday; you would meet at 3:00 at the snake house at the zoo.

Later on, of course, when she calmed down, she reread the letter and saw all the extra words that you had put in for personality, friendship, and self-expression.

If she were in the habit of taking notes on her letters, she would have written the main idea in the left-hand margin: "Anna's coming." Then she would have underlined the same words that you would have put into the telegram above.

Then she could have forgotten everything else in the letter, just as long as she remembered the *main idea* in the margin and the *underlined material*. Those were the two things she needed to store in her memory about that letter.

3. Here is another letter:

Dear Mr. Sage:

Thank you for your letter of November 17. I am very interested in your job offer, and I am agreeable to coming to Portland for an interview with the Board of Directors, as you suggested in your letter. Please expect me Monday, November 21, at 11:00. I will bring my drawings, as you requested, so that you can see more of the work I am doing at this time.

Suppose this information had to get to Portland immediately and a letter would take too long to be delivered. You have to send a telegram instead. To do this you will have to streamline and reduce the letter to only a few words. Your intention is to give the prospective employer information about the *main idea,* which is that you want the job and are coming for an interview. The information that you need to give him *to support* this main idea must include the date and time.

Do **For Practice** on page 92 before you read on.

For Practice

Go back and underline the letter to Mr. Sage, underlining the words that you will read over the phone to the telegraph office. Compare your underlining with your classmates'.

Here is a possible telegram: "Interested in job. Coming for interview Monday, November 21, 11:00. Will bring drawings."

When Mr. Sage gets this telegram he will know everything he needs to know. He knows that you want the job, when you are coming, and that you are bringing your drawings. If you were too poor to afford such a long telegram, you probably could even have left out the words, "Interested in job," because that's obvious. You could probably have also left out the words about bringing the drawings.

"Coming for interview Monday, November 21, 11:00." Maybe this telegram would be enough to give Mr. Sage all the information he needs to know. You would have to decide whether you want him to be *sure* you are interested in the job. You would have to decide whether he needs to know beforehand whether or not you are bringing the drawings (maybe he has to fly in a drawing expert from Alaska to evaluate them).

The other words in your original letter can be thrown away now that you have sent the telegram. All the other words in that letter are nonessential. You had put them in for smoothness and politeness. The telegram, which contains only the most important material, doesn't need those words. The telegram is clear, understandable, to the point, complete. That is how underlining should be.

4. But suppose you had sent the letter instead. And suppose that Mr. Sage was in the habit of taking notes on his letters. He would have written in the left-hand margin: "Clarke wants job. Will interview." Then he would underline the same important details you would have sent in the telegram above: <u>Monday, November 21,</u>

<u>11:00. Will bring drawings</u>. He doesn't need to store in his memory anything else in your letter.

5. Now observe the underlining in the following paragraph. You already know its main idea from the last chapter. I have written the main idea in the right-hand margin and then underlined only the most important pieces of information or details or examples.

Our college is not very old. It was <u>built</u> in <u>1970</u>. It is <u>one of three campuses</u> that make up *in* <u>one large college</u>. Our campus is the <u>most beautiful</u> of the three and has <u>won</u> a <u>prize for architectural design</u>. There are both <u>vocational and college transfer programs</u>. The <u>average age</u> of our students is <u>twenty-seven</u> and there are <u>many veterans</u> and <u>people returning to school after ten, twenty,</u> or even <u>thirty years</u>. We believe <u>most</u> of our <u>teachers</u> are <u>dedicated</u> and truly want to help their students.   *the college*

You could have written in the margin "our college" or "author's college." Remember, you can state it any way you prefer, as long as you have your finger on the actual main idea.

I did not underline "college not very old" because "built 1970" says the same thing better. I also did not have to underline "our college" because that idea is in the margin and I did not want to duplicate my efforts. Notice that I wrote in the word "in" before "one large college." I decided I wanted to make my "telegram" read more smoothly and clearly for when I would read it later during review. So I "rewrote" it a bit. Now when I review later and read the "telegram," it will read easily and make good sense.

Don't forget, *the reason for underlining is to prepare material for review.* Your main idea in the left margin plus the underlined supporting material are what you will review and store from the paragraph. When you review your textbook, you will read *only* the main ideas in the margin and the underlinings. (You will not have to read or review anything else in the textbook.) Therefore, you want to prepare the smoothest, most easy to read "telegrams" that you can. This will make your later reviewing more efficient and effective. Keep this in mind as you do your underlining.

6. Now look at the underlining and main idea statement in the next paragraph.

trol.
in signs
em to
fluence
racter
don't
gree!)

I believe that astrology has some value—but only in a very limited way. The only part of astrology that I believe in at all is that a person's sun sign really does seem to influence a person's character. For example, my friend <u>Jennifer</u> is a <u>typical Aquarius</u>, idealistic and unconventional. <u>Gene</u> is the <u>perfect Sagittarius</u>: independent, outspoken, gregarious. <u>James</u> is quite <u>clearly</u> the intense, self-improving, private <u>Scorpio</u>. <u>Not one of these people could fit under any other sun sign</u> but the one he or she was born with!

In the margin I added my own opinion of the paragraph's main idea. You can (and should) talk to the author this way. It is a way of expressing the result of your reality check. On the other hand, perhaps I am close-minded and did not give a complete enough reality check! Maybe if I checked out the subject more, I would find that I agreed, that sun signs really *do* seem to influence a person's character. In any case, you should certainly put your own comments next to the main idea in the margin. This makes the material even more familiar and interesting to you.

Following is another way this same paragraph could have been prepared for review:

un
igns
obably
fluence
aracter
raits

I believe that astrology has some value—but only in a very limited way. The only part of astrology that I believe in at all is that a person's sun sign really does seem to influence a person's character. For example, my friend Jennifer is a typical <u>Aquarius</u>, <u>idealistic</u> and <u>unconventional</u>. | Gene is the perfect <u>Sagittarius</u>: <u>independent</u>, <u>outspoken</u>, <u>gregarious</u>. | James is quite clearly the <u>intense</u>, <u>self-improving</u>, <u>private</u> <u>Scorpio</u>. Not one of these people could fit under any other sun sign but the one he or she was born with!

While the main ideas are almost the same (just stated differently), the underlinings are different. The difference between these two underlinings is that one of the students was preparing the paragraph for study and review in a *sociology* course while the other student was preparing the same text for study and review in an *astrology* course. Can you tell which one is prepared most appropriately for a sociology course on "beliefs through the ages" and which one is prepared most appropriately for an astrology course on "sun signs and their nature and influence"?

The first paragraph is being prepared by the sociology student. This student is underlining

material that demonstrates the main idea in a more *general* way, showing, simply, that these people are typical of their sun signs and could be under no other sun sign. In the sociology course, all the nitty-gritties about what the sun signs stand for and the actual, specific influences they have are not necessary.

But it is precisely this kind of nitty-gritty information that is appropriate in an astrology course. The astrology student wants to learn all about the exact influence each sun sign has. This student does not have to be convinced that certain people are typical of their sun sign. This astrology student wants to know what the influence is, what those character traits are.

Thus, when you underline, you must be careful to *underline the material that will be most appropriate for your purposes,* for your particular course. Remember, when you underline you are preparing material to store and review. What you write in the margin and what you underline are what you are going to remember from your reading. Make sure you are going to remember the material that is most relevant to your course.

By the way, the vertical lines in the second underlining above are there to make the meaning of the "telegram" clear when the student goes back to review it. Without the lines separating the different signs and their characteristics, the student might get them all mixed up when he or she just reads through the "telegram."

You can concoct your own ways to make your "telegram" clear so that later when you go back to read it for your review it will make good sense to you.

Do **For Practice** on page 94.

7. You will need to gain experience at this selective kind of underlining. When you get your tests back you will be able to judge whether you have been underlining and storing the *appropriate* material for that *particular* course and teacher.

As you gain more experience in school you will improve your ability to select the most appropriate details to underline and store in your memory for any particular course.

As with taking notes in class, you can't take notes on and store everything. When taking lecture notes you have to *select* what is important to *take* notes on. Then you have to *select* what notes

---

For Practice

Go back to the **For Practice** on page 81 in Chapter 12. Underline paragraph **(a)**. Underline it for a course in childhood education. Discuss your underlining with a classmate or in a small group. Perhaps your instructor will want to check your work.

Now underline paragraph **(b)** on page 81. This is for a course on women in education. Discuss as above.

Go on to paragraph **(c)**. Underline it for a course on interpersonal communications. Discuss as above.

---

you want to put into your mnemonic arrangements to *store* in your memory.

The same is true with underlining. You have to *select* which material you will *underline* and *store* in your memory.

8. Now observe the main idea and the underlining in this next paragraph:

How Phipps prepares a meal for friends

There are many ways to prepare a meal for friends. But I have my own personal method. First I <u>spend days looking through</u> all my <u>cookbooks for</u> a special <u>dish</u> that inspires me. Then I sit around <u>thinking</u> of <u>what would go with</u> the main dish. I think of the <u>colors and textures</u>. For a <u>day or two</u> I keep <u>reviewing</u> my <u>menu</u>, <u>daydreaming about</u> how it will all <u>look and taste</u>. Finally, <u>on</u> the <u>day of</u> the <u>dinner party</u>, I rush around like mad, <u>cleaning</u>, <u>shopping</u>, <u>cooking</u> and, at the last minute, <u>when</u> the <u>guests</u> are actually <u>arriving</u>, I throw on something clean and <u>hurry out</u> to meet them, <u>breathless and flushed</u>. But they expect this of me and <u>no one minds</u>—<u>because</u> they always enjoy the <u>delicious</u>, <u>artistic</u> dinner.

And here is another way to view underlining:

spend days looking through   cookbooks for   dish thinking   what would go with   colors and textures   day or two   reviewing   menu, daydreaming about   look and taste   on   day of   dinner party cleaning, shopping, cooking   when   guests   arriving hurry out   breathless and flushed   no one minds because   delicious, artistic

As you read this over you can easily get the gist of the meaning. It reads like a shorthand (or telegram) message.

9. Another possible way to state the main idea could be: "How Phipps prepares delicious, artistic dinner for friends."

If this had been in the margin, then you would not have had to underline these words at the end of the paragraph. *You do not want to duplicate your efforts.* If you want to have a longer statement of the main idea, then you will have less underlining. But if you want a short main idea statement, then you will have to do more underlining.

The point is that you want to be *efficient.* *Therefore, you do not want to repeat words from the underlining in the main idea, and you do not want to underline words you have already written in your main idea.* Just as long as all the appropriate information appears somewhere—either in the main idea or in the underlining—you are all right.

As you gain more experience, you can decide which style is best for you. Each person eventually will develop his or her own best style. Some people end up with very short main idea statements and lots of underlining. Other people prefer to write a long main idea statement, even including in it some of the supporting material. These people, then, do not underline very much.

Do **For Practice** at the top of page 95.

This is how I have underlined the **For Practice** paragraph for a labor unit in a United States history course:

For Practice

Try the next one on your own before seeing how I have done it.

People often wonder what we really mean when we say we are on strike. The dictionary says a strike is a work stoppage. Yes, it is that. But that word also means something more to us. When we hear that our brothers and sisters are on strike we understand it to mean that these people ae suffering and they have taken the only, last way left to them to protect themselves from an unfair or cruel employer. Of course this was more true fifty years ago, but it still has this same meaning for not only the old-timers but also for some of the younger people who have had rough experiences in some industries.

Compare your underlining with your classmates'.

People often wonder what we really mean when we say we are on strike. The <u>dictionary says</u> a strike is a <u>work stoppage.</u> | Yes, it is that. But that word also means something more to us. When we hear that our <u>brothers and sisters</u> are on strike we understand it to mean that these people <u>are suffering</u> and they <u>have taken</u> the <u>only, last way</u> left to them <u>to protect themselves from</u> an <u>unfair or cruel employer.</u> Of course this was <u>more true fifty years ago, but</u> it <u>still has</u> this <u>same meaning</u> for not only the old-timers but also <u>for some</u> of the <u>younger people</u> who have had <u>rough experiences in some industries.</u>

"Strike" (margin)

For the main idea I put the word in quote marks because this indicates to me that the word itself, its meaning, its definition, is the main idea of the paragraph. I could also have written in the margin as the main idea: "definition of <u>strike</u>."

Notice the various ways I concocted to make my "telegram" read more smoothly. I did those things so that when I go back to reread it, it will be easy to read and understand.

Do **For Practice** below.

This is my version of the main idea statement and underlining in the **For Practice** paragraph:

My house is often a big mess. My children are very <u>busy with</u> their <u>projects</u> and are always <u>leaving</u> the <u>sewing machine, thread, half-sewn material, drawing pads, crayons, jigsaw puzzles, games</u> lying around. Not to mention their <u>coats, school books, sweaters, scarves, gloves,</u> and <u>boots.</u> I think if I had the guts to <u>throw out everything</u> that they didn't put away <u>they'd soon learn</u> not to leave things lying around!

Kids make mess at home (margin)

For Practice

Now do the same with the next paragraph.

My house is often a big mess. My children are very busy with their projects and are always leaving the sewing machine, thread, half-sewn material, drawing pads, crayons, jigsaw puzzles, games lying around. Not to mention their coats, school books, sweaters, scarves, gloves, and boots. I think if I had the guts to throw out everything that they didn't put away they'd soon learn not to leave things lying around!

Compare your underlining with your classmates'.

I could have written a longer main idea statement: <u>Kids make mess at home—if I threw stuff out they'd stop.</u> If I'd had this longer statement (including the problem, the cause, *and* the solution), I wouldn't have had to underline any words in the last sentence of the paragraph. I preferred to have a shorter main idea statement and more underlining. Perhaps you preferred to include the solution in the main idea statement and do less underlining. Both methods are fine, just as long as all the information is included one way or the other. (I didn't underline "children" because I put "kids" in the main idea statement.)

10. Also, in this paragraph, I might not have had to underline all thirteen examples of what the author's children leave lying around.

If a particular paragraph has eight to ten or thirteen different examples or pieces of information you do not need to underline *all* of them. For example, if in the astrology paragraph there had been twelve examples of sun signs and their character traits, you would not have had to underline all twelve examples, unless you were taking an astrology course!

You need to select only *three or four of the most appropriate and strongest examples.* If all the examples are equally strong and appropriate, then pick the examples that strike your fancy as most memorable. (So you will be able to remember them better!) If there had been twelve examples in the astrology paragraph and you need only three or four sun signs and their character traits, then you might have picked your own, your best friend's, your mother's. All twelve signs would have been equally appropriate and strong, but these three will be the easiest for you to remember.

In the paragraph about the children's mess, you could have underlined only sewing machine, crayons, coats, books. Or you could have chosen any other four of the thirteen items given in the paragraph. You just need to be sure that you pick the ones that seem the strongest. The four I suggested above (sewing machine, crayons, coats, books) seem to give a good *variety* of the types of things left around. Four *different types* of things will be a strong support to the main idea that the cause of the problem is that the children leave things lying around.

The reason you need only three or four examples or pieces of information is that on a test you may want to support an answer with specific examples. You will need only three, four at the most. Two examples might even do. This is what you are preparing the paragraph for. This is why you want to select and store the material, why you want to be able to review it. It is because you may need to use the material on a test (or for your own research or in discussions, etc.)

Since you will not often need more than three or four pieces of supporting material for any point you want to make on a test or in a paper or discussion, that is all you need to select for underlining and storing.

As with the other skills you have been learning, once you get the hang of underlining you will be able to find your own best way of using this skill.

Continual practice and experience in this course and in your other courses will help you develop your own most effective and efficient way to prepare your reading for storage and review through main idea statements and underlining.

11. In the following article (left-hand column of page 97), the student prefers the style of having short main idea statements and a little more underlining.

For the same article (right-hand column of page 97), you will see that the student prefers the style of having longer, fuller main idea statements and less underlining. Both the following paragraphs and those above are completely and effectively prepared for study and review. The only difference is the style the student prefers.

Selecting which information you will include in your main idea statement and which you will underline will take time, effort, thought. Is this a waste of time? Definitely not! All this work is what you are *supposed to do* for study. It is *processing* the material—and processing the material always helps you to understand and remember it better. It is because you must take the time to do this during study that you need to schedule two hours a day to study for each course you have.

Do **For Practice** on page 98.

ALCOHOLISM*

The Department of Health, Education and Welfare (HEW) issued a <u>121-page</u> report <u>May 1, 1976. Congress recently passed a law</u> which <u>requires</u> the department to issue a <u>report</u> on alcoholism <u>each year,</u> and this was the <u>first</u> such <u>report.</u> The report was <u>prepared by a committee of 11 within HEW.</u>

The report said losses caused by alcoholism are high. It said alcohol <u>causes 28,000 traffic deaths a year,</u> and the deaths <u>cost</u> the <u>nation</u> a total of <u>$15 billion.</u> Nearly <u>9 million persons suffer from alcoholism or lesser drinking problems,</u> and they constitute <u>10 per cent of the work force</u> within the United States.

The report also contained some statistics about the use of alcohol. It said that in the <u>last year,</u> the <u>average American drinker drank the equivalent of 44 fifths of whiskey.</u> The report concluded that alcohol is "<u>the major drug problem</u> in this country." It said <u>HEW will spend $200,000 next year</u> to pay <u>for advertisements</u> to warn the public <u>about the dangers of excessive drinking.</u> The <u>liquor industry has endorsed the campaign.</u> The advertisements will be used on radio and television and in newspapers and magazines. But an official added, "<u>HEW will not tell people not to drink.</u> That is a <u>personal decision.</u> What we are saying is that <u>citizens have a responsibility not to destroy themselves or society.</u>"

The 121-page report suggests that the problem of alcoholism is not adequately understood by most Americans, who seem <u>more concerned about other drugs,</u> such as <u>marijuana and heroin,</u> even though those drugs <u>do not cause as many problems</u> as alcohol. To prove that point the report pointed out that <u>New York City has an estimated 600,000 alcoholics but only 125,000 heroin users.</u> Yet the <u>city spends 40 times more to fight narcotics addiction</u> than it does to fight alcoholism. The report explained that most persons do not know much about alcoholism and do not consider alcohol a serious problem. <u>People</u> also are <u>reluctant to admit</u> that they have a <u>drinking problem</u> or are alcoholics.

*In Fred Fedler, *Reporting for the Print Media* (New York: Harcourt Brace Jovanovich), p. 73.

ALCOHOLISM

The Department of Health, Education and Welfare (HEW) issued a 121-page report May 1, 1976. Congress recently passed a law which requires the department to issue a report on alcoholism each year, and this was the first such report. The report was <u>prepared by a committee of 11 within HEW.</u>

The report said losses caused by alcoholism are high. It said <u>alcohol causes 28,000 traffic deaths a year,</u> and the deaths <u>cost</u> the nation a total of <u>$15 billion.</u> Nearly <u>9 million persons suffer from alcoholism</u> or lesser drinking problems, and they constitute <u>10 percent of the work force</u> within the United States.

The report also contained some statistics about the use of alcohol. It said that in the <u>last year,</u> the <u>average American drinker drank the equivalent of 44 fifths of whiskey.</u> The report concluded that alcohol is "the <u>major drug problem</u> in this country." It said <u>HEW will spend $200,000</u> next year to pay <u>for advertisements</u> to warn the public about the dangers of excessive drinking. The <u>liquor industry has endorsed the campaign.</u> The advertisements will be used on radio and television and in newspapers and magazines. But an official added, "<u>HEW will not tell people not to drink.</u> That is a personal decision. What we are saying is that <u>citizens have a responsibility not to destroy themselves or society.</u>"

The 121-page report suggests that the problem of alcoholism is not adequately understood by most Americans, who seem more concerned about other drugs, such as <u>marijuana and heroin,</u> even though those drugs <u>do not cause as many</u> problems as alcohol. To prove that point the report pointed out that New York City has an <u>estimated 600,000 alcoholics but only 125,000 heroin users.</u> Yet the city <u>spends 40 times more to fight narcotics addiction</u> than it does to fight alcoholism. The report explained that most persons do not know much about alcoholism and do not consider alcohol a serious problem. <u>People</u> also are <u>reluctant to admit</u> that they have a <u>drinking problem</u> or are alcoholics.

[Handwritten margin notes, left column:] EW sued port on coholism

lc. = big roblem

EW will warn ublic

eople norant of anger

[Handwritten margin notes, right column:] HEW issued 1st report on alcoholism — required by law

Alc. affects many people + costs alot

Next year HEW will advertise to warn people that alc. is U.S.'s major drug problem

People mistakenly think other drugs worse than alcohol

For Practice

In the following essay, for each paragraph write your main idea statements in the margin and then underline the most appropriate and strongest supporting materials. Pretend you are preparing this material for a general English composition course (*not* for a library technician course). *Be sure to ask the six intention questions and the appropriate main idea questions to help find the main ideas quickly and easily.* Compare with your classmates.

WHAT'S IN A WORD*

Introduction to the Dictionary

In a word, a dictionary is a wordbook. With the aid of a good dictionary you can get the word or give the word, pass the word or spread the word, have words with someone or find words for what you want to say.

A word can be a message (*And now . . . a word from our sponsor*), a brief conversation (*I'd like a word with you*), a promise (*Do I have your word?*), news or a rumor (*What's the latest word?*), or even a quarrelsome remark (*They had words, and now they are not speaking*). In its basic sense a word is a sound or combination of sounds that symbolizes and communicates a meaning. Whether we use the written word or rely on word of mouth, words are our chief means of exchanging information with other people. To a large extent we pinpoint our perceptions, formulate our ideas, express our opinions, and convey our knowledge by means of words.

The best aid to the study of words and language is a dictionary. In a dispute over spelling, or meaning, or pronunciation "the dictionary" usually has the last word. Actually, though, there are many different dictionaries, of various sizes and types and varying degrees of usefulness.

The English language grows and changes so rapidly—with words coming in from different countries and regions and from special areas of activity and interest—that no dictionary could embrace the whole of it. The most highly detailed dictionaries of English are called unabridged dictionaries and usually contain at least 400,000 entries. These extensive and expensive reference books are used chiefly for research. Narrower in scope are specialized dictionaries, which may deal with one aspect of language (such as usage or etymology), with one class of words (such as slang or synonyms), or with terms used in one field (such as law or medicine).

What most people need is a good all-purpose dictionary that will fit easily into a budget and onto a shelf. A college dictionary, containing around 150,000 entries and providing a number of special features, is the best type of dictionary for high school, college, and adult use.

*Publisher's material for *The American Heritage Dictionary*, W. Morris ed., 1970.

Below I have written main idea statements for and underlined the same essay.

WHAT'S IN A WORD

Introduction to the Dictionary

Dictionary is book of words

In a word, a dictionary is a wordbook. With the aid of a good dictionary you can get the word or give the word, pass the word or spread the word, have words with someone or find words for what you want to say.

Words are used to communicate what we feel and know

A word can be a <u>message</u> (*And now . . . a word from our sponsor*), a <u>brief conversation</u> (*I'd like a word with you*), a promise (*Do I have your word?*), news or a rumor (*What's the latest word?*), or even a <u>quarrelsome remark</u> (*They had words and now they are not speaking*). In its basic sense a word is a sound or combination of sounds that symbolizes and communicates a meaning. Whether we use the written word or rely on word of mouth, words are our <u>chief means of exchanging information</u> with other people. To a large extent we pinpoint our perceptions, formulate our ideas, express our opinions, and convey our knowledge by means of words.

Dictionaries help us study and know words

The best aid to the study of words and language is a dictionary. <u>In a dispute over spelling, or meaning, or pronunciation</u> "the <u>dictionary</u>" usually <u>has</u> the <u>last word.</u> Actually, though, there are <u>many different dictionaries, of various sizes and types and varying degrees of usefulness.</u>

Too many Eng. words for any one dictionary

The <u>English language grows and changes so rapidly</u>—with <u>words coming in from different countries and regions and from special areas of activity and interest</u>—that no dictionary could embrace the whole of it. The <u>most highly detailed</u> dictionaries of English are <u>called unabridged dictionaries</u> and <u>usually contain</u> at least <u>400,000 entries.</u> These extensive and expensive reference books are used <u>chiefly for research.</u> <u>Narrower</u> in scope <u>are specialized dictionaries,</u> which <u>may deal with</u> one aspect of language (such as usage or etymology), with one class of words (such as slang or synonyms), or with terms used in <u>one field (such as law or medicine).</u>

People need all-purpose dict.

What most people need is a good all-purpose dictionary that will <u>fit easily into a budget and onto a shelf.</u> A <u>college dictionary,</u> containing around <u>150,000 entries</u> and providing <u>a number of special features,</u> is the <u>best type</u> of dictionary for high school, college, and adult use.

I didn't underline anything in the first paragraph because the main idea statement included everything that I thought was important.

In the second paragraph I could have written a shorter main idea statement: "words are used to communicate." If I had done that, I would have had to underline most of the last sentence, which says the same thing but with more specific words.

The first sentence in the fourth paragraph might be misleading. A student might make the mistake of thinking the main idea has to do with the growing language. But that is not what the paragraph is all about. The paragraph is giving us information about the topic of *dictionaries* and *not* about the topic of language.

12. To make sure that you have prepared a paragraph for good storage and review, look back and forth between your main idea statement and the underlinings. Have you got all the important material in one place or the other?

One warning: as you start underlining with more expertise, you may have the temptation to underline the main idea if it is written clearly in the paragraph itself. It may seem a way to save time— "I'll *underline* the main idea rather than write it in the margin since the author has written it down here very clearly." But don't do it.

Be sure you write the main idea down in your own words in the margin. It is important to do this for three reasons: (a) the paraphrasing (translating the author's statement into your own words) starts your *proper* storage process; (b) the physical writing of the main idea in the margin starts the nerve grooving or *firm* storage process; (c) the clear separation of the main idea, written in the margin, and the supporting material, underlined in the paragraph itself, will make your later review easier to do.

That is, if both the main idea and the supporting material are *all* underlined, later when you go back to review you will once again have to pick out the main idea and then separate it once more from its backup material. But if when you first study the paragraph you separate the two you are making it easy for yourself later. This method is more effective and efficient in the long run even though it may, at first, not seem so.

C. How to Summarize

1. *The main idea plus the underlined supporting material make up the summary.* In other words, if you need to have a summary of a chapter or section or article, all you need to do is write down the main idea and three or four of the most important pieces of supporting material. And there you have your summary!

For example, here is my summary for the article above on dictionaries (notice that in some cases I am paraphrasing):

Summary in Outline Form

A. Dictionary is book of words

B. Words are used to communicate what we feel and know
   1. Message
   2. Brief conversation
   3. News
   4. Quarrelsome remark
   5. Chief means of exchanging information

C. Dictionaries help us study and know words
   1. In spelling, meaning, pronunciation dispute, dict. has last word
   2. Many different areas of study

D. Too many words for any one dictionary
   1. Because Eng. language changes and grows rapidly
   2. Because words come from different places and areas of interest

3. Most highly detailed dictionaries are "unabridged"
   a. Contain about 400,000 words
   b. Used mainly for research
4. Narrower are the "specialized" dictionaries for one field
   a. Law
   b. Medicine

E. People need all-purpose dict.
   1. Cheap and small
   2. College dict. best
      a. Around 150,000 words
      b. Many special features

This same summary can also be written in paragraph form:

Dictionary is book of words. Words are used to communicate what we feel and know (message, brief conversation, news, quarrelsome remark, or chief means of exchanging information). Dictionaries help us study and know words (in a dispute over spelling or meaning or pronunciation, dictionary has last word; many different kinds of dictionaries). Too many Eng. words for any one dictionary (Eng. language grows and changes so rapidly, words come in from different countries and regions and from special areas of activity and interest; most highly detailed called unabridged dictionaries, usually contain 400,000 entries, used chiefly for research; narrower are specialized dictionaries, may deal with one field, such as law or medicine). People need all-purpose dict. (fit easily into a budget and onto a shelf); college dictionary, with 150,000 entries and number of special features, best type.

The above summaries are merely copies of all the main ideas and all underlined supporting materials (compare the summaries with the main idea statements and the underlinings). *Together they summarize the whole article in a short form.* All I need to do now is remember the information in my short summary. I do need to *prepare* the summary for easier storage—I may need to reduce it further, perhaps put it into a different form (Chapters 15, 16, and 18 will show you how to do this). Then, when the summary is ready for storage, I will copy, check, and correct it.

2. Remember, the combination of all the main idea statements in the margin and the underlinings is going to be your study and review version of the article, chapter, or individual paragraphs; it is the *summary* (the piece of writing in a neat little nutshell). Be sure you include all the important information either in the main idea statement or in the underlinings.

3. Unfortunately, few students have time to do a summary of every paragraph! A person should not feel he or she has to write the main idea of every single paragraph in the margin and underline every supporting idea of every paragraph. Of course, this would be the ideal situation—but time limits our ability to achieve the ideal.

Practicing doing this *here*, however, *is important to gain an understanding of these skills.* Remember, the work you do in connection with this book is *to help you learn skills.* Later, as you apply these skills to your regular classes and to your regular textbooks, you will *modify* the method learned here to suit your own needs and time limitations.

Do **For Practice** below.

4. Why should you learn how to underline or summarize or find main ideas in your reading when you learned earlier that all you need to do is incorporate your reading with your lecture notes? Why go to all this bother, especially learning how to write main ideas in the margin and underlining in the book or article itself?

There are two reasons: (a) *Not all of your reading can be directly related to your class lecture notes.* (b) Finding main ideas, underlining, and summarizing your reading are the ways you process (understand and learn) the material in your reading; *you must do this processing in any case, even when you add it to your notes.*

Chapter 19 will show you how to relate lecture

For Practice

Take the same paragraphs in parts 5 and 8 of Section B (pages 92 and 94) and write your summary for each one here *in outline form.*

College paragraph:

Dinner party paragraph:

Compare your summaries with your classmates'.

notes with that reading which cannot be directly related to and incorporated into your class lecture notes.

D. How a Whole Article Is like a Single Paragraph

It is important for you to realize that *the overall pattern of an essay or article or chapter is similar to the pattern of a single paragraph.* That is, in a whole chapter or article there is (as in a single paragraph) a main point or topic or idea. This main idea is frequently given at the beginning of the chapter or article, usually in the first paragraph or first few paragraphs. Then the rest of the chapter or essay gives (as in a single paragraph) supporting material or fill-in or backup material for that main idea.

Sometimes in a chapter or article the main idea is also restated or summarized in the last paragraph.

Thus, if you read the first and last paragraphs of a chapter or essay, you will, in many cases, get the main or overall idea or point of that chapter or essay or article. The material in between, in these cases, will basically be the supporting or background material.

If the last paragraph simply repeats or sums up the main point that you noted in the first paragraph, you save time and energy by *not* summarizing that last, repetitive paragraph. Why write a main idea statement for and underline material that you have already prepared in an earlier paragraph? Remember, you don't want to repeat or duplicate your efforts. You want to be efficient.

Your Summary

Items   *Page Number(s)*

Compare your list with your classmates'.

CHAPTER 14

General Categories and Specific Examples:

Outlining

A. How to Get a Lot of Work under Control

1. You are in charge of doing the laundry in your house. The three other people in the house are willing to help fold the clean laundry if you prepare the pile of laundry each one is supposed to do. One person even said he'd do the ironing if you gave him the pile of laundry that needed to be ironed.

Okay, you have a big pile with everyone's clothes jumbled together in it. Included in the pile are sheets, towels, tablecloths. The other three people are waiting for you to give them their pile of laundry so they can get to work on it. How will you divide the laundry?

How about giving each person his or her own laundry? That means you yourself have also to do all the linen besides your own clothes. That's not fair.

How about giving all the socks and underwear to Elaine, all the pants and shirts to Barbara, all the linen to Larry? Then you won't have to do any more work. That's fair, since you already did the washing.

But what about the ironing? How about first dividing the laundry into the ironing pile and the nonironing pile? Give the ironing to Larry. Then you can divide the nonironing pile as you

planned to before: socks and underwear to Elaine, the pants and shirts that don't need ironing to Barbara, and you could do the linen that doesn't need ironing.

A picture of that division of the laundry would look like the drawing below.

However, it is not always convenient to draw actual pictures of material that you want to divide up in a logical, orderly way. Therefore, you might wish to make an outline instead. An outline draws a word picture of how you want to divide your material. It is usually more convenient. See, for example, Outline 1 on page 104.

Outline 2 on page 104 presents another way you could show the division of the laundry.

Spend some time looking at these two different ways (Outlines 1 and 2) of outlining the same jobs. Both outlines do a good job. There are probably even other good ways to outline the division of the laundry, all of which could be equally correct.

2. How do you know which is the best way to arrange your material into an outline? It is just a matter of outlining in the way that is most useful and convenient and appropriate for your own purposes. You can outline study material in a way that makes it *easy for you* to understand and

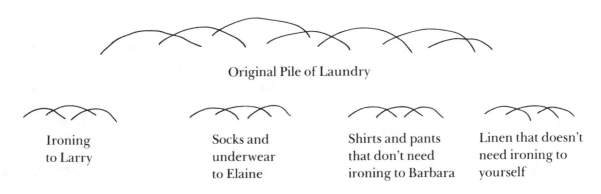

Original Pile of Laundry

| Ironing to Larry | Socks and underwear to Elaine | Shirts and pants that don't need ironing to Barbara | Linen that doesn't need ironing to yourself |

Outline 1

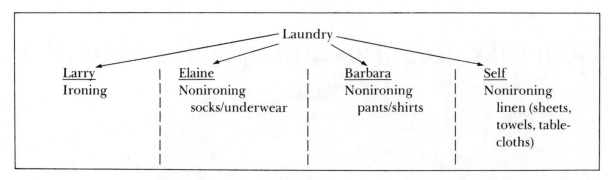

Visual Outlines

Outline 2

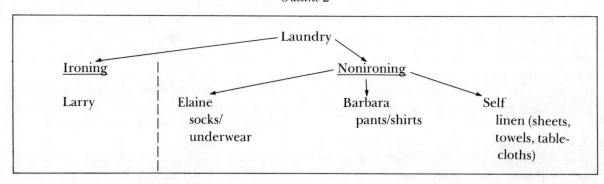

List Outlines Based on the Visual Outline

Dividing the Laundry: Outline 1
    A. Larry
       Ironing
    B. Elaine
       Nonironing
         Socks
         Underwear
    C. Barbara
       Nonironing
       Pants
       Shirts
    D. Self
       Nonironing
       Linen
         Towels
         Tablecloths
         Sheets

Dividing the Laundry: Outline 2
    A. Ironing
       Larry
    B. Nonironing
       Elaine
         Socks
         Underwear
       Barbara
       Pants
       Shirts
     Self
       Linen
         Towels
         Tablecloths
         Sheets

store it! You can depend upon your own inborn sense of logic. As you gain experience through practice you will improve your outlining ability.

Of the two outlines above (1 or 2) which one would you choose as more useful for your own purposes?

I think Outline 2 would be better as my own

worksheet for how I should divide up the laundry to give to the others. I would keep this tacked up on the laundry room wall so that I would remember how to divide the laundry: first I would separate out all the ironing; then it would be easier to divide the rest.

Outline 1 would be a good worklist for the

others, so they would know what they have to do. This list I would keep tacked up in the kitchen so each person would know what laundry he or she has to do: each person would look up his or her name to see what kind of laundry he or she had to fold.

3. The idea of an outline, then, is to arrange a lot of material in a logical, orderly way, showing which are the larger "piles" or categories and which are the smaller ones or the more specific ones under or in the larger or more general ones.

B. How to Write Out an Outline

1. In an outline you want to indicate which are the bigger, more general categories and which are the smaller or more specific ones inside them or subcategories beneath them. This

is the method: you alternate numbers and letters, getting smaller and smaller, and indenting more and more.

I. This is the biggest category.
  A. This is the next biggest one. It fits in or under the biggest one.
    1. The category of the next smaller size.
      a. The smaller one that fits into or under the one above.
        i. An even smaller one to fit in or under the one above.
          (a) And yet an even smaller one, if there is one.

If you have several categories of equal size or on the same level, then they must have the same letter or number designation.

We can see how this works in the expanded version of Outline 1 below.

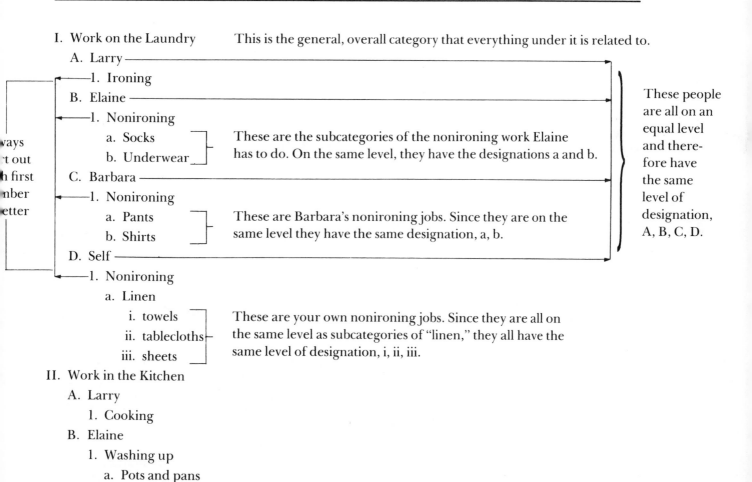

I. Work on the Laundry   This is the general, overall category that everything under it is related to.
  A. Larry
    1. Ironing
  B. Elaine
    1. Nonironing
      a. Socks
      b. Underwear   These are the subcategories of the nonironing work Elaine has to do. On the same level, they have the designations a and b.
  C. Barbara
    1. Nonironing
      a. Pants
      b. Shirts   These are Barbara's nonironing jobs. Since they are on the same level they have the same designation, a, b.
  D. Self
    1. Nonironing
      a. Linen
        i. towels
        ii. tablecloths   These are your own nonironing jobs. Since they are all on the same level as subcategories of "linen," they all have the same level of designation, i, ii, iii.
        iii. sheets
II. Work in the Kitchen
  A. Larry
    1. Cooking
  B. Elaine
    1. Washing up
      a. Pots and pans
and so forth.

These people are all on an equal level and therefore have the same level of designation, A, B, C, D.

[v]ays [s]t out [h] first [n]mber [l]etter

You might be interested to know that the correct style of outlining says that you don't need to put a letter or number if there is only one item in a category. Thus, under "A. Larry," since he only cooks as his kitchen work, we don't really need to put "1." We can just write "Cooking." If he had two tasks, we'd write:

> A. Larry
>   1. Cooking
>   2. Shopping

The division of a different kind of material is shown in the outline of foods below. Notice that for each letter and number there are at least two items in the same category.

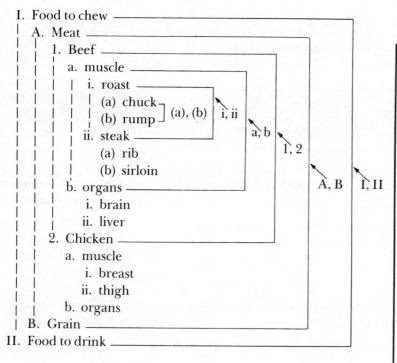

and so forth.

Notice that the numbers and letters of items that are on the same level of size or importance are lined up with each other. This has been indicated by the dotted lines on the left side in the outline. The lines on the right indicate the boxes that might be drawn (if we were to put these items in boxes) so that the smaller, more specific categories are inside the boxes of the bigger or more general categories.

Each category is more general (larger) than the category below it. And the one below is a

specific example or subcategory of the one above. For example, "food to chew" is a more general (larger) category than "meat." "Meat" is only one specific example or subcategory of "food to chew." But then "meat" is a more general category than "beef." In other words, beef is a kind of meat (meat is not a kind of beef). "Beef" is a specific example or category of "meat," and yet "beef" itself is more general than "muscle," which is a subcategory or specific example of a part of "beef." That is, a muscle is one kind of beef (beef is not a kind of a muscle). And so on. Look at the outline again and see that, except for the largest and smallest items, every other item is both a specific example of the item above it and more general than the one below it.

Do **For Practice** below.

<hr>

For Practice

Try making an outline on your own to see whether you are getting the idea. Take the category "car." Now fill in the blanks. Note that even though there is only one item at each level and ordinarily we wouldn't use the "I" or "A" or "1," I have included them here for clearness of the outline.

I._____

  A. Car

    1. _____

      a._____

Fill in these blanks, and discuss with your classmates, before you read on.

<hr>

Here is one possible correct outline of the **For Practice** material:

I. Transportation
  A. Car (one kind of transportation)
    1. Ford (one kind of car)
      a. Galaxie (one kind of Ford)

Except for the first and last items, each item is a specific example or subcategory of the level above it and more general than the one beneath it.

"Transportation" is a more general (larger) category than "car." And yet "car" is more general (larger) than "Ford." And "Ford," in turn, is more general (larger) than "Galaxie," which is just one specific example of a Ford. Just as Ford is just one specific example of a car. And car is just one specific example of transportation.

2. Here is another division of material. Notice the general categories and specific examples.

I. Transportation (the most general, largest category in this outline)
  A. Car (a specific example of a kind of transportation)
    1. Sports (a specific example of a car)
    2. Luxury (another, different specific example of a car)
    3. Economy (and yet a third, different specific example of a car)
      a. Volkswagen (a specific example of an economy car)
        i. camper (a specific example of a Volkswagen)
          (a) pop-top (a specific example of a VW camper)

In other words, in the above outline, each of the items is both general and a specific example, except the first item (which is not a specific example since it is the most general) and the last item (which is not a general category of anything else since there is nothing inside or beneath it or a subcategory or a specific example of it).

In the next column are some other ways to divide this material.

I. Motor Vehicles
  A. Car (one kind of motor vehicle)
    1. Sedan (one kind of car)
      a. 4-door (one kind of sedan)

Yet another correct outline is:

I. Transportation
  A. Car (one kind of transportation)
    1. Sports (one kind of car)
      a. MG (one kind of sportscar)

Or another:

I. Transportation
  A. Car
    1. Import (one kind of car)
      a. Datsun (one kind of imported car)

And so on. Remember, there are innumerable ways to divide your material. The way you choose to divide it should be the way that is most useful, convenient, and appropriate for your own particular use.

3. The idea of outlining is to divide the material in the way that will show the material in the most logical and orderly manner for your particular purposes. At the bottom of the page are three different outlines. If you were a travel agent, which of the three outlines would be most useful or appropriate? Yes, the one that divides the material into land and water modes of transportation. Your customers might need that kind of information.

If you were the owner of a carpentry shop and wanted to let your investors know what kind of work there is available, which outline would be the best for your purposes? Yes, the last one.

And if you were deciding which kind of vehicle to buy and you were not very happy with noisy, mechanical things, the second outline would be useful for you.

Do the first **For Practice** on page 108.

I. Transportation
  A. Land
    1. Bus
    2. Train
  B. Water
    1. Ocean liner
    2. Ferry

I. Transportation
  A. Motor driven
    1. Car
    2. Motor boat
  B. Not motor driven
    1. Bicycle
    2. Rowboat

I. Transportation
  A. Metal body
    1. Car
    2. Bus
  B. Wooden body
    1. Rowboat
    2. Wagon

For Practice

Just to make sure you are getting the idea, fill in the following:

I. Furniture

   A._____

      1. Couch

      2._____

   B._____

      1._____

      2._____

   C. Kitchen

      1._____

      2._____

Fill in the outline, and discuss with your classmates, before you read on.

For Practice

Try one more outline:

I._____

   A. Outdoors

      1._____

      2._____

   B.

      1._____

      2. Slippers

Here is one way to fill in the **For Practice** exercise:

     I. Clothing
       A. Outdoors
         1. Overcoat
         2. Hat
       B. Indoors
         1. Lounging robe
         2. Slippers

Notice that in the **For Practice** outlines, all items on the same level of size or importance or generality have designations of the same type (A. Outdoors; B. Indoors; 1. Overcoat; 2. Hat; etc.).

Also notice that these levels are lined up under each other so that the smaller ones or the specific examples are *indented* under the more general categories. This *indentation* indicates that the indented items are examples or subcategories of the item above, that they are smaller or more specific than the one above.

Do **For Practice** on the next page.

Here is one way to fill in the **For Practice** outline:

     I. Furniture
       A. Living room
         1. Couch
         2. Easy chair
       B. Bedroom
         1. Bed
         2. Dresser
       C. Kitchen
         1. Table
         2. Chairs

Do **For Practice** in the next column.

For Practice

Here is an outline that has some mistakes in it. Try to identify the mistakes and correct them before going on.

I. Balanced diet
  A. Protein
    1. Eggs
    2. Meat
      a. Pork
      b. Chicken
      c. Bacon
      d. Beef
        i. Roast
        ii. Chuck roast
        iii. Rump roast
        iv. Steak
          (a) Sirloin steak
  B. Milk

Discuss with your classmates before continuing.

Were you able to see that some of the examples and categories in the **For Practice** outline were not logically placed? Here is a way to correct the outline:

I. Balanced diet
  A. Protein
    1. Milk
    2. Eggs
    3. Meat
      a. Pork
        i. Bacon
      b. Chicken
      c. Beef
        i. Roast
          (a) Chuck roast
          (b) Rump roast
        ii. Steak
          (a) Sirloin steak

In the corrected outline, each subcategory is a specific example of the more general category above it. For example, bacon is a specific kind or example of pork so it belongs under pork, as in the corrected version. Also, in the incorrect version, chuck roast and rump roast are on the same level as roast. But this is not logical because chuck and rump roasts are specific examples or kinds of the more general category of roast. This has been corrected in the second version. Finally, in the first version, milk has been put at the same level as protein. Actually, milk is a specific example of a food that is a kind of protein. Thus, milk belongs under protein, as it is in the second version.

C. Outlining Helps You Remember Your Material

1. An outline, as you probably have already guessed, is a mnemonic device. It is a way to organize your material in an orderly, logical way, thus making it easier for you to remember. *The time spent working on your outline is time well spent because you are thinking about the material and are processing it in your mind. In this way you are getting familiar with the material; you are starting to make the nerve grooves.*

Go back to page 100 and see that the reading summaries are in the form of outlines. Study the outlines on page 100 and notice how the material is categorized into general and specific.

Outlines can also be less formal than the types presented so far. An informal outline would not have the letters and numbers and might be written in phrases or sentences. For example:

—people need a balanced diet that includes
  —protein
  —sources are milk
    eggs

2. In order to make your outline mnemonic device more effective, you should try to arrange the items as logically as possible. For example, in the Clothing outline on page 108, notice that the subitems under Outdoors and Indoors are arranged with the larger, outer garment listed first and then the smaller garment listed second. This logical reason for arranging your material will give you one more memory aid. (Be sure to flip back and look at that outline to see specifically what I am saying here.)

In the Furniture outline on page 108, the subitems under Living Room, Bedroom, and Kitchen are all listed with the larger piece first (couch, chair; bed, dresser; table, chairs). (Page-flip back to that outline.)

Notice on Outline 1 on page 104 how the items are arranged. The laundry items are all in order from small to large or from bottom to top: socks, underwear, pants, shirts; towels, tablecloths, sheets. Arranging the items this way is also part of your mnemonic device because it helps you remember the items more easily.

3. Now let us see how outlining helps you in your school work. See, for example, the class notes on the history of the English language below. These are the notes you take during the class lecture. You leave room to add information from your textbook.

When you go to study, you will read the text (if the teacher assigns reading in your textbook)

Eng. 112 - 10/22 - p. 3

<u>History of the Eng. Language</u>

Around 4000-2000 B.C. a certain tribe spoke lang. we now call "Indo-European Mother Language." Tribe split up around 2000 B.C. — members went to all parts of Europe + also to India (France, Italy, Spain, Germany, England, Scandinavia, etc.) Over the centuries orig. mother lang. changed in each country + today are diff. from each other but are all descendants of "mother lang."

and add to or correct these class lecture notes, as in the second version of the notes.

A second version of your notes (below) has the additions from your textbook assignment. (Page-flip to Chapter 1 if you need to refresh yourself about how to take notes, and remember to give the material a reality check as you read your text and review your notes.)

Now, after adding your new information and doing a reality check, you have a set of notes that is as complete as you can make it for your present studying purposes. (If you were doing a big research project or were especially interested in the subject, you might go to the library and get even more information to add to what you heard in class and read in your textbook.)

You are now ready to outline these lecture-plus-text notes. The outlining will go in the left-hand margin that you have been leaving blank. Use scrap paper first to figure out the best outline for you. Remember, time and effort spent figuring out your most logical mnemonic arrangement will help you understand the material even more. (*Processing* is good!) This is when you prepare your material for *proper* storage in your memory. The mnemonic order (logical and/or tricky arrangement) you make at this time is what you will then copy, check, and correct for *firm* storage in your memory. See the final version of the notes on the history of the English language on the next page.

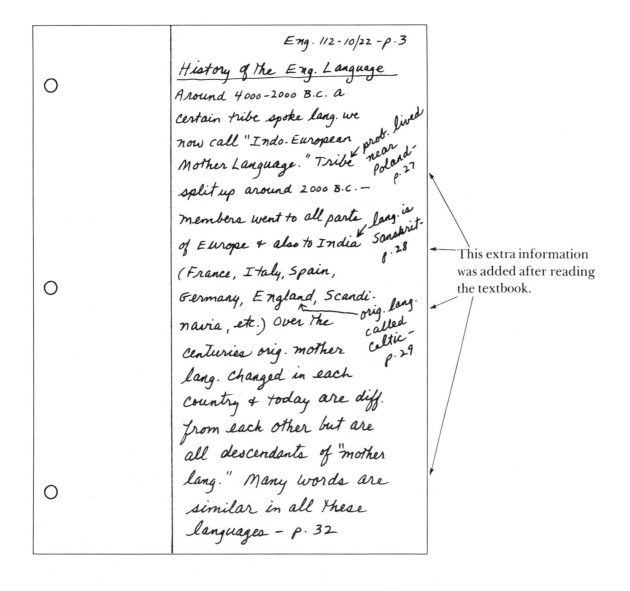

This extra information was added after reading the textbook.

This is the kind of logical arrangement mentioned in Chapter 4. Developing this kind of arrangement is one of the most important activities you should do during your study time. Doing this is really studying! And it will take a lot of time. Now can you see why you should schedule two hours of study for every hour in the classroom? *But this is how you learn and remember your material.*

Do **For Practice** on the next page.

As you gain more experience outlining your notes, you will be able to do it more quickly and easily. At first, however, you may need to use a lot of scrap paper and do a lot of trial and error thinking and planning before you decide on the most logical and appropriate outline (mnemonic arrangement) for yourself. *This is thinking!*

D. Outlining Skills Help You Answer Test Questions

1. There is yet another reason for knowing the difference between general categories (or general information) and the specific examples of the general. That reason has to do with tests.

When you are asked a certain type of test question, you need to give both the general answer and also a specific example of that general answer. For example, here is such a test question: <u>Explain what "peak energy time" means and how it is related to a student's schedule. Give an example.</u>

Here is one student's answer: "My energy is highest in the morning so I will schedule two hours of study from 6:00 A.M. to 8:00 A.M."

The letter "c." means "around" and is used as an abbreviation for that word.

These countries are mnemonically arranged in alphabetical order.

Hist. Eng. Lang.

I. Indo-European Mother Lang.
  A. One tribe
    1. near Poland
    2. c. 4000-2000 B.C.
II. Tribe splits up c. 2000 B.C.
  A. to Europe
    1. England
      a. Celtic
    2. France
    3. Germany
    4. Italy
    5. Scand.
    6. Spain
  B. Asia
    1. India
      a. Sanskrit
III. Many words similar in all these languages

Eng. 112 - 10/22 - p. 3

History of the Eng. Language

Around 4000-2000 B.C. a certain tribe spoke lang. we now call "Indo-European Mother Language." Tribe prob. lived near Poland - p. 27 split up around 2000 B.C. — members went to all parts of Europe & also to India lang. is Sanskrit - p. 28 (France, Italy, Spain, Germany, England, Scandinavia, etc.) Over the orig. lang. called Celtic - p. 29 centuries orig. mother lang. changed in each country & today are diff. from each other but are all descendants of "mother lang." Many words are similar in all these languages - p. 32

For Practice

The outline shown on page 112 is only one of many possible ways to outline the history of the English language material. How would you do it differently? (Chapter 15 will show you other, different ways to arrange lecture notes. *Outlining* is only one way to do it. The main consideration in arranging your notes is whether it is logical to *your* own way of thinking.)

Compare with your classmates.

Is this answer to the exact point of the question? No. This answer gives only the specific example. It does not give the *general* answer. The question has two parts; the first part asked you to give an explanation of what the term means and how it is related to a student's schedule. This part of the question is asking for a *general* explanation. It is asking what, *in general*, is a "peak energy time" and how, *in general*, this relates to a student's schedule. The second part of the question, then, asks for a specific example of what you have given *in general*. (Page-flip to Chapter 7 to refresh your knowledge of test-taking, if necessary.)

Do **For Practice** on page 114.

For Practice

How would you answer the question in Section D, giving both a general and a specific answer? Write your answer before going on.

Compare your answer with your classmates' answers. Try to see the difference between the general and specific parts of each one's answer.

Here is an answer that would receive full credit: "Peak energy time is when a person has the most energy, is able to concentrate best and work best. In terms of scheduling, a student should schedule time for study at his or her own peak energy time. For example, if a student has his or her peak energy time early in the morning, that student should schedule time for study at that time, perhaps from 6:00 A.M. to 8:00 A.M. Then that student will be able to do the best studying." (Can you see the difference between the general and specific parts of this answer?)

2. Sometimes the question does not so clearly ask for both a general and a specific answer, as in the example above. But you should always be aware that to give the most generous, the fullest, answer, you should try to give both a general answer as well as specific examples, whenever possible.

Do **For Practice** on page 115.

Here is one good answer to the **For Practice** question: "The Indo-European Mother Language was spoken by one tribe which lived near Poland around 4000-2000 B.C. Around 2000 B.C. this tribe split up and members went to all parts of Europe (England, France, Germany, Italy, Scandinavia, Spain) and to India. Over the centuries the languages in these countries have changed but there are still many words that are similar in these languages, which are all descen-

For Practice

Here is another question: "What is the Indo-European Mother Language?" Can you answer this question giving both general and specific information? Write your answer before reading further. (Please go back and use the information given in the student's notes above.)

Compare your answer with your classmates' answers and try to identify the general and specific parts of each one's answer.

---

dants of the original Indo-European Mother Language." If you wanted to give an even more generous answer you could add the information about the Celtic and Sanskrit languages. (Can you see the difference between the general and specific parts? Can you see that the outline—in the notes above—has helped you get both the general and specific information into the answer?)

3. If you do not have time on a long test to give all of the above information in a good sentence format, then at least briefly jot down the information on your answer paper. It is important to let the teacher know you know both the general and specific information even if you do not have time to express yourself in complete sentences in good essay style. An outline is especially useful for this purpose. It will help you organize and briefly state what you know.

4. Studies have shown that people tend to understand and remember material better when they think about material in terms of general categories (or general information) and specific examples of the general. This chapter has given you a start on this kind of thinking. But only you yourself, by practicing this kind of thinking on your own, can improve your ability to do it. The better you get at this kind of thinking, however, the better you will be able to understand and remember material.

Your Summary

Items   *Page Number(s)*

CHAPTER 15

More on Note-Taking

Using the Left-Hand Margin of Your Notebook

A. Why You Should Use the Left-Hand Margin

1. As you saw in Section C, part 3, of Chapter 14, the left-hand margin of your lecture notebook is where you will write your properly prepared mnemonic arrangements for your lecture-plus-text notes.

There are two main reasons why you should write your mnemonic arrangements in the left-hand margin of your notebook. (a) *You will have your messy lecture-plus-text notes converted into a neat, streamlined, organized mnemonic arrangement in a handy, convenient place.* You could, of course, write all your mnemonic arrangements in another notebook. But it is more convenient to have the mnemonic arrangements on the same page as the original material. (b) *You can then, later, go through your notebook and conveniently read over those mnemonic arrangements to review them.*

That is, instead of having to reread and review all your original notes, *you can simply glance down the left-hand margins of your notebook, page by page, for a quick and easy review of all your properly prepared material.* And as you are glancing down the left-hand margin reviewing your mnemonic arrangements, you can mentally copy, check, and correct to make sure the nerve grooves for the material are still strong. You should do this kind of review at least once a week to make sure the material remains firmly stored.

2. By now you have had a number of days of practice in taking lecture notes on the right two-thirds of your notepage and then filling in and correcting with additional notes from your textbook readings if there are any such readings. Chapter 1 said that though this method was useful for actually taking and correcting your notes, it would, unfortunately, create a rather messy set of notes. The main problem with messy notes is that when you want to review your notes it is not easy because of the messiness and lack of organization. (Neat notes are better but not always possible.)

As you have probably found out by now—since you have been taking notes in class—it is hard to organize and be neat when you are trying to write notes during a lecture. So how do you get notes that are organized, logical, and easy to read? This way: you take messy notes in class, correct or add to them as you study, and then, after that, you figure out your best mnemonic arrangement; finally, you write this arrangement over neatly in the left-hand margin of your notepage. See Section C.3 of Chapter 14 for an example of this process.

While many skillful and experienced students use this method, others develop their own different and unique method of taking and organizing notes. Some of them develop the ability to organize while they are actually taking the lecture notes! But this requires many years of practice. As you learn, you will probably do better to follow the method given here: (a) take complete, though possibly messy, notes in class, (b) complete them when reading the text, and then (c) clean them up later in the left one-third of the notepage. *As you gain experience, you, too, can develop your own method.*

B. How to Put Material in the Left-Hand Margin

1. In the left-hand margin you will not want or need to copy over every single word you wrote during the lecture or added from your reading. You will want to *select* the best and most important material from your notes. You will want to weed out repetitions and wordiness. In other words, you are going to *streamline* your messy and full lecture-plus-text notes.

But more than that, you will want to *organize* the *selected* material into a logical and/or tricky mnemonic arrangement for proper storage. As was pointed out in Chapter 14, the *activity* you go through in preparing these mnemonic devices *will help you better understand* the material. It will also start making the nerve grooves so that the storage process can begin, which, of course, is what you want. Then, after you have your mnemonic device, copy, check, and correct it for firm storage in your memory. (Page-flip to Chapter 4.)

2. So far we have talked about using an outline or the general/specific type of arrangement. That is, Chapter 14 showed you how to outline material using general categories and specific examples, designated by alternating numbers and letters.

The end of Chapter 14 said studies show that people tend to understand and remember better when they think in this general category/specific example way.

This is true; however, there are also other ways to arrange material. While the outline format is often the most appropriate way to arrange many kinds of material, sometimes there is material that can be more appropriately arranged in a different way.

You must, with your own inborn sense of logic (and every person has an inborn sense of logic), figure out what you yourself think is the most appropriate way to arrange your material. You can create any kind of arrangement that makes sense to you. It doesn't matter if you are the only person in the world with that particular mnemonic device. *You* are going to be studying (processing and storing) your own mnemonic devices, not somebody else. Your arrangements have to make sense to *you*. In other words, there is no one perfect way to organize or arrange a body of information (see Chapter 14).

You can use the general category/specific example outline form with alternating numbers and letters if that seems to you the best way to arrange one part of your notes. Or you can make diagrams or boxes or circles or charts if any one of these seems the most appropriate and logical way to arrange your particular material for proper storage.

One student (see illustration on page 118) thought that putting a circle in the middle and then having arrows going out of it was the best

way for her to arrange the information in her notes about the history of the English language.

Another student could have outlined it as on page 112. And there are probably many other ways to arrange this same material. Each student must figure out his or her own most logical way. The individual student must find the most logical and, therefore, for him or her, the easiest way to store the material.

Another possible way to arrange your material is to use a *time line* (see illustration below). This is often appropriate when you are studying dates and events.

Charts are also useful in some situations. When you have material that discusses the similarities or differences between two or more things, it can be appropriate to use a chart that clearly lays out the differences or similarities side by side. See the illustration on page 120.

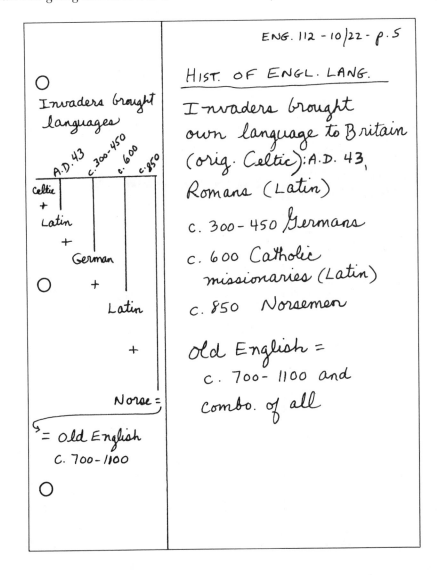

Some people like to draw pictures or maps or three-dimensional illustrations. As a student organizes the material in his or her notes first this way and then that way, trying to find the best way to arrange the material, he or she is gaining familiarity with the material. This, as has been mentioned before, helps the student understand and begin to remember the material.

You can make up a different logical and/or tricky arrangement for every different section of your notes. You do not always have to use the same kind of arrangement. For example, for some notes you may decide the outline form is most logical and appropriate. Then again, for other notes you may decide that a time line is the best way to organize that particular material. And so on.

C. What Studying Really Is

The search for the most logical arrangement is considered one of the most important parts of study. You should realize that you can expect to spend a good amount of time figuring out the best way to organize your material. Take as much time as you need to do this. I can't emphasize enough that this activity is at the very heart of studying. Unless you do this, you are not studying as you should. *This is real thinking!*

If you have two hours to study for a course, spend some time doing any reading assignment or exercises that have been assigned. Then spend a good amount of time reality checking and cross-referencing the new material (both the familiar and the unfamiliar). Then you are

---

ENG. 112 – 10/22 – p. 6

HIST. OF ENG. LANG.

O.E. c.700-1100	M.E. c.1100-1500
Celtic + Latin + German + Norse	O.E. + French (1066 invasion)
Beowulf (anon. c. 900)	Canterbury Tales (Chaucer 1343-1400)

Old Eng. — c. 700-1100

Beowulf — O.E. poem by unknown author

1066 – French invade

OE + French = Middle Eng. c. 1100-1500

Chaucer (1343-1400) wrote Canterbury Tales in M.E.

ready for the big, juicy part of study: figuring out the proper arrangement for your material. Spend a generous amount of time doing this. You might even spend one-half of your whole study time for that particular course making the proper arrangement of the material. Then, for the rest of the study time allotted for that course, copy, check, and correct the proper arrangement you have made.

Also, you will want to make a quick review, daily or weekly, of all these mnemonic arrangements, giving quick mental copy, check, correct reviews as you go through them.

And all that is really studying!

D. How Cross-Referencing/
Reality Checks Fit In

Before you begin to process your material (to try to find the most proper mnemonic device), you know you need to give the material a reality check. You know you should make an extensive search of all your knowledge and experiences related to the material being studied. (Page-flip to Chapters 5, 6 and 8 to refresh your memory on how and why to do these activities.)

Then, when you start to arrange the material (as discussed in the previous sections of this chapter), you may want to include some of what you came up with in your reality check and cross-referencing of your memory library.

For example, maybe you once studied, in a literature course, a poem about Beowulf (see notes on page 120) and remember part of it. Go ahead, put it into your mnemonic device as an example of what that material is talking about. Here is how you might do it:

Your Mnemonic Arrangement of Notes on Page 120
  Old English (O.E.): a combination of Celtic, Latin, German, Norse
    c. 700-1100
    Example: poem called *Beowulf* (Hwact! we Gar-Dena in gear-dagum—means—Listen [or Harken!] to old-time poem of the Spear-Danes)

Now you have not only prepared the material in your notes but made it *even better* by adding material you found in your memory (thanks to the cross-referencing you did). Chapter 6, Section A, part 5, discusses the benefit of good cross-referencing. Page-flip to that section to refresh your memory.

Your Summary

Items   *Page Number(s)*

CHAPTER 16

Preparing Textbook Notes
for Proper Storage

A. How to Study Your Textbook Notes

1. Now that you have your marginal notes (the main idea statements, as shown in Chapter 12) and your underlinings (as in Chapter 13) all done in your textbook, what do you do with this material?

It is good that you found and paraphrased the main ideas, and it is good that you underlined the supporting material. But you must do more with this textbook material if you want to store it properly and firmly in your memory.

2. If your textbook reading is coordinated with your class lecture, then you will need to match the textbook main ideas and underlinings with your lecture notes. You should then add to and/or correct your lecture notes, if needed. This activity was discussed in Chapters 1 and 15.

Then you will proceed, as discussed in Chapter 15, with rearranging your completed and corrected notes in the left one-third of your notepage.

In the present chapter, however, you will learn what to do with the textbook notes when they do *not* coordinate with your lecture material.

That is, for example, your teacher has lectured on the history of the Old Testament. This is what you took lecture notes on. The teacher then assigns you a chapter in your textbook on Buddhism to give you a broadened view of religious beliefs. The textbook reading on Buddhism cannot be matched up with your lecture notes on ancient Hebrew religious beliefs and writings. Therefore you cannot simply add a few facts here and there to your lecture notes. You will need a whole separate, different set of notes on Buddhism. You will need to take your main ideas and underlinings from your text-book and turn them into notes on separate, different note paper.

But how do you transfer your main idea statements and underlinings from your textbook to a notebook?

3. You will be pleased to know that you already have a good start with the main ideas you have written in the margins and with your underlinings. For example, look at the main ideas and underlinings I made for two paragraphs in my textbook assignment.

There are <u>now</u> rather <u>more than three billion people on earth. For the three leading nations of the</u> world, the population figures are now roughly <u>700 million for China, 250 million for the U.S.S.R.</u>, and <u>200 million for the United States.</u> *[world pop. today]*

What will the <u>situation</u> be a generation from now, say in <u>1990</u>, assuming that we avoid a thermonuclear war? It is virtually certain that the population will have <u>increased by at least 60 percent</u>. The population of the <u>United States</u>, for instance, <u>may have</u> reached the <u>320,000,000 mark.</u>* *[60% more in 1990]*

First of all, I found these to be information paragraphs. What are the topics I am getting the information about? "World population today" and "in 1990." These, then, are the main ideas. I wrote those main ideas in the margin.

Then I underlined the supporting material; that is, I underlined the pieces of information on the topics (main ideas) of "world population today" and "population in 1990."

Now I am ready for the next step. Unfortunately, my teacher did not give any lectures on population. My teacher has been lecturing on pollution and natural resources. In order to give

*Isaac Asimov, "Life in 1990," in *Science Digest*, August 1965.

us more background information, she assigned a reading in a resource book on population. Since I have no lecture notes on population, I will have to create my own new, separate set of notes on this extra reading assignment.

Where should I put this different set of notes? I could put it on the page following my most recent lecture notes on natural resources. Or I could put it in a different part of my notebook (maybe at the back). Or I could put it into a different notebook that I would buy just for outside reading notes. To do one of the first two options, you will need a loose-leaf notebook.

But how do I write down my main ideas and underlinings in a notebook?

Easy. They are already summaries that can quickly be put into outline form (page-flip to Section C of Chapter 13). See the following outline summary; compare it to the quoted paragraphs above. Notice that as I write the material down in my notebook I am paraphrasing it. To paraphrase at this time is to *process* the material even further. (Writing the main ideas in the margins and underlining the selected supporting details are also *processing*.)

A. World population today
   1. Over 3 billion
      a. China: 700 million
      b. U.S.S.R.: 250 million
      c. U.S.: 200 million
   2. 60% more in 1990
      a. U.S.: possibly 320 million

I write this down on a piece of scrap paper. I do not yet write it down in my notebook. The reason I don't write it down immediately in my notebook is that I am going to restate and rearrange it into a mnemonic device that seems more clear and logical *to me*. The arrangement I have on scrap paper is according to the *author's* sense of logic. I have simply copied down the book's arrangement of the material.

But I will want to rearrange the material according to my *own* sense of logic. I will also want to paraphrase it so that it is clear to *me*. I need to do this because I will be able to store it better if it is arranged and stated according to *my* understanding and *my* sense of logic and not the *author's* way of speaking and the *author's* sense of logic. This is the processing I spoke of in Chapter 15, Sections B, C, and D.

The author has the population of the countries in the order of *large* to *small*. I do not find this as logical as having them in the order of *small* to *large*. Thus, I will restate and rearrange the material on scrap paper so that it reads:

A. World population
   1. 3 billion plus
      a. U.S.: 200 million
      b. U.S.S.R.: 250 million
      c. China: 700 million
   2. 60% more in 1990
      a. U.S.: possibly 320 million

On the scrap paper I first had copied down the material *in order, exactly as I had underlined it.* This was to lay it out clearly in an outline form so that I could look at it and see what the *author's* logic was. Then I was able to think about what logic would be better. Then I copied over my better arrangement.

Did I waste time with all this copying, thinking, restating, rearranging? No, of course not. The *physical* repetition of the copying helped start making the nerve grooves to store the material firmly. The thinking and restating and rearranging helped me prepare the material for proper storage and helped make the material more familiar to me.

As has been mentioned before, a great deal of study time ought to be spent in this sort of rearranging of material and copying it over and then, perhaps, rearranging and restating it even more, trying to find the most perfect statement and logical arrangement *for yourself*. (At this time please page-flip back to Chapter 4, Section E, part 6.) You are now *really* thinking.

For example, after I had rearranged the material and copied it over, as above, maybe I would think about it some more and rearrange and restate it again:

World Population		
<u>Now</u> → 60% Increase → <u>1990</u>		
U.S.—200 million	→	U.S.—320 million
U.S.S.R.—250 million		
China—700 million		

In my final and most perfect (for me) restatement and rearrangement, I did not use the outline form; instead I chose to use the chart form, laying the two contrasting times (now and 1990) side by side so that the contrast would be very clear to me. This seemed, to me, the *most* logical way to arrange this particular material.

4. Okay, now I have my most perfect mnemonic rearrangement of the material from the book. I have transferred my main idea statements and underlinings to scrap paper, and I have rearranged and restated them so that they are in the most logical arrangement that I can make. Now what?

Now I copy this final, perfect mnemonic arrangement or device over into my notebook. I put it either on a page near my most recent class lecture notes, or I put it in that special place in my notebook that I have chosen for outside reading notes. Or I put it into the special notebook I have bought for outside reading notes that don't match with my class lecture notes. Now I have my material in a safe and convenient place and prepared for proper storage.

5. And then what? Then I will store this properly prepared material firmly in my memory. How? By using the copy, check, correct method.

If I had wanted to, I could have put this material *also* on flash cards. That is, first the material would be written in my notebook so that all my notes would be complete and together. Then, it could *also* be copied over on flash cards, if I felt that was appropriate or useful for this particular set of notes.

If the material had been also copied over on flash cards, then I would copy, check, and correct the flash cards. If, on the other hand, I had felt that using flash cards was *not* useful with this material, then I would have copied, checked, and corrected the notes as I had written them in my notebook.

Remember, when you make flash cards it is best to type them. If you can type your notes it will also make them easier to review later. If you can't type, then be sure to write clearly or print.

6. In the next column is another way to explain this whole process, starting with the text:

*things
kids leave
lying
around*

Sewing machine
crayons

coats   books

Paragraph in textbook
(showing only the underlining)
a. This textbook paragraph has four strong and appropriate supporting details underlined; and main idea is in margin.

A. *Things kids leave lying around:*
1. *sewing machine*
2. *crayons*
3. *coats*
4. *books*

Scrap paper
b. This is the first copying onto scrap paper of details as underlined (according to *author's* sense of logic).

A. *Kids leave lying around*
1. *books*
2. *coats*
3. *crayons*
4. *sewing machine*

Scrap paper
c. This might be the first rearrangement and restatement of material according to your *own* sense of logic—this is an *alphabetical* arrangement (as an example of a kind of logic).

A. *Kids leave lying around*
1. *crayons*
2. *books*
3. *coats*
4. *sewing machine*

Scrap paper
d. *This might be your more perfect* rearrangement with the items arranged from *small to large* (as an example of a kind of logic that you might like better).

Now you will copy over the last and best rearrangement into your notebook. Then, if you think it appropriate and useful, you can also recopy the material into flash cards:

```
┌─────────────────────────────────────┐
│                                      │
│                                      │
│                                      │
│                                      │
│       Kids leave things lying around │
│                                      │
│                                      │
│                                      │
│                                      │
└─────────────────────────────────────┘
```

One side

Other side

```
┌─────────────────────────────────────┐
│                                      │
│                                      │
│      1. crayons                      │
│      2. books                        │
│      3. coats                        │
│      4. sewing machine               │
│                                      │
│                                      │
└─────────────────────────────────────┘
```

Finally, you copy, check, and correct the material from your notebook or from your flash cards, if you made any.

Do **For Practice** on page 126.

B. An Example of How to Study Your Textbook

1. Here is how I prepared the **For Practice** paragraph for proper storage in my memory:

Water is inexhaustible but fresh water is not. The squeeze for fresh water is on already. However, it seems quite likely that before the quarter of a century is up there <u>will be practical methods for desalinizing ocean water</u> so that, in principle, fresh water will be inexhaustible. <u>But</u> desalinized ocean water is bound to be considerably more expensive than natural fresh water. It will still be <u>too expensive</u> in 1990 <u>for</u> any use

water in 1990

<u>other than drinking or cooking</u> and the <u>fight against water pollution will have to become strenuous</u> indeed.

Notice that I am going through all the procedures (**a** to **h**) as listed in the **For Practice**.

a. I know the meaning of every word so I do not need my dictionary; I give this paragraph a reality check and, from what I already know of this subject, I feel I can say that it seems pretty true to me.

b. The main idea is clearly *water in 1990* (this seems an *information* paragraph and perhaps has some *problem/solution* and *thesis/proof* intentions as well—in all cases I come up with the same main idea); I write this in the margin.

c. Then I select the supporting material that seems to support the main idea strongly, and I underline that material (it reads like an efficient telegram):

Will be practical methods for desalinizing ocean water—but too expensive for other than drinking or cooking—fight against pollution will have to become strenuous.

I could have left out the last underlining because I have several strong points already underlined. But I feel this is good information and I want to store it away in my memory just in case I might need it. Besides, my course is a political science course on "how citizens change their own society." For *that* course, the last underlining is especially appropriate (it tells what people will be doing about the problems in their society).

d. Now I am ready to copy that outline over onto scrap paper, paraphrasing it:

—water in 1990
 —desalinization of ocean water will be developed by 1990
 —but will not really work because too expensive
 —only for drinking and cooking
 —therefore, in 1990 people will still be fighting water pollution

e. I am not very satisfied with the way this is stated or the logic of this arrangement; so now I need to think about the material, which has been laid out in this clear form, and rearrange and restate it in a way that is more clear and logical to me:

For Practice

Now you need to practice this rearranging and restating of textbook material. Study the practice paragraph (below) by the following procedure:

a. Understand every word and give the paragraph a reality check.

b. Find the main idea and write it in your own words in the margin; if you have trouble finding the main idea, ask the questions you learned in Chapter 12.

c. Select three or four of the strongest, most appropriate supporting details and underline them; this and your main idea statement from above will be your summary or outline of the paragraph.

d. Copy over on scrap paper the outline that you have just made for the paragraph; you can forget about all the other material in the paragraph.

e. Rearrange and restate that outline according to your *own* best understanding and sense of logic and then copy onto more scrap paper. (Do you feel your mind working, thinking?)

f. Try to rearrange and restate that same material even better, if you can.

g. When you have finally found your most perfect rearrangement and restatement of the material, copy it over onto a flash card (since you don't have a special notebook for *this practice material,* we will, *just for this practice case,* go directly to the flash card).

h. Finally, copy, check, and correct the flash card.

When you have done all that, you will have stored that now well-understood, familiar material properly and firmly in your memory. Now you will be able to recall it should you have a test on the material in this practice paragraph. *Studying a paragraph means doing all of these activities.*

Practice Paragraph

Water is inexhaustible but fresh water is not. The squeeze for fresh water is on already. However, it seems quite likely that before the quarter of a century is up there will be practical methods for desalinizing ocean water so that, in principle, fresh water will be inexhaustible. But desalinized ocean water is bound to be considerably more expensive than natural fresh water. It will still be too expensive in 1990 for any use other than drinking or cooking and the fight against water pollution will have to become strenuous indeed.*

*Isaac Asimov, "Life in 1990," in *Science Digest,* August 1965.

Compare your flash cards with your classmates'.

A. Water in 1990
　1. Desalinization of ocean water will work but be too expensive
　　(a) Will be used only for drinking and cooking
　　(b) People will have to continue fighting water pollution

(I know I am not supposed to use an "A" unless there is at least a "B," or a "1" unless there is at least a "2." However, I choose to be a rebel and use these anyway because it clarifies the outline for me. Some people might use a dash or an arrow or an asterisk or some other pointer instead.)

f. That seems pretty good, but I think I can get the material arranged and stated even more clearly; besides, *by thinking about it further, I am getting even more familiar with it* and am, therefore, understanding and nerve grooving it even better.

Water in 1990
　1. Will be practical methods for desalinizing ocean water but too expensive for other than
　　(a) Drinking
　　(b) Cooking
　2. People will be strenuously fighting against water pollution

g. Now I am satisfied with having stated and arranged the material into a form that seems really logical and clear to me; I am ready to copy it over into my notebook, or, in this case, onto a flash card (see below).

Notice that I made some other, final changes as I copied the material from the scrap paper onto the flash card.

h. This way, I have my material in the most proper form for storage. Now I will want to store it firmly. Therefore, I will copy, check, and correct the flash card I have made.

2. After all the work I went through to get the material prepared and onto the flash card, I am already very familiar with it. The nerve groove in which I will store it has already been started. Thus after all the previous activities, my copy, check, correct work will not be very difficult or take very long. Soon I will have this material properly and firmly stored in my memory for future recall and use.

3. You may want to read your whole textbook assignment over before preparing it for storage part by part. Some people prefer to partially prepare it in the first reading and then go back to finish the processing. Each person needs to discover her or his own best method.

C. How to Skim and Scan

1. To skim means to read quickly, just looking for the main idea in a paragraph or for the supporting details.

Skimming should be done when you have a lot to read and much of the reading is all on the same subject or on a subject with which you are familiar.

Skimming should not be done when you are studying an important, unfamiliar subject. If you skim in this situation you will *not* store the material and will lose the trace of it because in skimming you go too quickly to give reality checks or summarize. And these activities are needed to make

Water in 1990

One side

1. desalinization of ocean water will be developed
2. but too expensive & only for:
　a. drinking
　b. cooking
3. therefore, people will still be fighting against water pollution

Other side

nerve grooves for firm storage, necessary with new material.

If, for example, you are studying Shakespeare and you come across a chapter about Queen Elizabeth and the Spanish navy and England's position in the world c. 1600, you can skim that chapter if you have already learned that material in your English history course. You are skimming just to see whether there is anything new there. Note the new facts.

However, if you did not take an English history course and the historical information is new to you, you should skim that chapter *only* if that material is not important to you, *only* if both you *and* the teacher think it is unimportant.

In this case, if the material is unimportant and unfamiliar, you can skim just to get the main ideas: King Philip II of Spain sent his navy against England; England won; England became the greatest sea and therefore world power; Queen Elizabeth was admired by all; golden age in all the arts flourished.

You will want to write down these main ideas in your notes, probably near the lecture notes on Shakespeare's England. But you will not need to arrange and rearrange and restate as you would for important material that you must learn and remember. You can skim a chapter, then go back and reread it more carefully and slowly if you decide you do want to firmly store the material.

2. To *scan* means to move your eyes quickly over a piece of reading material looking for one specific point (e.g., information about tests in the introductory handout for a new course you are taking). The great thing about scanning is that the words you are looking for just jump off the page at you.

Do **For Practice** below.

For Practice

Try this scanning exercise. You want specific information about quizzes and exams in a new course that you are taking. *Scan* the following description of the course given out by the instructor. Move your eyes rapidly over the lines, from left to right, just as fast as you can, looking for information about quizzes and exams. Don't worry about missing it by going so fast; you will be surprised to find that when you reach the place where this information is given, the words will suddenly jump into view. Just keep concentrating strongly on the information for which you are looking: repeat to yourself, "quizzes, exams."

Class Objectives

The instructor wishes to place within the grasp of students the skills and understanding needed to put ideas together logically and express these ideas in writing clearly, in correct grammar, and in the student's individual style.

Major activities will be class work on structure, analysis of readings, journal-writing. There will be time devoted to spelling, vocabulary, and grammar.

Rewriting of student papers is highly encouraged. All work, including quizzes and larger exams, may also be rewritten.

The purpose of the course is to provide students with the environment and opportunities for learning.

Class discussion and questions in class are urged.

Your Summary

Items   *Page Number(s)*

CHAPTER 17

Writing a Research Paper

A. What Is a Research Paper?

A research paper is a report you write about some research you have done.

This means that first you have to do some research.

B. What Is Research?

Research is searching for information about a subject. You can do the following different kinds of research:

1. Find out what is *already known* about your subject.

2. Find out something *new* about your subject. This is the *original research* that, for example, scientists conduct.

3. Combine both the above. (If you want to find out something new about a subject, first you should find out what others *already know* so that you do not have to waste time reinventing the wheel.)

C. Reporting Your Findings

After you have found out the already known information or discovered new information, you will want to see that your work and your efforts will not be lost or forgotten, and will be available to others who might want to profit from your efforts, learn from your research. To do this you need to *write a report on what you have done and have learned.*

The important aspect of writing a research paper is doing the actual research. The paper is only writing down, at the end, what you have found out. If you know how to write, the paper writing aspect is really a minor and relatively easy thing.

However, because people often have problems writing, they tend to feel that the writing is the major aspect. They feel they have to spend the majority of their time and effort and concern on writing the paper.

This is the opposite of what should be the case. The bulk of your time, effort, and concern needs to be on researching. This is the content, the substance. The paper only records and preserves the substance.

D. How to Conduct Research

Is there something you want to find out? Is there an answer you want to a problem? If not, then you have nothing to research. You should not be bothering yourself with how to conduct research. You will have nothing to write a research paper about, so you will not have to worry about writing the paper.

However, as a student, you will sometimes be asked by your teachers to do research. When you leave school, you may need to do research for your employer or for your own work. Therefore, you may want to know how to do research (and how to write a report on it) for these purposes.

The most unfortunate part about learning how to do research is that you may believe there is nothing you feel you want to find out. You will, of course, need to practice doing research in order to learn how to do it. So if you have nothing you feel you really want to find out about, you will have to cook something up just for practicing and learning the research skills.

E. Finding a Topic

Oh well, if there is no burning question or topic in your mind, then try to find some subject or area of life which interests you. Do you have a hobby? Is there something about your hometown or family or country or world or universe that makes you curious? (Have you ever heard of a black hole in space? Do you wonder what that is? Have you heard of the coal mine in Chicago? Do you know what it is, why it is, exactly where it is? Did your family come from Europe? When? Why? Was there a movement of many people to the United States at that time that included your family? What about the fall 1979 scare about Russians in Cuba? Was Fidel Castro right about their having been there for almost two decades and a number of U.S. presidents knowing all about it? After the 1979 pre-party convention vote in Florida, Jimmy Carter's people said his previous record would win him the 1980 election. What *was* his record? Was it better than Edward Kennedy's? What is really going on in the Mideast? Who or what is causing our economic ups and downs? What about a cure for cancer—is one almost here? Can vitamins prevent heart disease? Is pollution a real danger? And so on and so forth.)

F. Limiting Your Subject

1. Your subject should be small enough to research thoroughly in a relatively short time.

If you can and want to put in an indefinite length of time researching, then you do not have to limit your subject. Cancer scientists are committed to researching for the rest of their lives if necessary. If you don't have this commitment or time frame, you will want to get a subject you can do the full research on in a reasonable time (5–10 hours? 2–3 hours?).

The rule here, as you may have inferred, is that whenever you do research you must do *complete, thorough, full* research. What is the point of doing a half-baked job? You might as well not have bothered. What would be the point of it? And of then wasting your time writing up something that has no real substance and doesn't tell the real story?

Thus, if you are going to do a full and complete job and you have a limited time to do it in, the only conclusion is that you need to have a limited or narrow topic.

Black holes in space is obviously a very large topic. It might take several months or years to understand and get all the information on that.

Your family's coming to the United States? That might take at least a few weeks, what with the letters you'd want to collect and interviews you'd have to do. The Russians in Cuba? That might not take too long, if you want only a list of numbers and names of military stations. But if you want to list all the presidents who knew it, then you'd have to find out what they said about it; otherwise, how would you know they knew? And that might take a week or more, working at it part-time. Carter's record? If you want to find out about his presidential record in all areas, you would probably have to take a few days of part-time researching. If you want to contrast it to Kennedy's record during the same period, it would take part of another week as well. If you want to find out both their records from the time they both became public figures until the 1980 election, that would considerably lengthen the time needed. But what if you want to compare their records on health policies during a given time? You could probably do that in a few days. That would be a topic suitable for doing a thorough research job in a time span that is probably realistic for you.

2. Here's a rule of thumb that might be useful: after you decide on a topic, then make it smaller; and then make that smaller again. Shorten it at least twice. Maybe more.

Here's an example: *Topic*—black holes in space; *first limitation*—discovery of black holes in space; *second limitation*—what led up to the discovery of black holes in space. (What led up to this discovery in the United States is an even smaller topic.)

You can do a short but thorough research job on this limited topic of what *led up* to the discovery. You are searching, now, only for the phenomena that caused scientists to begin to look for what turned out to be black holes. And if you are still curious, you can do another research project on another aspect of black holes.

G. Doing the Research

First, go to the library. You will, to begin with, need to explore four sources of information. Be sure to ask the librarians for help if you have any problem finding the material.

1. *The reference section of the library.* Here you will find the encyclopedias. Look up "black holes" in a general encyclopedia and also in an encyclopedia of science and technology as well as in specialized encyclopedias in astronomy.

2. *Reader's Guide to Periodical Literature.* Here you will find a listing of all articles on your topic that have been published in the regular, popular magazines (ranging from *Hot Rod* to *Business Week* to *Esquire* to *Scientific American*). Read the articles that pertain to your subject.

3. *Indexes and abstracts section.* Here are booklets that contain lists and also short descriptions of the contents of all the books published on your topic; they also list and describe articles that have been published in the specialized or professional journals related to your area of interest. (Indexes in different fields have different formats.) Topics in *indexes* are usually listed with subtopics. For example, under "black holes" you might find the subtopic "discovery of" or some other subtopic that seems pertinent to your specific topic. Under the subtopic you will find a list (index) of the books and articles pertaining to that subtopic. Then you can look up in the *abstracts booklet* short descriptions (abstracts) of those books and articles that strike you as particularly relevant. When you do this, you can weed out the books and articles that, from their description, are probably not going to help you. It saves you from having to read *all* the books and articles. Thank goodness for those who thought up and who produce these indexes and abstracts!

Now you need to find those articles that you want. You can ask your librarian to help you find them.

4. *The card catalog section and the book collection.* In the card catalog section you will find a "subject catalog." Here all the books in the library are listed by *subject,* alphabetically. Look up your topic and find all the books in the library on your topic.

Below is a copy of a *subject* card for a book titled *Planetary Encounters.* Notice that the words "Planets—Exploration" at the top of the card are also listed at the bottom of the card (this subject is "1."). This list at the bottom of the card shows you all the subject cards filed on that book. The second card below is for the second subject listed, "Astronautics."

Thus, if you don't know a specific title or author and you want to read a book about planets or space exploration, you can, by going through the subject file, find these cards. In this way you can find a book on your subject.

A book is also, of course, always cataloged under its author's name and under its title, as in the examples on page 133. Notice that the author card has the author's name at the top and the title card has the book's title at the top.

Notice that all the cards are exactly the same, except for the heading at the top. (Yes, it *is* odd that the title is not spelled with capital letters!)

Do **For Practice** on pages 134-135.

PLANETS—EXPLORATION

QB
602.9   Powers, Robert M., 1942—
P68   Planetary   encounters/ Robert   M.
1978   Powers; original drawings by Helen
         Zane Jensen.—Harrisburg, Pa.: Stack-
         pole Books, c1978.
             288 p., [4] leaves of plates: ill.
         (some col.); 25 cm.
         Includes index.
         Bibliography: p. 283—284.
         ISBN 0-8117-1270-2

    1. Planets—Exploration. 2. Astronautics. I.
Jensen, Helen Zane. II. Title.

Subject Card 1

ASTRONAUTICS

QB
602.9   Powers, Robert M., 1942—
P68   Planetary   encounters/ Robert   M.
1978   Powers; original drawings by Helen
         Zane Jensen.—Harrisburg, Pa.: Stack-
         pole Books, c1978.
             288 p., [4] leaves of plates: ill.
         (some col.); 25 cm.
         Includes index.
         Bibliography: p. 283—284.
         ISBN 0-8117-1270-2

    1. Planets—Exploration. 2. Astronautics. I.
Jensen, Helen Zane. II. Title.

Subject Card 2

Catalog cards are filled with helpful information. They tell you the author, title, and subjects of the book. They tell you the number of pages in the book and also in the preface, if there is one. They tell you the city in which the book was published, the name of the publisher, and date of publication. They also tell you whether the book helps the reader find information in it (whether it has a bibliography and/or index). Finally, they tell you where you can find the book on the library shelves. This is the *call number* and is in the upper left corner. Ask your librarian to help you if you do not know how to use the location information on the catalog cards. Now you just need to get the books from the shelves.

By the way, librarians are there to help you, answer your questions, show you how to use the library, help you find the materials you need. Librarians are helpful and knowledgeable. Do not hesitate to ask them for any assistance you might need. If your college has a library skills or library use class, or if the library staff offers library tours, utilize these opportunities. Libraries are wonderful, especially when you know your way around them, how to use them, and all the riches they contain for you.

Do **For Practice** on page 136.

H. Other Library Services

Here are lists of some of the other services a library may offer. Both library and media services are included. Read through these lists.

Does your library offer some or all of these services? Does your library have other services that it offers you besides these?

Library Services
Information resources:
    Reference and general book collection
    Magazine subscriptions and microfilm holdings
    Reserve book collection
    Subject indexes for magazine articles
    Maps, globes, and atlases
    Local newspapers and selected national ones
    College catalogs, telephone books, zip code directory, and the current city directory
    Occupational information and other miscellaneous information sources
Instructional equipment:
    Typewriters, calculators, and adding machines
    Photocopy machines
    Cassette players for listening to instructional tapes
    Caramates for sound/slide program viewing
    Microfilm reader and copier
    Televisions
Reference and instructional services:
    General information and directions
    Assistance in doing research for papers
    Orientations in using the library
    Credit classes in library use and research skills
Additional services:
    Quiet study areas
    Small meeting and study rooms
    Language lab
    Tutoring Center
    Interlibrary loans

(continued on page 137)

Powers, Robert M.

QB
602.9
P68
1978

    Powers, Robert M., 1942—
      Planetary encounters/ Robert M. Powers; original drawings by Helen Zane Jensen.—Harrisburg, Pa.: Stackpole Books, c1978.
      288 p., [4] leaves of plates: ill. (some col.); 25 cm.
    Includes index.
    Bibliography: p. 283–284.
    ISBN 0-8117-1270-2

    1. Planets—Exploration. 2. Astronautics. I. Jensen, Helen Zane. II. Title.

Author Card

Planetary encounters

QB
602.9
P68
1978

    Powers, Robert M., 1942–
      Planetary encounters/ Robert M. Powers; original drawings by Helen Zane Jensen.—Harrisburg, Pa.: Stackpole Books, c1978.
      288 p., [4] leaves of plates: ill. (some col.); 25 cm.
    Includes index.
    Bibliography: p. 283–284.
    ISBN 0-8117-1270-2

    1. Planets—Exploration. 2. Astronautics. I. Jensen, Helen Zane. II. Title.

Title Card

For Practice

Following are all the cards in the subject, author, and title catalogs for a biography of a woman set designer who was the special friend of the famous novelist Thomas Wolfe.

Identify each card as subject, author, or title card. Then, when you are finished, compare answers with a classmate or in a small group.

1.

SET DESIGNERS—UNITED STATES—
BIOGRAPHY

PS
3503 Klein, Carole.
E727   Aline / by Carole Klein.—1st ed.—
Z75   New York: Harper & Row, c1979.
     xi, 352 p., [4] leaves of plates; 24 cm.
   Includes index.
   Bibliography: p. 345–346.
   ISBN 0-06-012423-7

   1. Bernstein, Aline Frankau, 1881–1955—Biography. 2. Wolfe, Thomas, 1900–1938—Relationship with women—Aline Frankau Bernstein. 3. Set designers—United States—Biography. 4. Novelists, American—20th century—Biography. 5. New York (City)—Intellectual life. I. Title.

Type of card_____

2.

Klein, Carole

PS
3503 Klein, Carole.
E727   Aline / by Carole Klein.—1st ed.—
Z75   New York: Harper & Row, c1979.
     xi, 352 p., [4] leaves of plates; 24 cm.
   Includes index.
   Bibliography: p. 345-346.
   ISBN 0-06-012423-7

   1. Bernstein, Aline Frankau, 1881–1955—Biography. 2. Wolfe, Thomas, 1900–1938—Relationship with women—Aline Frankau Bernstein. 3. Set designers—United States—Biography. 4. Novelists, American—20th century—Biography. 5. New York (City)—Intellectual Life. I. Title.

Type of card_____

3.

NOVELISTS, AMERICAN–20TH CENTURY—
BIOGRAPHY

PS
3503 Klein, Carole.
E727   Aline / by Carole Klein.—1st ed.—
Z75   New York: Harper & Row, c1979.
     xi, 352 p., [4] leaves of plates; 24 cm.
   Includes index.
   Bibliography: p. 345–346.
   ISBN 0-06-012423-7

   1. Bernstein, Aline Frankau, 1881–1955—Biography. 2. Wolfe, Thomas, 1900–1938—Relationship with women—Aline Frankau Bernstein. 3. Set designers—United States—Biography. 4. Novelists, American—20th century—Biography. 5. New York (City)—Intellectual Life. I. Title.

Type of card_____

4.

NEW YORK (CITY)—INTELLECTUAL LIFE

PS
3503 Klein, Carole.
E727   Aline / by Carole Klein.—1st ed.—
Z75   New York: Harper & Row, c1979.
     xi, 352 p., [4] leaves of plates; 24 cm.
   Includes index.
   Bibliography: p. 345–346.
   ISBN 0-06-012423-7

   1. Bernstein, Aline Frankau, 1881–1955—Biography. 2. Wolfe, Thomas, 1900–1938—Relationship with women—Aline Frankau Bernstein. 3. Set designers—United States—Biography. 4. Novelists, American—20th century—Biography. 5. New York (City)—Intellectual Life. I. Title.

Type of card_____

5.
Aline

PS
3503 Klein, Carole.
E727   Aline / by Carole Klein—1st ed.—
Z75   New York: Harper & Row, c1979.
     xi, 352 p., [4] leaves of plates; 24 cm.
   Includes index.
   Bibliography: p. 345–346.
   ISBN 0-06-012423-7

   1. Bernstein, Aline Frankau, 1881–1955—Biography. 2. Wolfe, Thomas, 1900–1938—Relationship with women—Aline Frankau Bernstein. 3. Set designers—United States—Biography. 4. Novelists, American—20th century—Biography. 5. New York (City)—Intellectual Life. I. Title.

Type of card_____

7.
WOLFE, THOMAS, 1900–1938—RELATIONSHIP WITH WOMEN—ALINE FRANKAU BERNSTEIN

PS
3503 Klein, Carole
E727   Aline / by Carole Klein.—1st ed.—
Z75   New York: Harper & Row, c1979.
     xi, 352 p., [4] leaves of plates; 24 cm.
   Includes index.
   Bibliography: p. 345–346
   ISBN 0-06-012423-7

   1. Bernstein, Aline Frankau, 1881–1955—Biography. 2. Wolfe, Thomas, 1900–1938—Relationship with women—Aline Frankau Bernstein. 3. Set designers—United States—Biography. 4. Novelists, American—20th century—Biography. 5. New York (City)—Intellectual Life. I. Title.

Type of card_____

6.
BERNSTEIN, ALINE FRANKAU, 1881–1955—BIOGRAPHY

PS
3503 Klein, Carole
E727   Aline / by Carole Klein.—1st ed.—
Z75   New York: Harper & Row, c1979.
     xi, 352 p., [4] leaves of plates; 24 cm.
   Includes index.
   Bibliography: p. 345–346.
   ISBN 0-06-012423-7

   1. Bernstein, Aline Frankau, 1881–1955—Biography. 2. Wolfe, Thomas, 1900–1938—Relationship with women—Aline Frankau Bernstein. 3. Set designers—United States—Biography. 4. Novelists, American—20th century—Biography. 5. New York (City)—Intellectual Life. I. Title.

Type of card_____

For Practice

As an exercise, use the library map below to show how you would follow the steps given above for using various sections of the library. As you find and select materials for a research project, you will have to move from one part of the library to another. Indicate as exactly, thoroughly, and specifically as you can where you would actually go to follow and carry out each of the activities outlined above, numbering each step, starting with the first step as (1). Finally, draw a line to connect the numbers to show your actual trip or route through the library. This will be a map of your library work.

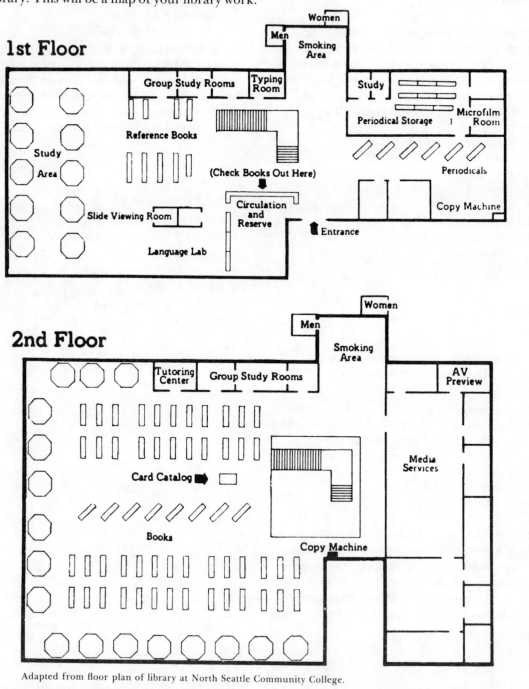

Adapted from floor plan of library at North Seattle Community College.

Media Services

Duplication of instructional cassette tapes

Viewing areas for non-print instructional materials

Consultation on media-oriented projects

Audiovisual equipment scheduling, distribution, and maintenance

    Motion picture projectors

    Slide and filmstrip projectors and viewers

    Videotape recording and playback equipment

    Record players

    Tape recording equipment

    Overhead projectors

    Opaque projectors

Access to commercially available instructional media. This includes a catalog collection, preview areas, and booking and rental service

Consultation for the selection, evaluation, and purchase of media resources and equipment

Instructional development assistance for the design and production of curriculum materials

Production service for audiovisual materials such as slides, photographic prints, overhead transparencies, video recordings, sound recordings, and graphic displays

Offset printing services for classroom materials

[Adapted from *North Seattle Community College Library Handbook*]

I. Reading Resources Material/ Doing the Research

Now you have a pile of books, journals containing your selected articles, and several encyclopedias. You know the specific, limited topic on which you are going to focus your research. You are ready to begin your investigation/research. Get lots of paper or cards; then select from all your reference materials what you believe may be the most general, basic treatment of your topic. Perhaps it will be an entry in one of the encyclopedias. This will give you an easy place to start.

Read the pieces you have selected. Write down on your paper or cards whatever, in your best judgment, gives you useful information about your topic. Be conscious that *you are a detective* looking for evidence, proof, information. This is what research is like. It is exciting, interesting, thought-provoking. After all, you are searching for *truth!*

You will now read the other materials and write more notes. No, you do not have to read whole books! Look up in the index and table of contents of each book the topic of your research. Then read only those sections of the book that relate to that topic.

Your curiosity, your search for more of the picture, for more of the story, for more of what is true, may lead you to read other sections, to find out other information. *But always keep in mind that you must bring everything back to the sharp focus of your topic.* Otherwise, your paper will ramble and your reader will lose your idea, will not be able to know exactly what you are writing about. (More on this in Section K, "Writing the Paper.")

J. Taking Notes

1. Your notes need to be in a format that will make *your* notetaking on *your* reading as easy as possible for *you.* As you read you will begin to see that certain names or ideas or facts keep recurring. You should then set up a separate sheet of note paper or a pile of note cards for recurring names or ideas or facts. Then, as you read on, list each further reference to that same fact or name on its appropriate sheet of note paper or on a note card in the appropriate note card pile.

Be sure to identify the piece of writing (give name of book and/or author) *and the page number* for each of these references as you write it down in your notes. This will prevent one of the most horrible experiences a researcher can have—that is, you start to write your paper; you have a reference you want to quote in your paper; you need, of course, to tell where you read it and who wrote it so that you can give credit where it is due (otherwise you are guilty of plagiarism, which is stealing others' ideas and work). But—oh, horrors!—you did not write down where you got the reference. And you have read eight different pieces. You cannot go back and reread them all, even by scanning, and you now have no idea where it came from. (You can try to scan, of course; but it may take a very long time—how much easier if you had written down the information to begin with.)

The only thing you can do now is not use that reference, even if it is just perfect and exactly what you need. What a misfortune!

Next time you will remember to give yourself the help you need by writing down the page and the work from which each reference came.

2. Your notes can be written in any way that is most convenient, understandable, and natural to you. Who cares if no one else in the world can make sense of it? No one else has to.

3. As you begin to increase your information, you will find that ideas or discoveries or understanding may start coming to you. At this point you will want to start another, separate, special sheet of note paper that will be for you to write down your *own* thoughts about the information, your *own* ideas about it, your *own* conclusions and understanding of the topic. Talk to yourself on this special idea sheet. Ask questions. Answer them. Refer to your other notes, to the ideas, facts, and references you have written down. *Be pulling it all together on this separate idea sheet.* At this point you can start getting very engrossed in your research, as you develop your *own* ideas.

As you are adding more information to your various reference note papers and note cards (as well as to the idea sheet referred to just above) you need to use your study skills of page-flipping and cross-referencing. These skills are discussed in Chapters 6 and 15; they are the magic keys to doing really good research and coming up with really thorough, well-thought-out, and perhaps even creative ideas and discoveries of your own!

4. Here is a brief review of page-flipping: when you are reading something and believe you recognize something about it, if even only vaguely (if it rings a bell, reminds you of something else you were reading), then stop, try to remember or find that other thing (in your notes perhaps, or earlier in the piece you are reading or in another piece you were reading previously).

Look back and forth through your notes or books or articles: page-flip. When you find the reference that you vaguely recognized, then you will have made a connection that ties information together. This cross-referencing, this tying together of information, is a key to successful research. *Make a note, on your separate reference note pages and/or idea sheet, of every relevant connection.*

5. Yes, as you may imagine, you will have to use a lot of note paper and/or many note cards. You should, as you go along, reorder or rearrange or rename your notes. You may want to transfer information from one category (or pile of note cards or notepage) to another. You may want to join two categories or groups (or piles or notepages). You may want to divide one notepage into two or three, separating the information into different subunits. You will keep making better notes, improving the ones you took at first. Put the old ones aside (discard them, but don't throw them into the garbage yet—who knows but that later you may want to go back and review your original ideas or arrangement). The following two chapters will give you help in acquiring this skill of consolidating material. Be sure to study those chapters before you begin your research project.

Is this rearranging and reordering a waste of time or is it good for you? Of course it is good for you. It is the very best thing you can do. This is the *processing* that is absolutely necessary for making sense of your research, of the information you are finding. (Review Chapter 15 on the good results of arranging and processing material.) It is only by doing this processing (thinking) that you can see and "hear" what the facts and ideas you have collected reveal about themselves. Only in this *active* way can you discover the truth about them.

Your reading, note-taking, arranging of your notes, page-flipping (cross-referencing), then doing more work on your notes, restructuring and rearranging them, and developing your ideas and theory (your conclusions) about the truth of the matter should take a lot of time. Expect to spend time on this; do not begrudge the time or regret it. This work is essential to the research task you have undertaken.

K. Writing the Paper

1. Now you have completed your research and investigation. All the information has been collected on your many notepages or note cards. Your ideas and theory (conclusion) have been developed on the special idea sheet. Now you need to look it all over, get an overview, and think about how it will be best to report on it— that is, how you are going to organize this material in the report, in the research paper you are now going to write on what you have discovered about the search for black holes.

Are you going to start out with your final idea or conclusions and then fill in with the information that led you there? Or will you start with the different pieces of information and then move along to the conclusions you came to? Or will you tell how you did the research and what you were thinking as you were going along? Do you need to have sections in which you explain or define for your readers some of the ideas or terms with which they may be unfamiliar? Should you try to make it suspenseful and exciting? Or should you be businesslike and scientific? Should you be personal? Should you give a historical perspective to it? Should you start out describing the phenomena? Should you include the problems and difficulties the scientists had? Should you go into detail about the equipment they used? Do you want to include the controversy and disagreements the scientists have with each other?

Will you end with a science fiction type of slam-bang ending? Perhaps you should start out with a science fiction type of slam-bang attention-grabber?

How in heaven's name should you organize and present your material? Who will give you the answer and tell you how?

You yourself! There is *no* one-and-only-one right way. Ten different people could organize and present the material in ten different ways, all equally correct. You yourself will have to decide how you are going to present your material.

2. To help you make your decision you can consider some of the following:

a. For whom are you writing the paper? Is your reader up on scientific matters or will he or she need explanations and other background information? That is, will you need to include a kind of catch-up mini-course so that the uninitiated reader can understand what you are talking about? Or can you jump right in and expect your reader to know what you are talking about? In other words, are you writing it for scientists or an English teacher? If you do need to add some background, where will you put it? At the beginning? When a specific idea or term comes up? In a special footnote (see Section L below on footnotes)?

b. Do you want to entertain your reader or do you want to inform in a serious way? Which feels more natural to you? Which seems more appropriate to the subject? You may start out one way, reread your paper, decide you have the wrong tone, and then decide to rewrite it with a different, more appropriate tone. Your judgment will guide you. You have no other choice but to develop, use, and rely on your own judgment. As you become more experienced, your judgment will, of course, improve. (Improving one's judgment is a lifelong process to which we all should commit ourselves!)

c. Will your readers be offended by your topic or ideas? Will they need to be prepared or softened up first? Or can you expect agreement—in which case you can just tell it as it is? You do want your readers to have a positive reaction, don't you? If you fear a negative attitude perhaps you will want to have a long background section to get your readers ready before you actually say what you know and think.

d. Do you need to prove what you are saying? Do you want to convince or persuade your readers to believe you? Do you need to assert (make) your point and then list the evidence or proof to back up your assertion so that your reader will agree—or at least not say, "I don't agree. I don't believe this. It is a bunch of half-baked, unproven assertions!"? I always prefer to have my readers say, "Okay, I may not totally agree, but I have to admit you have given some convincing evidence to back up your assertions (points)." (Remember the six intentions authors have? You are an author now yourself. What are *your* intentions?)

e. Perhaps you don't have assertions/points to make. Perhaps you want only to share information. In this case you don't need to line up your evidence and proof for the purpose of convincing or persuading your reader that what you are asserting is valid and believable. If you want only to share information, then you just need to present the information.

Yes, you are now one of the authors spoken of in Chapter 12, and you will want to get across your ideas, one main one in each of your paragraphs. You will have to be clear in your own mind what you want each paragraph to do (give information? prove a point? give a definition? discuss a problem?). Review Chapter 12 to see what supporting material you will have to put into each paragraph to get your idea across, to accomplish your purpose.

As you write, you may discover that some of your material is not related tightly or closely to your topic. Then, even though the information is interesting, you will have to cut it out. It is alway better to cut out unrelated material than leave it in and get your reader all confused and led away from your topic.

If you just haven't the heart to leave it out altogether, you can put it into a footnote (discussed below in Section L).

f. Now your problem is deciding which piece of information or what proof or piece of evidence you should put first and which second, and so on, and which last. Will you start out with the one that historically occurred first and work up, through time, to the last or most recent piece of information or piece of evidence? Or will you start with the smallest or least important? Or should you start with causes and then give the results? Or the other way around? Should you just follow your instinct and write down whatever pops into your head? (Please don't use this method! Others will find it hard to follow your logic and will find it hard to make sense of where you are going and where you are taking them! They will cry out in anguish: "What is this author's main idea here? I am all confused!")

Who can tell you which is the best way to order your facts and proofs? No one but yourself, using your own best judgment. You may even start with one order and then decide another is better for your material. Then you will have to reorder your material and start over. Is this a waste of time? Absolutely not. The more you explore and use your sense of logic and try to make good and then better judgments, the more your mind will develop, the better your work will become.

g. Be sure, after you have decided how best to order your material (which first, which next, which last), that you then add words and phrases to help guide or lead the reader from one point to the next. Use such words as "But more important than that is the fact that . . . ," or "The next fact that was discovered was . . . ," or "The result of this fact is that. . . ." These phrases or words, such as "second," "last," "more," "to the left," "just next to this," "to the right," "therefore," "consequently," "moreover," "however," "on the other hand," are called "transitions."

The word "transition" contains the word "trans," which means "across." Thus, a transition is something that takes or helps a person across or over, from one thing to the next.

Transitions are like road signs or a friendly hand leading your reader along so she or he won't get lost. Transitions keep your reader with you, close to your logic, not wandering off getting confused and lost. Reread your paper and be sure that each part is linked by a transition, a connector, a bridge, to the next part ("thus," "in connection with this," "finally," "despite this," "although," etc.).

Using transitions will also help *you* keep to your own logic! (Page-flip back to Chapter 13, Section A, part 1, for another use of transitions.)

h. Finally (notice the transition), you need to know how to write grammatically, in sentences, in paragraphs, with correct punctuation and spelling. If you are shaky about these skills, you might want to take a writing or specialized skill course or drop in at your school's communication skills lab (if there is one) or request a tutor (if your school has tutoring services).

It is not possible to teach you how to write correctly in one chapter of a book on the different subject of how to study.

If you are a competent writer, then after you have made all your decisions as listed above in items **a** through **g,** you can write your paper. Remember, you can expect that you may be wanting to change your mind, make different decisions, rip up all or part of what you have done and start over again—in order to *make your paper as excellent, as sharp, as tight, as to the point, as logical, as easy to follow as possible.* These activities are called revising and rewriting, and they are essential activities. Do a lot of them, with the commitment to do a job of which you can be proud.

L. Notes and Bibliography

1. The last thing you have to do (notice the transition) is give due credit to the authors whose ideas or words or works you used in your own work. You need to give each author's name, the work in which you found his or her words or ideas or information, certain publication information about that work, and the page from which the specific reference or passage was taken. This information is put into *notes*. There are different kinds of notes. For example, "footnotes" are notes at the bottom of a page that tell the reader where each quoted or borrowed item on that page came from. The footnote ("foot" because it's at the foot or bottom of the page) will include the name of the author from whom you are borrowing, the title of the piece, the publisher, and the page number. (See part 3 below.)

Sometimes these notes are not at the foot of each page but, instead, are all given together at the end of the paper and are called endnotes.

Sometimes the note is just the author's name and a date in parentheses right before or after the quoted words or borrowed ideas (see part 2 below). This date and name then can be looked up in the bibliography. The bibliography is on the very last page. It has all the same information as in the footnotes, endnotes, and parenthetical notes. But the notes now are in a slightly different format and are in alphabetical order by author's name. This is for the convenience of a reader who wants to look up easily any of the authors you have borrowed from in your paper. (See part 2 below.)

2. There are a number of different ways to write references/notes and bibliographies. Each of your teachers may want to assign the use of a different style. Here is an example of the style psychologists use:

Moore (1976) asks: "Can we accept the proposition that the age of two-year-college students, their mobility, employment, experience, learning, and other factors have no positive effect on them even if they were culturally disadvantaged as children . . . " (p. 6). We also might consider the idea that an adult is a constantly changing organism (Birren, 1964).

In the example above, the name of the author (of the information used by the writer of the paper) is followed by the year of publication of the article or book from which the information was taken. Then, at the end of the paper, there is the bibliography (see below), often called "References Cited." Each bibliographical entry has the author's name, the title of his or her work, certain publication information, and the date of publication. By referring to the bibliography, the reader of a psychologist's paper can find the work referred to in the text. (There is no separate footnote section in a paper using this style.)

References Cited

Atkinson, J. W., and Feather, N. T. *A Theory of Achievement Motivation.* New York: John Wiley and Sons, 1966.

Birren, J. E. *The Psychology of Aging.* Englewood Cliffs, N.J.: Prentice-Hall, 1964.

Cross, K. P. *Planning Non-Traditional Programs.* San Francisco: Jossey-Bass, 1974.

Cross, K. P. *Accent on Learning.* San Francisco: Jossey-Bass, 1976.

deCharms, R. *Enhancing Motivation: Change in the Classroom.* New York: Irvington, 1976.

Gehlbach, R. D. 1979. "Individual Difference: Implications for Instructional Theory, Research and Motivation." *Educational Researcher, 8,* April 1979.

Moore, W. "Community College Response to the High-Risk Student: A Critical Reappraisal." *Horizons Issues: Monograph Series.* American Association of Community and Junior Colleges/Council of Universities and Colleges/ERIC Clearinghouse for Junior Colleges, 1976.

3. Here is an example, in contrast (notice the transition), of the style a writer on literature might use—the numbers refer to footnotes, which will appear at the bottom of the page. (The footnotes contain the same information as the References Cited; the *format* for footnotes, however, is different.)

The literary critic François Jost believes that all the different European national literatures are really the same. To him, all these national literatures come from the same underlying culture, and this is why they are all essentially the same. "It is necessary . . . to study several national literatures in order to see their oneness and unity beyond all appearances."[1] He writes of a "cultural substratum common to all literatures,"[2] of a European culture that "forms an individual whole,"[3] and says that comparative literature's "fundamental principle consists of the belief in the wholeness of the literary phenomenon. . . ."[4]

_____

1. François Jost, *Introduction to Comparative Literature* (New York: Pegasus, 1974), p. 9.
2. Ibid., p. 20.
3. Ibid., p. 29.
4. Ibid.

_____

"Ibid." means "the same as above," or "ditto."

Notice above in the text that each piece of borrowed (referenced) material is followed by a raised number, with the same number and related reference material written out in the footnote section at the bottom of the page. This paper's *bibliography,* at the end of the paper, will be similar to the bibliography of a psychology paper.

References Cited

Anderson, G. L., ed. *Masterpieces of the Orient.* Enlarged ed. New York: Norton, 1977.

Birch, Cyril. *Anthology of Chinese Literature: vol. 2, From the Fourteenth Century to the Present Day.* New York: Grove Press, 1972.

Caudwell, Christopher. *Illusion and Reality: A Study of the Sources of Poetry.* New ed. New York: International Publishers, 1946.

Jost, François, *Introduction to Comparative Literature.* New York: Pegasus, 1974.

4. An *informational note,* on the other hand (notice the transition), is not like the *reference note* we discussed above. It is, instead, a place for you to add those interesting thoughts and pieces of information that you could not fit into the text itself. Here are two examples. They are placed at the bottom of the page and are indicated by an asterisk in the text:

Whenever faculty workload is increased, quality of education must necessarily go down. A teacher can simply not do as well for one hundred students as he or she can for fifty or even seventy-five students. A teacher can simply not do as well for two hundred students as for one hundred. And surely not as well for fifty as for twenty-five. This is a fact of education. One "solution" is the increasing use of temporary and underpaid part-time faculty. In a period of inadequate funds the colleges can either make each teacher's classes larger or hire part-time faculty at smaller salaries. But hiring many part-time teachers will also harm the quality of education because part-time faculty are often hired at the last minute, are not given time to prepare, have low morale* and are not encouraged to feel a commitment to the college** even though they might wish to do so.

_____

* When part-time faculty are paid less than full-time faculty and yet teach the same number of students in the same number of courses as full-time faculty, they, naturally, will feel underpaid and unfairly treated. This hurts morale.

** The college prefers the part-timers to be temporary and, therefore, does not want the part-timers to believe the college has a commitment to them. They do not want the part-timers to get their hopes up about one day becoming a more expensive full-timer.

_____

Because footnoting and bibliographic styles are so varied and numerous, and because there are a number of excellent handbooks in your library and bookstore which go into the many complex details at length, this chapter will end here, having introduced you to the general concepts of footnotes and bibliographies.

I wish you good research, good decision-making, and good writing (luck really doesn't have much to do with it)!

Your Summary

Items   *Page Number(s)*

CHAPTER 18

Consolidating the Paragraph Summaries

A. Making Paragraph Summaries in Your Textbook

1. In previous chapters you learned that studying a textbook paragraph includes writing your main idea statement in the margin and underlining some good supporting material.

This combination of (a) main idea statement and (b) underlinings is called the *paragraph summary.*

In other words: *A paragraph summary is the main idea statement plus the underlined material.*

One page of your textbook could look like the diagram below after you have finished making your individual *paragraph summaries:*

2. If every *page* of your textbook looks like this example you will have a great many little individual paragraph summaries to review and copy, check, and correct. In fact, there will be too many. On pages 146 and 147, section 2, is an example of what a whole page of paragraph summaries might look like when you copy them for studying.

Therefore, you will want to *consolidate* (combine) the many little individual paragraph summaries. That is, you will want to boil down the many little paragraph summaries into a smaller number of summaries so that the material is easier to copy, check, and correct.

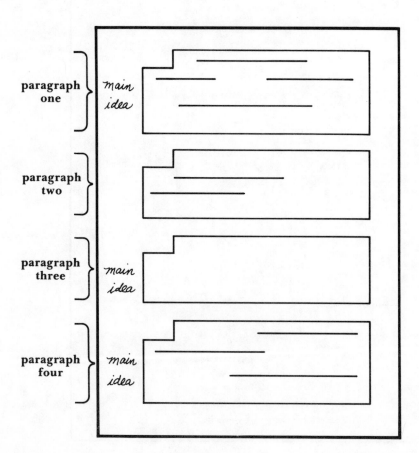

paragraph one

paragraph two

paragraph three

paragraph four

More pointers about making paragraph summaries:

This is the standard, typical paragraph summary — it includes main idea in the margin and several underlined details.

This has no main idea statement because the main idea is the same as in the first paragraph. This paragraph just contains more supporting material that has been underlined.

Nothing is underlined here because the main idea statement includes all the important material.

This is another standard, typical paragraph summary with both main idea statement and underlined material supporting it.

B. How to Consolidate Paragraph Summaries

1. The process of consolidating little individual paragraph summaries is done as follows. (You will again need lots of scrap paper—students, as you must have realized by now, need a great deal of scrap paper!)

Flip back to page 99. We will use that outline to demonstrate how you consolidate paragraph summaries.

Consolidation is done, as mentioned above, by combining several things into one. This will reduce the number of things you have. For example, if you have five main ideas it will be harder to remember them than to remember only one or two main ideas. Therefore, if you have five main ideas, you want to try to combine (consolidate) them into one or two. Look at the five main ideas on page 99:

1. Dictionary is book of words.
2. Words are used to communicate what we feel and know.
3. Dictionaries help us study and know words.
4. Too many words for any one dictionary.
5. People need all-purpose dictionary.

(Yes, first we consolidate the main ideas and then, *later,* we will consolidate the underlined supporting material.)

Can you combine (consolidate) any of those main ideas? Here is one example of how to combine main ideas 1 and 3: "Dictionary is book of words and it helps us study and know words." Or we can say it another way: "We study and know words with the help of dictionary." I like that. It is short and gets the ideas of both into one.

How about consolidating some others? Let's consolidate 2 and . . . no, I don't see how 2 can combine with any of the others. So I'll leave it as it is. But what about 4 and 5? "People need dictionary that is all-purpose and don't need to know all the words in the world." (That adds some words, but it gets the idea, doesn't it?) Or, "All-purpose dictionary has enough words for most people."

Let me try again, in other ways now, to get them even more consolidated. Let's try to combine 1 and 2 and 3 this time: "Words help us

communicate our ideas and feelings, and dictionaries help us study and know words." That's an improvement over my last attempt, but I want to improve it more. What are those main ideas saying? Do they make sense together? Yes, like this: "Dictionaries help us study and know the words we need for communicating our feelings and knowledge." Now, let's add that to consolidated 4 and 5: "A limited, all-purpose dictionary is what people need."

So here we have only two main ideas instead of the five we started out with. Two will be easier to study (copy, check, and correct) than five. And, perhaps even more important, *I have spent a lot of time and effort processing and reprocessing this material in my attempt to consolidate it.* The more I process and reprocess material, working it over, thinking about it, trying to put it together, the more my nerve grooves are deepening. In other words, *I am already a long way toward storing this material firmly in my memory as I work and work on it, trying to get it into a proper form.*

Now let us work on consolidating all the underlined supporting material. There are twelve items underlined (eighteen if we count all the subparts). This is too much to copy, check, and correct! So let's consolidate them. The way to do this is to super-select. This means, we pick out only two to five of the very strongest, to the point, memorable items for each of the consolidated main ideas.

Do **For Practice** on page 146.

Here are the items that I would have super-selected in the **For Practice** example.

1. Dictionaries help us with the words we need for communicating our feelings and knowledge (I improved it a bit more).
   a. In conversations
   b. For spelling and punctuation
2. People need all-purpose though limited dictionary (I improved it a bit more).
   a. Eng. language constantly grows (words come from diff. places and areas of interest)
   b. Big dictionaries can have 400,000 words and are used for research
   c. Cheap college dictionary has 150,000 words and special features

For Practice

Look at the outline on page 100 and pick out the few best items (strong, easy to remember, to the point) for each of our two main ideas. When you are finished, share with a classmate.

1. Dictionaries help us study and know the words we need for communicating our feelings and knowledge.

   a.

   b.

   c.

   d.

2. A limited, all-purpose dictionary is what people need.

   a.

   b.

   c.

   d.

The diagram on page 147 will show the above process in another way.

On your scrap paper, then, you will have the following consolidated summary:

The one *consolidated main idea*
   1. Super-selected supporting material
   2. Super-selected supporting material
   3. Super-selected supporting material
   4. Super-selected supporting material
   5. Super-selected supporting material

2. That summary (in the form of an outline) is the consolidated summary of those three separate paragraph summaries. If you had *not* consolidated the three separate paragraph summaries, you would have had to study all of the following:

   A. Main idea
      1. Underlining
      2. Underlining
      3. Underlining

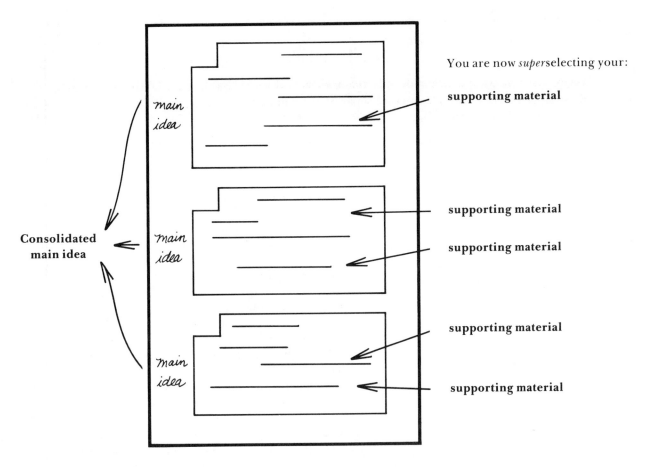

B. Main idea
  1. Underlining
  2. Underlining
  3. Underlining
C. Main idea
  1. Underlining
  2. Underlining
  3. Underlining

Obviously, the short consolidated summary is much more efficient for studying than the many separate paragraph summaries.

3. But how do you know which and how many of all the underlined details you should select for your own consolidated summary? As with your selections for the original paragraph summaries themselves—you will have to use your best judgment. You will try to select *the strongest, a good variety, and those most appropriate to the course or your purposes.*

For each original *paragraph* summary you selected only three or four details or pieces of supporting material *to underline.* In your *consolidated summary* you will also want to select only some of the details. The principle is the same: *you want to store in your memory only enough material to support your ideas.*

When studying and storing material for a particular course, you will know better what and how much to select for storage when you get your first test back. Then you will know whether your teacher wants lots of facts or whether your teacher prefers that you understand the ideas and back them up with only two or three good details or pieces of information.

Some people study for their own purposes—they may have a special interest in a certain topic, or they even may wish to do serious research on a topic of their own choice. These people will know themselves what and how much they need to study and store.

As you gain experience and practice, you will improve your judgment about what and how much to include in your summaries for the purpose of storing it for future use, as on a test.

Do **For Practice** on page 148.

4. Compare what you just did on page 148 with what I've done on pages 149 and 150.

For Practice

Process the following article. Identify main ideas and underline here. Then make paragraph summaries and consolidation on a separate sheet of paper.

ALCOHOLISM

The Department of Health, Education and Welfare (HEW) issued a 121-page report today. Congress recently passed a law which requires the department to issue a report on alcoholism each year, and this was the first such report. The report was prepared by a committee of 11 within HEW.

The report said losses caused by alcoholism are high. It said alcohol causes 28,000 traffic deaths a year, and the deaths cost the nation a total of $15 billion. Nearly 9 million persons suffer from alcoholism or lesser drinking problems, and they constitute 10 percent of the work force within the United States.

The report also contained some statistics about the use of alcohol. It said that in the last year, the average American drinker drank the equivalent of 44 fifths of whiskey. The report concluded that alcohol is "the major drug problem in this country." It said HEW will spend $200,000 next year to pay for advertisements to warn the public about the dangers of excessive drinking. The liquor industry has endorsed the campaign. The advertisements will be used on radio and television and in newspapers and magazines. But an official added, "HEW will not tell people not to drink. That is a personal decision. What we are saying is that citizens have a responsibility not to destroy themselves or society."

The 121-page report suggests that the problem of alcoholism is not adequately understood by most Americans, who seem more concerned about other drugs, such as marijuana and heroin, even though those drugs do not cause as many problems as alcohol. To prove that point the report pointed out that New York City has an estimated 600,000 alcoholics but only 125,000 heroin users. Yet the city spends 40 times more to fight narcotics addiction than it does to fight alcoholism. The report explained that most persons do not know much about alcoholism and do not consider alcohol a serious problem. People are also reluctant to admit that they have a drinking problem or are alcoholics.

HEW issued 1st report on alcoholism

Alcoholism is big problem

HEW will advertise to warn public about excessive drinking

People don't know how serious a problem alcohol is

ALCOHOLISM

The Department of Health, Education and Welfare (HEW) issued a 121-page report today. Congress recently passed a law which requires the department to issue a report on alcoholism each year, and this was the first such report. The report was prepared by a committee of 11 within HEW.

The report said losses caused by alcoholism are high. It said alcohol causes 28,000 traffic deaths a year, and the deaths cost the nation a total of $15 billion. Nearly 9 million persons suffer from alcoholism or lesser drinking problems, and they constitute 10 percent of the work force within the United States.

The report also contained some statistics about the use of alcohol. It said that in the last year, the average American drinker drank the equivalent of 44 fifths of whiskey. The report concluded that alcohol is "the major drug problem in this country." It said HEW will spend $200,000 next year to pay for advertisements to warn the public about the dangers of excessive drinking. The liquor industry has endorsed the campaign. The advertisements will be used on radio and television and in newspapers and magazines. But an official added, "HEW will not tell people not to drink. That is a personal decision. What we are saying is that citizens have a responsibility not to destroy themselves or society."

The 121-page report suggests that the problem of alcoholism is not adequately understood by most Americans, who seem more concerned about other drugs, such as marijuana and heroin, even though those drugs do not cause as many problems as alcohol. To prove that point the report pointed out that New York City has an estimated 600,000 alcoholics but only 125,000 heroin users. Yet the city spends 40 times more to fight narcotics addiction than it does to fight alcoholism. The report explained that most persons do not know much about alcoholism and do not consider alcohol a serious problem. People are also reluctant to admit that they have a drinking problem or are alcoholics.

For this one-page article I have four separate paragraph summaries with four main ideas and fifteen details. Now, in order to prepare this article for more efficient copy, check, correct study, I will want to combine these many summaries into one consolidated summary.

HEW's 1st report says: Alcoholism is biggest drug problem in the U.S., but people don't know it. HEW will advertise to warn people.

1. Alcohol causes 28,000 traffic deaths/year
2. Costs $15 billion
3. 9 million (10% of work force) suffer from drinking problems
4. Average U.S. drinker drinks c. 44 fifths of whiskey
5. Alcohol is major drug problem
6. Citizens should be responsible to self and society.
7. Worse than other drugs (e.g., grass and heroin)
8. NYC has 600,000 alcoholics/125,000 junkies
9. NYC spends 40 times more on junkies!
10. People won't admit they have a drinking problem

Clearly this consolidated summary will be quicker and easier to store in my memory than four separate paragraph summaries! It has streamlined the article down into a handy, convenient form.

For Practice

Rearrange and reconsolidate your work in the previous **For Practice** on page 148. When you have finished making your reconsolidated summary, share with your classmates.

Did you feel your mind thinking?

5. What is your next step? Yes, you will want to try to restate and rearrange your consolidated summary in order to find the most perfect statement and arrangement for yourself.

In other words, in Chapter 16 you learned how to restate and rearrange an individual paragraph summary many times until you found your own best statement and arrangement. Now you will want to carry out the same activity on your consolidated summary.

Remember you are preparing this material for proper storage. Therefore, you need to work on restating and rearranging the material so that it is in the clearest and most logical form for you. Then you will be able to copy, check, and correct it most effectively and efficiently for proper and firm storage. Be sure to study for your own particular course or purpose.

Here is a possible restatement and rearrangement that might be better for storage than the arrangement found in the actual article itself.

HEW'S 1st report on alcoholism states it is biggest drug problem in U.S. but people don't know it. Therefore, people need to be warned.
1. 9 million (10% of work force) suffer from drinking problem
   a. Average U.S. drinker consumes c. 44 fifths/ whiskey
   b. 28,000 traffic deaths/year
      (i) Costs $15 billion
   c. NYC has only 125,000 junkies but 600,000 alcoholics
      (i) But spends 40 times on junkies!
2. HEW will have advertising campaign
   a. Citizens should be responsible to self and society
   b. People with drinking problem don't want to admit it

But let's try to improve this summary outline even more to make it even more perfect for storage; *we need to rethink the ideas and try to be as clear and logical as we can.*

overall main idea { HEW's 1st report on alcoholism states it is biggest problem in U.S. but people don't know it. Therefore, people need to be warned.
cause to effect {
1. Average U.S. drinker consumes c. 44 fifths/whiskey
   28,000 traffic deaths/year
      Costs $15 billion
2. 9 million (10% of work force) have serious drinking problem

NYC has 600,000 alcoholics
   (NYC has 125,000 junkies but spends 40 times more on them!) } *contrast*
3. People with drinking problem don't want to admit it
   But citizens should be responsible to self and society
4. HEW will warn the public with ad campaign

I've left out the length of HEW's first report, the cost of HEW's advertising campaigns, and the fact that the liquor industry will support the advertising campaign. They didn't seem important enough facts to try to remember for my course, Social Problems.

Do **For Practice** on page 150.

6. You will not need to put your logic in words, as I did above in the left margin. I put that there just to let you see the logic I was using in making this summary outline. All you will need to do is try to make sure *that there is logic to* what you are doing.

The *overall* logic to my *whole* outline above is to go from large (*all* U.S. drinkers) to smaller (those with an actual drinking *problem*) to smaller (won't admit it). There is also an *overall* logic of *cause* (the drinking problem and people not being aware of it) to *effect* (what HEW is going to do about it). Now when this summary is copied, checked, and corrected and stored, it will be properly stored for the easiest possible recall.

7. In the process of writing and rewriting, rethinking, restating, and rearranging this material into the best possible summary outline, we have become very familiar with the topic or material. We understand it better, and our nerve grooves have been started. *After this work, we almost have all the material already properly and firmly stored in our memory!* Now when we start the serious, formal copy, check, correct activity, our job will go quickly and easily.

Do **For Practice** on page 152.

8. This may all seem like a lot of work. Yes, you are right. It *is* a lot of work. That is why you need at least two hours outside class to study for every hour in class. That is why you need to be sure to schedule sufficient time for study. And why you need to be motivated.

For Practice

Create four self-test questions, two short answer and two essay, based on the "Alcoholism" essay. Then, without looking at the material, answer the questions on a separate sheet of paper.

Trade questions with a classmate and answer each other's questions. Then go over the answers with each other.

All this work is what you will be doing during those hours you have scheduled for study. *All these activities discussed here and in previous chapters are studying.* And thorough, successful studying takes time and perseverance.

C. How to Consolidate Summaries of Several Pages

1. You have summarized this one-page article. But what if your article or chapter is *several pages* long?

You will use the same summarizing process that you just learned, except that for a several-page reading you will have more than just one or two consolidated summaries.

Each page may have one or two summaries, as we had for the article "Alcoholism." After you have summarized *each page,* you will then need to take the summaries from *all the pages* and consolidate them! It is a narrowing and streamlining process and will look something like the diagram on page 153.

Original text with each of its paragraphs summarized:

The first attempt to consolidate the paragraph summaries:

A later attempt to refine and streamline the material into an even more efficient and effective summary:

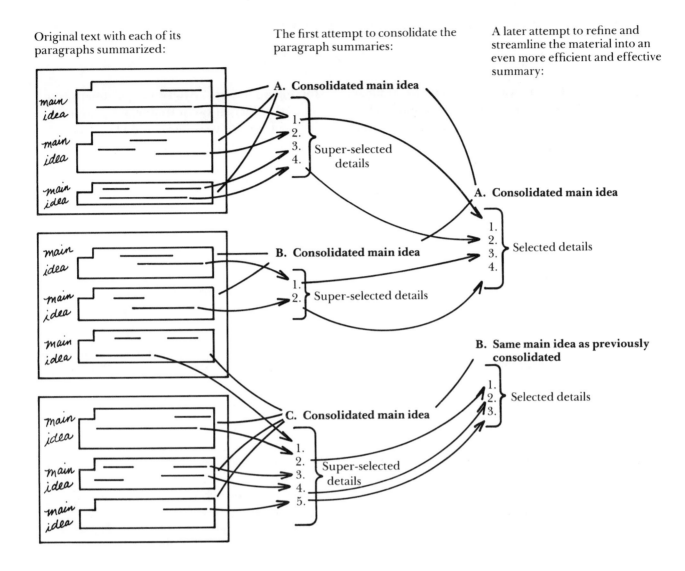

When you consolidate *several pages,* you may find that the main idea of some paragraphs consolidate best with the main ideas of paragraphs *on a different page.* This is what happened with the third paragraph's main idea on page 2 in the diagram above.

Thus, this *three-page* reading assignment with nine paragraphs and nine different main ideas has been streamlined and consolidated down to two main ideas. And the underlinings from all the nine paragraphs have been selected down to only seven pieces of information. Obviously, this consolidated and streamlined summary is more efficient and effective for storage than the original nine paragraph summaries (or even the three consolidated summaries you came up with in your first attempt, before you found the most streamlined summary).

Now, of course, you will need to rethink, re-

state, and rearrange the final summary that you have made. You do it just the same way you restated and rearranged the paragraph summaries for the "Alcoholism" article earlier in this chapter. When you have developed your best summaries, you put them into your notebook where you have your notes on outside reading.

Not every reading can be streamlined down this much. But you should try. It is good to struggle to select and to consolidate it. It will take a long time and will take a lot of thinking. But will that be wasted effort and wasted time? Of course not! *Every minute and every thought put into the struggle to select and consolidate and to restate and rearrange are increasing your deep and complete understanding of the material.* These moments and thoughts are also helping to make nerve grooves to store the material firmly in your memory.

Do **For Practice** on pages 154-155.

For Practice

Try to make a consolidated summary for the following essay. Afterwards, compare your final summary with those of others in the class. (Since the first two introductory paragraphs simply tell us about his writing the article, they do not need to be summarized.) On page 156, paragraphs 2–8 are summarized for you. (Do not read ahead. Try it yourself first.) Write your main ideas in the margin and underline the main supporting material right here in this book. Do your consolidating in the space provided following the essay.

*Life in 1990**

Isaac Asimov

Predicting the future is a hopeless, thankless task, with ridicule to begin with and, all too often, scorn to end with. Still, since I have been writing science fiction for over a quarter of a century, such prediction is expected of me and it would be cowardly to try to evade it.

To do it safely, however, I must guess as little as possible, and confine myself as much as possible to conditions that will certainly exist in the future and then try to analyze the possible consequences. Consider, for instance, our planet's population.

There are now rather more than three billion people on earth. For the three leading nations of the world, the population figures are now roughly 700 million for China, 250 million for the USSR, and 200 million for the United States.

What will the situation be a generation from now, say in 1990, assuming that we avoid a thermonuclear war? It is virtually certain that the population will have increased by at least 60 percent. The population of the United States, for instance, may have reached the 320,000,000 mark.

Very well, then, let's get down to cases. How will everyday life here in America be lived in 1990 in the light of the population explosion? An obvious consequence is an overwhelming appreciation of the necessity of conserving the planet's resources—not out of idealism, but out of sheer self-love.

Air is inexhaustible, for instance, but to be useful it must be clean. The problem of polluted air is already serious and, by 1990, it will be as unthinkable to dump untreated smoke and exhaust into the atmosphere as it is now unthinkable to dump sewage into a city reservoir.

It is possible that this will impinge on the average human being most directly in the form of bans on smoking in the open air. It will probably be discovered that air pollution (including the tobacco smoke discharged from the lungs of hundreds of millions of smokers) contributes to lung and skin cancer even among nonsmokers. Smoking may therefore be restricted to "smokatoriums" where smokers can give themselves and each other lung cancer without affecting the rest of the population.

By 1990 more and more apartments will be outfitted with devices for circulating filtered air. The old-fashioned phrase "fresh air" will be replaced, perhaps by the phrase "raw air," and this will be considered increasingly unsuitable for delicate lungs, especially in urban areas.

Again, water is inexhaustible but fresh water is not. The squeeze for fresh water is on already. However, it seems quite likely that before the quarter of a century is up there will be practical methods for desalinizing ocean water so that, in principle, fresh water will be inexhaustible. But desalinized ocean water is bound to be considerably more expensive than natural fresh water. It will still be too expensive in 1990 for any use other than drinking or cooking and the fight against water pollution will have become strenuous indeed.

Energy sources will not yet present a serious problem in 1990. With luck, this may be no problem at all. Oil and coal will still be with us and nuclear fission plants will have become common. The great problem of disposing of atomic wastes safely will, in all likelihood, be solved. (My guess is that it will be done by

*Isaac Asimov, "Life in the 1990," in *Science Digest*, August 1965.

mixing the wastes into glass blocks which can then be dumped into salt mines or the ocean deeps.) There will even, I suspect, be an experimental power plant or two, based on hydrogen fusion, somewhere on the planet, and considerable talk about solar power plants.

Minerals are less easy to be optimistic about. The world need will rise sharply and some mineral supplies are already critically short. Great sources, as yet untapped, are the bottoms of the continental shelves where, in some cases, nodules of metal compounds lie for the taking. Ocean dredges should be exploiting this resource by 1990.

What will impinge most directly upon the average man, however, will be the pressures on soil and living space. There are no easy solutions to the problem of crowding more and more people into the cities, but I think that by 1990 we will plainly see the direction of forthcoming change. The movement will be no longer upward into skyscrapers as has been true for the last two generations, but downward. This is not necessarily a welcome thought to those used to living in the open, but it may be inevitable and people will come to see advantages in it.

People already work and live in beehives, surrounded at all times by artificial light and conditioned air. They would scarcely know the difference if they were suddenly transported underground. Consider, too, that underground temperature changes are minor so there would be less problem of cooling in the summer or warming in the winter. If a whole city were built underground, then transportation would never be upset by rain or snow. Production would increase in efficiency, since round the clock shifts would be easy to set up in surroundings in which the difference between day and night is minimized.

Furthermore, the earth's surface will not be directly encumbered by the city. The ground above a large city may be devoted in part to park land for recreation and in part to farming or grazing. However, even in 1990, this kind of plan will still be in the reasonably distant future. Increasing numbers, though, of individual houses and factories will be built underground by then.

The population pressure will make the less desirable areas of the earth's surface seem more desirable, particularly for people who wish to get away from crowds. Those who can afford it will retreat into the isolation of the mountains, where the transportation and communication methods of 1990 will keep them in touch with humanity without subjecting them to physical crowding.

2. As was noted above, the first two paragraphs in the **For Practice** essay do not need to be summarized. The next six paragraphs, after the main idea statements are written in the margin and the most important supporting material is underlined, can be outlined on scrap paper this way:

A. Population today . . . . . Main idea
   1. 3 bil. in world . . . . . General information
     a. 700 mil.—China ⎫ Three items of
     b. 250 mil.—USSR ⎬ . .   more specific as-
     c. 200 mil.—US ⎭   pects of that gen-
                       eral information

B. Pop. in 1990 . . . . Main idea
   1. 60% increase . . . . . General information
     a. 320 mil.—US . . . . More specific aspect
C. Will need to conserve ⎫ Main idea says it all;
   resources   ⎬ . .   no underlining
                       needed

D. Air in 1990 . . . . Main idea
   1. Will be unthinkable ⎫
     to pollute air   ⎬ . . General information
E. Ban on smoking in open air ⎫
   1. Will find smoke from
     smokers' lungs causes
     cancer in nonsmokers   ⎬ Same as for D
   2. Smokatoriums for
     smokers
F. "Raw air" will be unsuitable ⎫
   to breathe
   1. Especially in cities   ⎬
   2. Most apts. will have   Same as for D
     devices to circulate
     filtered air

Now you can think about this arrangement (presented according to the author's logic) and try to consolidate and rearrange it further to make it more logical and more effective *for yourself*. I will consolidate and rearrange only four of these paragraph summaries. You can do the rest of the article yourself later.

C. Will need to conserve resources in 1990
   1. Air
     a. Will be unthinkable to pollute air
       (i) Ban on smoking in open air
          (a) Smoke from smokers' lungs causes
              cancer in nonsmokers
          (b) Smokatoriums for smokers
     b. "Raw air" will be unsuitable for breathing
       (i) Especially in cities
          (a) Apts. will have devices to circulate
              filtered air
   2. Water

But this material can be rearranged and restated even more logically and clearly for me:

C. Will need to conserve resources in 1990
   1. Air
     a. "Raw air" will be unsuitable for breathing
       (i) Especially in cities
          (a) Apts. will have devices for filtered
              air
       (ii) Smoke from smokers' lungs will be caus-
           ing cancer in nonsmokers
     b. Further pollution of air will be unthinkable
       (i) Smokers will have to smoke in smokato-
          riums
   2. Water

And so on.

Note that when you rearrange you can move material around, as, for example, putting part of the material on smokers under 1a and part under 1b—if this seems logical to you.

The overall logic is now *cause* (air unsuitable for breathing) *to effect* (further pollution is unthinkable). This kind of overall logic is especially appropriate for these problem/cause/solution paragraphs.

Notice that some details were omitted (e.g., ban on smoking in the open air) because that same information was implied elsewhere (smokers will *have to* smoke in smokatoriums).

All this thinking, rethinking, arranging and rearranging, and restating and copying (physically repeating) has already started strong nerve grooves for firm storage.

Do **For Practice** on page 157.

3. Your teacher might want you now to summarize one of the chapters in this book. It will be good practice.

Perhaps you will come up with your own better way of stating and arranging the material than I did when I wrote this book!

4. Finally, to repeat what I have said in other chapters about other skills: when you gain experience with this skill you may want to develop your own unique method of using it. Some students do not go through all the steps outlined above for every textbook reading assignment. Some students do not copy over the final result into a notebook. Some students do this type of work only when they are preparing for a test.

You yourself will have to find your own best and most convenient way to use this skill. How- ever, *as you begin to learn this skill it will be to your advantage to follow the steps suggested in this chapter.*

For Practice

Now go ahead and further consolidate and rearrange the main ideas and supporting materials until you have a streamlined, efficient outline for the entire essay. At this point you can forget about the original long article. You will have to store only your final efficient, short mnemonic arrangement (which will probably be in outline form for this particular article).

Use your *own* logic, even if it is different from the author's. Write your final consolidation (mnemonic device) here. Discuss with your classmates.

Your Summary

Items   *Page Number(s)*

CHAPTER 19

Consolidating Lecture Notes and Outside Reading Notes

A. How to Consolidate Outside Reading Notes

1. You learned in Chapter 1 how to combine your lecture notes and your textbook reading when the two materials *coordinate*. You learned that by combining the two kinds of information you are able to create lecture-plus-text notes that are complete. These notes, then, are transformed by you into your organized, clear *lecture note summaries* for review and written in the left one-third of your notepage.

Chapter 16 described what to do when your teacher lectures on a certain subject and then assigns a reading on material that was not directly covered in the lecture.

Chapters 16 and 18 showed you how to make summaries on the outside reading and told you to write them in a special notebook for outside reading or in your regular notebook, either near the lecture notes or in a separate part of the notebook.

2. In order to understand your subject completely and to prepare for a test thoroughly, you will want, at some point in your studying, to consolidate these *lecture note summaries* and the *non-coordinated outside reading summaries*.

Some students do this coordination regularly as they study. Other students do it only when preparing for a test. You will have to decide which is best for you.

3. On page 160 is a sample page from a student's notebook on a lecture about education in the United States. These notes were taken in an American history course.

4. The teacher then assigns outside readings in two books, one a sociology book and the other a psychology book. The teacher does this in order to give the students the opportunity to get a broader and more controversial view of the topic of education in the United States today.

As you read your assignment, always try to read paragraph by paragraph, writing the main idea in your own words in the margin and underlining the strongest and most appropriate material to remember for your particular course.

Do **For Practice** on page 161.

On page 162 is my version of this same material. While I was reading the sociology text, I was giving the material my own reality check. I did not totally agree with the sociology text. In my own experience I know that, indeed, some teachers and many students *do* play these games. But I also know many teachers and many students do *not* play these games. I know many teachers who want to teach students to think and to help them learn. Also, I know some students who go to school to learn. I do agree, however, that the grade game is played all too often, especially in elementary school and high school. I agree that this game is very bad.

Do **For Practice** on page 163.

My version is on page 164. In giving the psychology text my reality check, I agreed that what students learn in the classroom does influence their values and ideas. I also agreed that it is easy to confuse outward appearances with true inner intelligence. I did *not* agree, however (based on my own experience and other things I have studied and researched), that IQ tests are especially objective or can accurately tell what a person's IQ is. I do agree, though, with Binet's and our own modern definition of "intelligence."

(text continued on page 165)

Education in U.S.

Before Rev.
○ Education for _religious_ purposes

New England:
- under Puritan influence
- all colonies (except R.I.) had compuls. elem. ed.
- Harvard (1636), Mass.
- Wm. + Mary (1693), Va. (to train ministers)
○

After Rev.
Education for _public_ purposes.
Public demanded free public ed. because wanted educated citizens in the new democracy
○

Am. Hist. 104 - 3/4 - p. 4

Education in U.S.
Earliest Puritan settlements had schools with heavy religious influence.
First higher ed.: Harvard U. (1636), Mass. 2nd was Wm. + Mary in Va. (1693) and was to train ministers.

Most New Eng. colonies had schools.
Elem. school compulsory in N.E. (except R.I.)
After Rev., there was demand for free public schools to have educated electorate in this new democracy.

For Practice

Prepare the following textbook selection for study: main ideas, underlining, and, on another sheet of paper, your paragraph summary.

School is one of the major areas of modern life in which games dominate relationships. When a person becomes a student, as we all must the way society is set up today, he quickly learns that his well-being in the educational institution centers around the "grade game." Students find that they must regurgitate materials assigned them or about which they have been lectured. Whether they believe or assent to the materials is deemed irrelevant in most of our testing procedures: Students are simply held accountable for familiarity with certain facts. If they reproduce those facts, they receive a good grade. If they do not, they receive a low grade or fail. Because the game is played by professors and students alike, the question that is seldom asked is whether the students' regurgitating of lectured or assigned materials has any bearing whatsoever on their learning. In many cases the teacher does not want to give exams any more than students want to take them, but the educational administration requires the assigning of grades, and examinations turn out to be a handy way of separating the sheep from the goats.

One of the major educational games is the "degree game." In this game a college degree is pursued for its own sake, without regard for learning: The degree simply represents a marketable product and is valued for what it brings in terms of status and money. Sometimes students become so caught up in this game and become such good game players that one degree leads to another without any specific purpose. I have known students, for example, who initially attended college because their fathers expected it. After graduation, they entered graduate school because of vocational uncertainties or because of a desire to avoid the draft. By the time they received their master's degrees, they had done so well the faculty encouraged them to continue their studies. They did so, but by the time they received the highest degree possible, the Ph.D., they did not know why they had the degree. They had indeed played the degree game excellently, and if the game could have continued until the end of their lives, they might have been content to continue playing it. But once they reached "home," as it were, they were at a loss regarding what to do. They did not particularly want to do research and they certainly did not want to teach. . . .

From James Herslin, *Introducing Sociology* (New York: Free Press, 1975), pp. 148-50.

Here is my version of the **For Practice** exercise. Compare with yours.

*Today students
and teachers
play
"grade game"
and learning
isn't important*

*College students
play
"degree game"
and learning
isn't important*

School is one of the major areas of modern life in which games dominate relationships. When a person becomes a student, as we all must the way society is set up today, he quickly learns that his well-being in the educational institution centers around the "grade game." Students find that they must regurgitate materials assigned them or about which they have been lectured. Whether they believe or assent to the materials is deemed irrelevant in most of our testing procedures: Students are simply held accountable for familiarity with certain facts. If they reproduce those facts, they receive a good grade. If they do not, they receive a low grade or fail. Because the game is played by professors and students alike, the question that is seldom asked is whether the students' regurgitating of lectured or assigned materials has any bearing whatsoever on their learning. In many cases the teacher does not want to give exams any more than students want to take them, but the educational administration requires the assigning of grades, and examinations turn out to be a handy way of separating the sheep from the goats.

One of the major educational games is the "degree game." In this game a college degree is pursued for its own sake, without regard for learning: The degree simply represents a marketable product and is valued for what it brings in terms of status and money. Sometimes students become so caught up in this game and become such good game players that one degree leads to another without any specific purpose. I have known students, for example, who initially attended college because their fathers expected it. After graduation, they entered graduate school because of vocational uncertainties or because of a desire to avoid the draft. By the time they received their master's degrees, they had done so well the faculty encouraged them to continue their studies. They did so, but by the time they received the highest degree possible, the Ph.D., they did not know why they had the degree. They had indeed played the degree game excellently, and if the game could have continued until the end of their lives, they might have been content to continue playing it. But once they reached "home," as it were, they were at a loss regarding what to do. They did not particularly want to do research and they certainly did not want to teach. . . .

For Practice

The following selection is from a psychology textbook. Prepare this selection for study: main ideas, underlining, and, on another sheet of paper, your paragraph summary.

To an important degree, schools shape the future. The skills, ideas, and values children acquire during their long years in the classroom exert a powerful and lasting effect upon the course of their later lives. And since the vast majority of individuals now remain in school at least through their teens—and increasingly on into their twenties—the collective impact of our educational system upon changes in the structure of society is truly immense.

Given the many complex problems involved in educating the young, it is not surprising that teachers, principals, and school superintendents have often found it necessary to call upon psychologists for important practical assistance. In answer to their pleas for aid, educational and school psychologists have undertaken many diverse tasks including the design of more effective methods of instruction, the diagnosis and treatment of school-related behavior disorders, and both the planning and assessment of special educational programs for the culturally disadvantaged (DeCecco and Crawford, 1974). Perhaps their most important—and certainly most controversial—contributions to the field of education, however, have involved the development and use of objective measures of intelligence. Because such tests have been so widely employed, and also because they have recently become the subject of intense criticism and debate, we will focus most of our attention upon this important topic.

We often make informal judgments about the intelligence of others. After observing their behavior or listening to their words in a number of different settings, we label some as "bright," others as "average," and still others as "slow." Given the speed and apparent ease with which we draw such conclusions, it might seem at first that our informal system for assessing the intelligence of friends—and even casual acquaintances—is quite a good one. Unfortunately, though, it often leads us into error. For example, it is easy to confuse high verbal output with brilliance, fluency with comprehension, and an imposing physical appearance with wisdom.

Given the unreliability of our informal system for assessing the intellectual capacity of others, the need for more objective methods of drawing such conclusions is readily apparent. Surprisingly, though, no techniques of this type were available until the first decades of the present century, when, largely in response to practical problems arising in the field of education, psychologists began the task of developing practical tests of mental ability.

In 1904, a time when psychology was just getting started, school authorities in Paris approached Alfred Binet and asked him to develop an objective method for detecting mental retardation in children. In effect, they requested that he devise a simple, workable test of intelligence. Before he could devise such a test, of course, Binet first faced the task of deciding exactly what it should measure—that is, what would be meant by the term intelligence. Rejecting an earlier approach suggested by Sir Francis Galton, in which intelligence was equated with superior sensor and motor performance, Binet chose instead to focus primarily upon intellectual abilities. Together with his colleague, Theodore Simon, he finally settled on the view that intelligence refers primarily to the ability to judge, comprehend, and reason well. It is interesting to note that today, more than 70 years later, modern definitions of intelligence retain much of the same flavor, often relating this characteristic to the abilities to adapt to new circumstances, deal with complex or abstract materials, and solve intellectual problems. . . .

From Robert A. Baron et al. *Psychology: Understanding Behavior* (Philadelphia: W. B. Saunders Co., 1977), pp. 510-11.

Here is my version of the **For Practice** exercise. Compare with yours.

Education influences a child's life

educational school psychologists help — most important, they develop objective I.Q. tests, which are widely used + controversial

We informally judge others' I.Q. but are often mistaken

To an important degree, schools shape the future. The skills, ideas, and values children acquire during their long years in the classroom exert a powerful and lasting effect upon the course of their later lives. And since the vast majority of individuals now remain in school at least through their teens—and increasingly on into their twenties—the collective impact of our educational system upon changes in the structure of society is truly immense.

Given the many complex problems involved in educating the young, it is not surprising that teachers, principals, and school superintendents have often found it necessary to call upon psychologists for important practical assistance. In answer to their pleas for aid, educational and school psychologists have undertaken many diverse tasks including the design of more effective methods of instruction, the diagnosis and treatment of school-related behavior disorders, and both the planning and assessment of special educational programs for the culturally disadvantaged (DeCecco and Crawford, 1974). Perhaps their most important—and certainly most controversial—contributions to the field of education, however, have involved the development and use of objective measures of intelligence. Because such tests have been so widely employed, and also because they have recently become the subject of intense criticism and debate, we will focus most of our attention upon this important topic.

We often make informal judgments about the intelligence of others. After observing their behavior or listening to their words in a number of different settings, we label some as "bright," others as "average," and still others as "slow." Given the speed and apparent ease with which we draw such conclusions, it might seem at first that our informal system for assessing the intelligence of friends—and even casual acquaintances—is quite a good one. Unfortunately, though, it often leads us into error. For example, it is easy to confuse high verbal output with brilliance, fluency with comprehension, and an imposing physical appearance with wisdom.

Given the unreliability of our informal system for assessing the intellectual capacity of others, the need for more objective methods of drawing such conclusions is readily apparent. Surprisingly, though, no techniques of this type were available until the first decades of the present century, when, largely in response to practical problems arising in the field of education, psychologists began the task of developing practical tests of mental ability.

In 1904, a time when psychology was just getting started, school authorities in Paris approached Alfred Binet and asked him to develop an objective method for detecting mental retardation in children. In effect, they requested that he devise a simple, workable test of intelligence. Before he could devise such a test, of course, Binet first faced the task of deciding exactly what it should measure—that is, what would be meant by the term intelligence. Rejecting an earlier approach suggested by Sir Francis Galton, in which intelligence was equated with superior sensor and motor performance, Binet chose instead to focus primarily upon intellectual abilities. Together with his colleague, Theodore Simon, he finally settled on the view that intelligence refers primarily to the ability to judge, comprehend, and reason well. It is interesting to note that today, more than 70 years later, modern definitions of intelligence retain much of the same flavor, often relating this characteristic to the abilities to adapt to new circumstances, deal with complex or abstract materials, and solve intellectual problems. . . .

Psychologists develop objective I.Q. tes in ear 1900's

Psychologist Alfred Binet defined "intellig in term of intellec ability still useful today

Having given these two texts a reality check, I understand them well, and *because I have been relating them to my own sense of reality, I am finding the subject very interesting.*

5. The paragraphs in the above two outside reading assignments have been summarized; i.e., the main idea statements have been written in the margin and the most important supporting material has been underlined.

The next step is to transfer those separate paragraph summaries onto scrap paper.

From the sociology text:

A. Today students and teachers play "grade game" and learning isn't important
   1. Students must regurgitate lecture and reading material
   2. Reality checks not considered relevant
   3. Get good grades for just repeating
B. College students play "degree game" and learning isn't important
   1. College degree pursued for its own sake
   2. It gives student ability to get status and money
   3. Students go from one degree to another without any specific purpose
   4. By the time they get Ph.D., don't know why
      a. Don't want to do research or teach

From the psychology text:

A. Education influences child's future life
   1. Skills, ideas, values are acquired in the classroom
B. Educational and school psychologist help—most importantly develop IQ tests, which are widely used and controversial
   1. Many complex problems in educating children
   2. School personnel call in psychologists for practical help
      a.Design more effective teaching methods
      b.Diagnose and treat school-related behavior disorders
      c.Plan and assess special ed. programs for culturally disadvantaged
C. We informally judge others' IQ—often are mistaken
   1. Observe their behavior or listen to their words
   2. Easy to confuse lots of words with brilliance
   3. Easy to confuse imposing physical appearance with wisdom
D. Psychologists developed objective IQ tests c. 1900
E. Psychologist Alfred Binet defined "intelligence" in terms of intellectual ability—still useful today

   1. Ability to judge, comprehend, reason well
   2. Today we add ability to adapt to new circumstances, deal with complex or abstract materials, and solve intellectual problems

Go back to the two previous **For Practice** sections and compare the paragraph summaries you wrote with mine.

6. Now we should try to *consolidate* each of these sets of notes, first getting the two sociology paragraph summaries into one consolidated summary and then getting the five psychology paragraph summaries streamlined into a more efficient and shorter consolidated summary.

Do **For Practice** on page 166.

After arranging and rearranging this material several times on more scrap paper, I have finally come up with these two consolidated summaries.

From the sociology notes:

A. Today students play "grade game" and "degree game"
   1. Must repeat what they are told to get good grades
      a. Thinking and understanding are not important
   2. College degrees are only for status and money
      a. After getting Ph.D., student wonders why
         (i) Didn't want to do research or teach

This consolidated summary is clearly more efficient than the two paragraph summaries in part 5 above. (I have put an "A" by the first line because, if I were really studying, there would be other parts coming up to be designated as "B," "C," etc. I have "a" without "b" and "(i)" without "(ii)." This is not considered correct—but I like to do it anyway because it helps me think more clearly!)

From the psychology notes:

A. Since education is important to future and is a complex process, psychologists help, especially by developing IQ tests
   1. Skills, ideas, values learned in classroom have long-lasting influence on students
   2. Objective tests are needed to help educators
      a. First objective IQ tests developed c. 1900
         (i) Alfred Binet, in 1904, defined "intelligence"

For Practice

Consolidate the sociology and psychology paragraph summaries (from part 5 above):

1. *Consolidated sociology summary:*

2. *Consolidated psychology summary:*

Do you feel your mind thinking?

(a) Ability to judge, comprehend, reason well
(ii) Our definition today is like his, only adding some things
(a) Ability to adapt to new circumstances, deal with complex or abstract materials, solve intellectual problems

This consolidated summary is clearly more efficient than the five separate paragraph summaries in part 5 above. I have left out some of the supporting materials that I had underlined in the original paragraph summaries. This is because as I consolidate I must be more *selective* in what I choose to include. (Page-flip to Chapter

18's discussion of super-selecting supporting material. Review it quickly before you go on.)

As a result of all the work I have put in on rethinking, restating, and rearranging, I understand this material much better than I did, and I already have this material partially stored in my memory. As I copied the material over and over on scrap paper, as I tried to restate and rearrange it better and better, I was already beginning to make nerve grooves for this material.

I also tried to be very accurate, exact, and precise as I made my summaries. I wanted to be sure to get the author's ideas paraphrased as correctly as possible. Then if I want to disagree I will know what the author really said so that my disagreement will be right on target. This gives me credibility.

B. How to Consolidate Reading and Lecture Notes

1. Now we are ready to get these two consolidated outside reading summaries coordinated or consolidated with the original lecture note summary, on education in the United States (on page 160, in the notebook's left-hand margin).

Let's go back and look at the lecture note summary and see whether we can fit that material together in some way with the non-coordinated outside reading material.

As I read over the lecture summary, I try to figure out what in it can be related to what I found out in the outside reading assignment. I think and think and flip back and forth between the lecture summary and the reading summaries. *Then I see it!* In the lecture summary is the idea that "the public demanded free public education because wanted educated citizens in the new democracy."

In the sociology text it says that people don't go to school to learn; they only play games. Well, to the extent that that's true, then the hopes of the people after the Revolution to have an educated citizenry have been unfulfilled! Those people back then took the democracy seriously; they demanded free education so that people could become educated enough to be responsible voting citizens. But if education today is just a game for many people then it shows we are not taking our democracy seriously and are not preparing people to be responsible citizens.

On the other hand, the psychology text seems to agree that education *is* important for people, because it influences their values and ideas of later life. Thus, *if* schools can teach the students well, these students should end up as responsible citizens. However, as the psychology text points out, teaching is full of complex problems. One way to help overcome these problems is to have IQ tests to determine a student's intellectual abilities. The text hasn't proved that IQ tests will really help schools teach better, but I assume this is what they are implying or suggesting.

If psychologists can develop truly objective IQ tests *and* if these tests actually do help schools educate students well, then perhaps the students *will* end up as the early U.S. citizens hoped they would: able to be an educated electorate in this democracy.

As I flip back and forth among these three summaries *and do a lot of thinking about them,* I come to the conclusion that the sociology text doesn't say whether education is or could be important for teaching people ideas and values and thus making people better citizens. It only talks about how bad schools are because they are not really educating people. I suppose I can assume from this that the sociology text would *like* students and teachers to stop playing games and get down to the important business of true teaching and true learning.

2. Having done a lot of thinking, I am now ready to begin to write down a consolidation of the three sets of summaries; after several rewrites, my final version is as follows:

a. After the Revolutionary War, people demanded free public education so that citizens could be educated and responsible in the democracy.

b. Today, however, according to the sociology text, schools mainly play games so that people are not getting educated to be responsible citizens—students just learn to repeat and not to think.

c. Psychologists, though, according to the psychology text, are helping schools improve their ability to teach people to develop their intellectual abilities to judge, comprehend, reason, adapt, deal with complex materials, and solve problems. IQ tests help them do this.

d. If the psychologists and the schools can actually teach students to do this rather than just play "grade and degree games," then the original purpose for having free public education will be fulfilled.

This is the best result of *my* own studying. How would *you* do it?
Do **For Practice** below.

3. Finally, to prepare for the test on this subject, I will copy, check, and correct my three note summaries (one from the lecture, one from the sociology text, and one from the psychology text) and also the consolidation of all three—the a, b, c, d points given above.

Then I will give myself a self-test or dress rehearsal. This is the first question I decide to give myself:
—Who is Alfred Binet? What did he do?

When? Why is it important to us today?
Do **For Practice** on page 169.

I try to answer this question as fully and thoroughly as I can. Then I look back at my notes to check and, if necessary, correct my answer, as you just did above.

Then I go on to my next self-test question:
—What is the definition of "intelligence" that we use today?

And so on, through as many fact and thought questions as I can think up for my dress rehearsal.

When I get through with all this studying, I will be full of knowledge and understanding and I will be prepared to take any test the teacher might give; I will probably get an A, maybe even an A+.

This amount of studying takes a lot of time. Only someone with a schedule that provides for adequate study will be able to do this kind of quality work. Remember, going to school full-time is a full-time job!

For Practice

Write your own consolidated summary here:

Discuss with your classmates.

For Practice

Without looking back, answer the questions in part 3 (be sure to answer *all* the questions). When you are finished, check and then, if necessary, correct your answers.

Your Summary

Item   *Page Number(s)*

CHAPTER 20

Checklist

What You Should Be Doing from Start to Finish

Lecture Notes

1. Take notes—pay attention
2. Add or correct from textbook assignment if it coordinates with lecture notes
3. Give reality check, cross reference
4. Process, arrange, rearrange into mnemonic devices, and put in left margin of lecture notebook
5. Make flash cards if appropriate
6. Copy, check, correct in writing
7. Review mnemonic devices and flash cards for tests
8. Give dress rehearsal self-test

Textbook

1. Read paragraph by paragraph, understanding every word, giving reality checks, page-flipping, and cross referencing
2. Summarize each paragraph by paraphrasing main idea in margin and underlining several of the best supporting materials—or skim if appropriate
3. Add to or correct *lecture* notes if text coordinates
4. Coordinate or consolidate with other outside reading and with related lecture notes if possible
5. Consolidate paragraph summaries if text doesn't coordinate with lecture notes

6. Rearrange and restate until you find best mnemonic devices
7. Write final best mnemonic devices in notebook (in special place or in separate notebook)
8. Make flash cards if appropriate
9. Copy, check, correct these mnemonic devices
10. Review mnemonic devices and flash cards for tests
11. Give dress rehearsal self-test in conjunction with material from lecture notes

General Activity for All Studying

1. Give reality checks as much as possible
2. Page-flip and cross-reference as much as possible
3. Pay attention—focus—concentrate
4. Review regularly

These are the study skills and the order in which they should be used. As you gain experience, however, you may find that you will want to use these skills in a different way and in a different order.

Each student eventually must find his or her own best way to use these skills. But until you have reached that stage, you may find it helpful to use the order outlined above.

Index

NOTE: Numbers in boldface refer to complete chapter treatment of a topic.

Abbreviations, 12
Absences, 12
Attention span, 30
Attitude, 7, 17

Breaks, 29-30

Carefulness, 7, 63, 66
Checklist, **73, 170**
Concentration, 7, 12, 29, 31, 40, 45
Confidence, 3, 42, 59, 67
Consolidating: page summaries, 152-56; lecture and reading notes, **159-69**
Copy/check/correct, 42-45, 111
Cross-referencing, 38-39, 47, **52-58**, 121. *See also* Page-flipping

Dictionaries, 73, 99
Dress rehearsal. *See* Self-testing

Education: early U.S., 160
English language: history of, 112, 114-15

Flash cards, 43-45, 124
Footnotes, 141-42
Forgetting curve, 41
Formulas: memorizing them, 37, 39-40, 45; understanding them, 40; mnemonic devices for, 45

Grades, 163; on tests, 63-65

Index, 10
Intelligence: definition of, 164

Knowledge: using it in life, **71-72**

Lecture notes: how to take them, 7-10; how to study them, **117-21**
Libraries, 131-37
Logical arrangement: of lecture notes, **117-21**; of reading notes, **122-29**; of paragraph summaries, 151, 156

Main ideas: only one in a paragraph, 77-78; six kinds, 78-86; difficulty in finding them, 78, 86-87; what to do with them, 89, 90-99; in articles, 102

Memorizing: lists, 37; terms, 37; repetition needed for, 39-40; physical activity needed, 40, 43, 45, 113; recalling as, 42; items of interest, 46; copy/check/correct method for, 111, 115; with categories and examples, 115. *See also* Memory grooves; Mnemonic devices
Memory: how it works, **35-46;** short term, 41; long term, 42; sabotaging it, 42
Memory grooves, 39, 40, 41, 100, 109, 151
Mnemonic devices, 3, 36-37, 40-41, 43, 45, 54; outlines as, 100, 109-12; diagrams as, 118-20; time line as, 119
Motivation, **15-18,** 30, 32; having none, 16; increasing it, 17

Nerve grooves. *See* Memory grooves
Notes: consolidation of, **159-69.** *See also* Lecture notes; Summaries; Textbook
Nutrition: students' need for, 19

Outlining: for summaries, 100, **103-16;** indenting in, 108
Overstudy, 65

Page-flipping, 10, 38-39, **52-58,** 138. *See also* Cross-referencing
Paraphrasing, 10, 99-100
Peak energy level, 22, 31, 112-14
Problems: emotional, 3; physical, 3; with teacher, 11. *See also* Test anxiety
Processing, 37, 40, 42, 55, 59, 101, 109, 111, 123, 138, 145
Procrastination, 14

Questions: asking them, 10-11

Reading: SQ3R used in, 4-5; reality check used for, 48; cross-referencing in, **52-58;** page-flipping in, **52-58;** understanding words in, **74-76;** understanding sentences in, **74-76;** understanding paragraphs in, **77-89;** finding main ideas in, **77-89;** taking notes while, **122-29;** understanding chapters and articles in, 153. *See also* Dictionaries; Textbook
Reality check, 5, **47-51,** 75, 78, 111, 121. *See also* Cross-referencing
Recalling, 59-61, 68, 70. *See also* Memorizing
References Cited, 141-42
Relaxing, 29; before tests, 66

Research paper, **130-43;** finding a topic, 130-31; limiting the subject, 131; doing the research, 131-33, 137-38; taking notes, 137-38; writing the paper, 138-40; bibliography, 141-42; footnotes and endnotes, 141-42; references cited, 141-42. *See also* Libraries

Reviewing, 29, 39, 46, 59

SQ3R, 4-5

Scanning, 128

Scheduling, **19-34;** for full-time students, 20; with full-time job, 20; with part-time job, 20; daily, 21-24, 29; realistic, 22; flexible, 23; for day person, 23; for night person, 23; weekly, 24-28, 29; regular, 26, 27, 31; daily lists for, 27, 29

Self-testing, **68-70**

Skimming, 127-28

Sleep: students' need for, 19

Spelling, 3, 7

Study breaks. *See* Breaks

Study: review, 23, 29; extra, if needed, 26, 29; regular, 29; unexpected or long-range, 29

Studying: before sleeping, 23; music with, 31; proper place for, 31; getting ready for, 31-32; activities during, 45, 73, 152

Summaries: of paragraphs, 100-1; of articles, 100, 102, 152; consolidation of, **144-58;** of pages, 152-56; of chapters, 156

Table of contents, 10

Tape recorder: use of, for taking lecture notes, 10

Test anxiety, 39, 52-54, 65-66

Test questions: different kinds of, 60-63

Tests: fear of, 54; how to take them, **59-67;** grades on, 63-65. *See also* Test anxiety

Textbook: how to study, **122-29;** taking notes, **122-29;** organizing reading notes, 122-29. *See also* Reading; Summaries

Time line, 119

Time management. *See* Scheduling

Transitions: in writing research papers, 140

Underlining, **90-102;** appropriate material for, 93; for remembering material, 94; strongest examples for, 96; variety of examples for, 96; to make reading notes, 122, 124